INDIA AS AN EMERGING POWER

Of Related Interest

Decentring the Indian Nation
edited by Andrew Wyatt and John Zavos

Constitution and Erosion of a Monetary Economy: Problems of India's Development Since Independence
by Waltraud Schelke

Future Trends in East Asian International Relations
edited by Quansheng Zhao

India
as an
Emerging
Power

Editor

SUMIT GANGULY

FRANK CASS
LONDON • PORTLAND, OR

First Published in 2003 in Great Britain by
FRANK CASS PUBLISHERS
Crown House, 47 Chase Side
Southgate, London N14 5BP

and in the United States of America by
FRANK CASS PUBLISHERS
c/o ISBS, 920 NE 58th Avenue #300,
Portland, Oregon, 97213-3786

Website: www.frankcass.com

Copyright © 2003 Frank Cass Publishers

British Library Cataloguing in Publication Data

India as an emerging power
1. India – Foreign relations – 1984–
I. Ganguly, Sumit
327.5'4

ISBN 0-7146-5386-1 (cloth)
ISBN 0-7146-8321-3 (paper)

Library of Congress Cataloging-in-Publication Data

India as an emerging power / editor, Sumit Ganguly.
p. cm.
Includes bibliographical references and index.
ISBN 0-7146-5386-1 (cloth) – ISBN 0-7146-8321-3 (pbk.)
1. India–Foreign relations–1984– 2. National security–India.
I. Ganguly, Sumit.
DS480.84.I54 2003
327.54–dc21

2002153167

This group of studies first appeared in a Special Issue on
'India as an Emerging Power' of *The Journal of Strategic Studies* (ISSN 0140 2390)
25/4 (December 2002) published by Frank Cass.

Printed in Great Britain by MPG Books Ltd, Bodmin, Cornwall

Contents

Acknowledgements and Dedication

The workshop that preceded this special issue was supported by a generous grant from the Cooperative Monitoring Center, Sandia National Laboratories in Albuquerque, New Mexico. Additional assistance for this workshop was also provided by Richard Lariviere, the Dean of the College of Liberal Arts and Kathryn Hansen, the Director of the Center for Asian Studies at the University of Texas at Austin. Major Kent Breedlove and Captain Larry Smith, students in the Foreign Area Officer program, provided substantial and invaluable logistical assistance. This volume is dedicated to my friend, Jack Snyder of the Department of Political Science, Columbia University.

1

Introduction

SUMIT GANGULY

Issues of regional security in South Asia have received considerably greater attention since the September 11, 2002 terrorist attacks on the United States. Such a focus on the region is hardly unwarranted. Even though the majority of the perpetrators of the acts of terror were Saudi nationals, it is all but certain that the infrastructure of terror that supported and abetted them was located athwart South Asia, in the dens of the Taliban regime of Afghanistan.

Despite the renewed focus on South Asian regional security, knowledge of and interest in the principal player in the region, India, still remains limited in the Western world. Yet India's role is of paramount significance for the long-term security and stability of the region. It is not merely the most populous state in the region but also has a number of other important attributes that undergird its strategic significance in the region and beyond. It has a substantial military apparatus,[1] a growing economy with some world-class sectors,[2] and democratic political institutions that have withstood countless vicissitudes.[3] Consequently, India's place in the global order at the Cold War's end merits careful scrutiny.

The end of the Cold War necessitated fundamental changes in India's security and foreign policies. In the initial years of its independence, India's leadership propounded and promoted the doctrine of nonalignment. This doctrine, among other matters, sought to steer India away from the emergent, titanic superpower struggle.

In keeping with the expectations of this doctrine, its principal proponent, Prime Minister Jawaharlal Nehru, sought to dramatically limit defense expenditures. His interests in limiting the scope and dimensions of India's military were manifold. Domestically, he was acutely cognizant of India's endemic poverty and also feared of possible Bonapartist ambitions on the part of the Indian military.[4] Internationally, he was determined to forge a world order that eschewed, or at least hobbled, the use of force in international politics.

Nehru's stature in the Indian political arena enabled him to pursue these ends despite criticism and opposition from some quarters. But Nehru's hopes were dealt a devastating blow in 1962 with the Chinese attack on India's northern frontiers. The Indian military, largely unprepared for this onslaught, was easily routed.[5] This military debacle led to a fundamental shift in India's security policies as the country lurched forward with a major program of military modernization.

Although Nehru's successors continued to invoke the precepts of nonalignment, Indian defense policy increasingly came to embrace a Realist outlook. In the absence of reliable, powerful patrons, India, its decision-makers came to realize, would have to resort to strategy of self-help to protect its security interests. Even though the United States was keen on protecting India from Chinese military pressures, its support was not forthcoming. The American military dependence on Pakistan for bases, coupled with India's neuralgic insistence on nonalignment, foreclosed the prospects of an Indo-US security relationship.[6] The considerations of nonalignment also inhibited the emergence of an Indo-Soviet security nexus.

India's costly commitment to the principles of nonalignment became more diluted as it perceived a growing threat from China in the wake of the Sino-American rapprochement. Accordingly, India forged an alliance of convenience with the Soviet Union in 1971. This relationship held India in good stead for nearly three decades. Soviet intransigence toward China dovetailed with India's misgivings about a renewed Chinese threat.[7] The Indo-Soviet relationship was not without cost, however. India's ties to the Soviet Union, coupled with its feckless anti-American rhetoric, stunted the any meaningful improvement in Indo-American relations.

The Cold War's end, however, also brought an end to the Indo-Soviet relationship, forcing India's decision-makers to find new means to assure their country's security. To this end, India assigned greater significance to its nuclear weapons program as a hedge against strategic uncertainty and the possibilities of future Chinese nuclear blackmail. The inexorable progress of its nuclear weapons program was demonstrated to the world by the controversial tests of May 1998. Ashley Tellis' article in this special issue sketches the likely evolution of the Indian nuclear weapons program in the foreseeable future. Tellis persuasively argues that the program will evolve in an incremental, cautious, and circumscribed fashion.

India's decision to forthrightly challenge the existing global nuclear order initially led to a significant setback in its relations with the United States. This relationship had seen some limited improvements in the 1990s as a consequence of India's hesitant embrace of the free market, the abandonment of its reflexive anti-American rhetoric and the end of its close ties to the Soviet Union. Adroit diplomacy enabled India's leadership over the course of the next year to repair much of the rift that the nuclear tests had generated.

As Robert Hathaway's article argues, the relationship has gathered greater strength under the George W. Bush administration. The administration's willingness to adopt a less rigid policy on the question of India's acquisition of nuclear weapons, among other matters, removed a key irritant in the relationship.

Despite the warming trend, Hathaway appropriately cautions that the relationship is far from robust and important differences persist in such areas as global trade negotiations, the pace of economic reform within India and the question of India's hoped-for membership on the United Nations Security Council.

India's relationship with the principal successor state to the other former superpower, the Soviet Union, has also undergone profound changes. Nevertheless, as Deepa Ollapally argues, the bonds, though significantly attenuated, have not been entirely sundered. India can no longer rely on Russia to militarily pin down a recalcitrant China, nor can it count on Russian support on the Kashmir issue in the UN Security Council. Yet because India possesses a very substantial Soviet-made military arsenal, India maintains a substantial arms purchase relationship with Russia. India has, however, rebuffed Russian overtures for the formation of an Indo-Russian-Chinese diplomatic bloc as a bulwark against overweening American power. Given India's recent efforts to court the United States, its reluctance to participate in such a dubious enterprise is hardly surprising.

In the absence of a post-Soviet security guarantee against future Chinese malfeasance, India's decision-makers still remain wary of Chinese intentions and capabilities. More to the point, as John Garver's contribution to this special issue reveals, a considerable gap exists between China's public rhetoric and its internal assessments of India's capabilities and intentions. Given the history of past mistrust, divergent regional security goals and interests, and the persistence of a border dispute between the two powers any improvements in Sino-Indian relations will be incremental.

India's relations with its other contentious neighbor, Pakistan, are the subject of Stephen Cohen's analysis. Cohen argues that the Indo-Pakistani relationship constitutes a 'paired minority' conflict, one in which both sides tend to see themselves a members of a besieged minority, the actual circumstances notwithstanding. Accordingly, they devise a range of strategies, from attempts at accommodation to assimilation to cope with the unique security problems that stem from this self-definition. After discussing a variety of possible scenarios of conflict resolution, Cohen argues that little progress is likely without the involvement of a powerful external actor, namely the United States.

Although the Cold War's end has done little to ameliorate India's relations with two of its fractious neighbors, it has opened opportunities for better ties with other states, such as France and Israel. During the Cold War, Indo-French relations, though hardly hostile, lacked diplomatic or cultural ballast. With the Cold War's end and the seeming emergence of American uni-polarity, as Jean-Luc Racine shows, India and France have drawn together.

One of the principal factors underlying this new convergence of interests is the common concern about American hegemony. Both sides have therefore repeatedly expressed an interest in the formation of a more multipolar world, one that would give greater weight to their interests and interests of other mid-level powers.

During much of the Cold War, fearful of offending its Muslim minority population and seeking nonaligned solidarity with the Arab world, India maintained the most limited diplomatic contacts with Israel. With nonalignment having lost all vestiges of vitality, and with Third World solidarity with the Muslim Arab world at bay, India's leadership has chosen to enhance relations with Israel. As P. R. Kumaraswamy shows in his contribution, the long-feared backlash from India's Muslim community failed to materialize. Since the initial decision to improve the Indo-Israeli relationship in 1992, it has flourished. Today, as Kumaraswamy demonstrates, robust bonds have been fashioned in areas ranging from trade to arms transfers.

This special issue would be incomplete without some discussion of India's new economic trajectory. As is well known, India's pathway of economic development after independence long led it down the road of import-substituting industrialization. This regime, despite some limited initial success, did little or nothing to ameliorate mass poverty or promote significant economic growth.

Since 1991, India has been involved in a fitful process of economic reform which triggered a severe economic crisis involving a deep balance of payments crisis. The subsequent progress of reform was in large part driven by the significant benefits that the efforts toward economic liberalization had already generated. Shortly after embarking upon its reforms, India's growth rate climbed from about 5 per cent or less to about 7 per cent per annum.

This process of economic reform, as Sunila Kale shows, is still far from complete, and important barriers remain. At a material level, these bottlenecks involve weak infrastructure in the pivotal areas of transportation, telecommunications, and power. At the socio-political level, critical reforms, especially in the labor and financial sectors, remain in abeyance.

It remains to be seen if India's political leadership can grasp these nettlesome issues and thereby complete the process started more than a decade ago. The ability to complete the reform process will, in considerable measure, shape India's economic future. More to the point, unless India can achieve sustained economic growth at around 7 per cent annually for the next decade, it will not be able to make a significant dent on endemic poverty. Nor, for that matter, will it be able to sustain the defense expenditures commensurate with addressing its perceived security concerns.

NOTES

1. International Institute for Strategic Studies, *The Military Balance, 2000–2001* (London: OUP for IISS 2001).
2. Joydeep Mukerji, 'The Indian Economy: Pushing Ahead and Pulling Apart', in Alyssa Ayres and Philip Oldenburg (eds.), *India Briefing: Quickening the Pace of Change* (Armonk: M.E. Sharpe 2002).
3. Stephen P. Cohen, *India: Emerging Power* (Washington DC: The Brookings Institution 2001).
4. Sumit Ganguly, 'From the Defense of the Nation to Aid to the Civil: The Army in Contemporary India', in Charles H. Kennedy and David J. Louscher (eds.), *Civil-Military Interactions in Asia and Africa* (Leiden: E.J. Brill 1991).
5. Steven A. Hoffmann, *India and the China Crisis* (Berkeley: University of California Press 1990).
6. Dennis Kux, *Estranged Democracies: India and the United States* (Washington DC: National Defense University Press 1993).
7. Linda Racioppi, *Soviet Policy Towards South Asia Since 1970* (Cambridge: Cambridge University Press 1994).

2

The US-India Courtship:
From Clinton to Bush

ROBERT M. HATHAWAY

*'It's like boy meets girl. We have tried to hold hands but the
kissing hasn't started.'*[1]

*Former Indian foreign secretary S.K. Singh,
on the US-India relationship*

Preparing to take up his duties as the new American ambassador in India a
quarter century ago, William Saxbe met with the US secretary of state for
final instructions. Henry Kissinger's directive, Saxbe would later recall, was
simple and to the point: 'The less I hear from you and the less I hear about
India, the happier I will be.'[2]

How times have changed. In early April 2001, two months into the
administration of George W. Bush, India's external affairs and defense
minister journeyed to Washington. During his one-day visit, Jaswant Singh
met with the US secretaries of state and defense and the national security
advisor, Condoleezza Rice, all of whom emphasized that the new
administration had high expectations for US-India relations. During Singh's
meeting with Rice, President Bush dropped by and, in a gesture accorded
signal importance by Indian analysts, invited the minister for a stroll in the
Rose Garden and further discussion in the Oval Office. The president asked
his Indian visitor to brief him on the situation throughout Asia. New Delhi
was elated: Washington, at last, now regarded India as a country whose
power and influence extended beyond the subcontinent, and whose
cooperation and advice were being sought on issues far removed from
South Asia.

Five months later, New Delhi repaid the compliment. Following the
September 11 terrorist attacks in New York and Washington, the Indian

government stepped forward with remarkable speed to extend, in the words of one New Delhi official, 'unconditional and unambivalent support' to the United States.[3] Going well beyond the perfunctory offer to share intelligence with Washington, India volunteered its military bases as a staging ground for US forces preparing to strike targets in Afghanistan. Such an offer would have been unthinkable a few years earlier. It was even more extraordinary when one recalled how during the Persian Gulf war, New Delhi retracted its permission for American warplanes to refuel at Indian airfields just as soon as the public got wind of such activities.

The contrast with past practices and patterns of Indo-American interaction could not have been more stark. Moral indignation and mutual incomprehension, even at times a sense of betrayal, have been the defining characteristics of relations between India and the United States over the past half century. Historians exploring this troubled relationship have written of *Estranged Democracies*, *Comrades at Odds*, and *The Cold Peace*.[4] Although seemingly linked by common values and a shared commitment to democratic pluralism, the two countries frequently found more reason to quarrel than to collaborate. Even on those relatively rare occasions when the two worked in tandem, bruised sensibilities and bitter recriminations soon regained the upper hand in the relationship.

The Clinton Legacy

Only in the mid-1990s did this depressing pattern begin to change. Over the course of the decade, the end of the Cold War (and its confining bipolar world view that led Americans to lump India in the Soviet camp), a new commitment to economic reform in India, and the growing political clout of the Indian-American community combined to shift American thinking about India and gave Indo-American relations a new importance in Washington. By the time Bill Clinton started his second presidential term, the administration had resolved to seek a healthier US-India relationship.

In late 1997, Madeleine Albright became the first US secretary of state in fourteen years to visit India. Planning for a presidential trip to India – the first since Jimmy Carter visited in 1978 – also got underway. These plans were thwarted, however, first by political instability and a change of governments in New Delhi, and then, more seriously, by India's decision to conduct five nuclear tests in May 1998. The Indian detonations were followed by the imposition of American military and economic sanctions, as required by US legislation commonly known as the Glenn amendment.[5] Bilateral relations seemed headed back into deep freeze.

Except that this did not happen. Though angered by the Indian tests and the setback to US nonproliferation hopes they appeared to represent, the Clinton administration opted to engage rather than isolate India. Over the following two years, there ensued a remarkable series of high-level discussions between Jaswant Singh and the US deputy secretary of state, Strobe Talbott. Not since the early 1960s had the two countries engaged each other in such a serious and sustained fashion. New Delhi in particular valued these meetings; according to one well-placed Indian analyst, they served to 'transform' the bilateral relationship. The Americans were at last taking India seriously, recognizing its role as an emerging great power.[6]

Other developments in 1999 and 2000 helped override the sting of the Glenn amendment sanctions. Indians viewed Clinton's role during the 1999 Kargil crisis in persuading Pakistan to withdraw its troops from the Indian portion of Kashmir as an important milestone, since the American president appeared to have acknowledged the justice of India's Kashmir stance. That fall the US Congress moved to ease some of the sanctions against India, following more limited waivers enacted the previous year. A wildly successful Clinton visit to India in March 2000, followed six months later by a more sedate but still productive state visit to Washington by Indian Prime Minister Atal Behari Vajpayee, underscored the new vitality in bilateral relations. Reciprocal visits by lower level officials and the creation of joint working groups on counter-terrorism, peacekeeping, and energy and the environment promised to provide an institutional framework to complement the high-level summitry.

Yet, for all the warm glow surrounding US-India ties by the end of Clinton's presidency, it remained in many respects a stunted relationship. Take, for instance, the joint statement issued after the Clinton-Vajpayee summit in September 2000. What was absent from this document is as telling as what it contained. In celebrating a 'closer and qualitatively new relationship', the two leaders 'reiterated their conviction that closer cooperation and stronger partnership between the two countries will be a vital factor for shaping a future of peace, prosperity, democracy, pluralism and freedom'.

The communiqué 'welcomed the progress' achieved by various joint consultative and working groups; 'reaffirmed' the leaders' confidence that economic dialogues and a coordinating group would strengthen economic links between the two countries; 'noted the opening' of an American legal attaché's office in New Delhi; 'welcomed the establishment' of a science and technology forum; 'noted the contribution' of science and technology roundtables; and 'welcomed' recent initiatives in the health sector.

The statement also indicated that the two leaders had agreed that their countries 'must build upon this new momentum in their relationship to further enhance mutual understanding and deepen cooperation across the full spectrum' of issue areas. In the security realm, the two leaders 'recalled the long history' of Indo-American cooperation in United Nations peacekeeping; 'agreed to broaden their cooperation in peacekeeping and other areas of UN activity'; and reiterated 'their common desire to work for stability in Asia and beyond.'[7]

These were all admirable sentiments. But none of these expressions and re-affirmations and agreements, by themselves or in combination, signified a shared strategic purpose, or anything more than a routine bilateral relationship. Indeed, their prominence in the joint statement demonstrated just how thin the relationship had been in the past, and suggested that the two countries had yet to agree upon a common vision for the future. Cooperation in the fields of biotechnology and civil aviation, telecommunications and health care, no matter how promising, is not the stuff of 'strategic partnership.'

Moreover, major differences over nuclear issues persisted – symbolized in the US hope that India would become a signatory to the Comprehensive Test Ban Treaty (CTBT), and New Delhi's reluctance to do so. Thomas Pickering, US undersecretary of state and a former ambassador to India, candidly summarized the administration's priorities when he noted that the United States would not be able to upgrade military ties with India in any significant fashion 'until there is substantial progress on nonproliferation'.[8]

Clinton's public designation of the subcontinent as 'the most dangerous place in the world', and the resentment this statement occasioned in India, also illustrated the differing perceptions in the two capitals and the obstacles impeding the establishment of a broad and deep bilateral relationship. Nor could a genuinely collaborative partnership be formed so long as one party still imposed economic sanctions against the other. The two-and-a-half years after the May 1998 tests witnessed a remarkable transformation in the tone and content of US-India ties. Nonetheless, the declarations about the existence of a new 'strategic partnership' that one heard from analysts, journalists, and politicians in both countries wildly overstated the congruence of interests and outlooks that linked the two nations as the United States prepared to inaugurate a new president.

The Bush Team Takes Charge

The US presidential election of 2000 featured two major candidates with widely divergent stands on nonproliferation issues. Vice President Al Gore, the Democratic standard bearer, fell very much within the mainstream of his party's approach to nonproliferation, and in particular felt a keen commitment to the CTBT. Texas Governor George W. Bush, on the other hand, harbored considerable skepticism about multilateral arms control agreements and the international arms control regime. Candidate Bush opposed the CTBT, arguing that further testing was required in order to ensure the reliability and safety of the US nuclear stockpile. Turning to another venerable arms control pact, he called the Anti-Ballistic Missile (ABM) Treaty a 'Cold War artifact' and pledged that the agreement would not constrain his actions as president.

Bush did not have much to say about South Asia during the campaign, but what he did say seemed calculated to win support from the affluent Indo-American community rather than to raise unpleasant questions about India's nuclear ambitions. India is 'emerging as one of the great democracies of the twenty-first century', noted the Republican Party platform. Nowhere was there any hint of anger or disappointment over the 1998 tests. Instead, the candidate called for the removal of all Glenn amendment sanctions against India.

A Bush administration, the *Telegraph* informed its Indian readership, would have a 'less absolutist view' of New Delhi's nuclear aspirations. The nettlesome nuclear issue would no longer be permitted to dominate the relationship, or to impede cooperation. Respected analyst Raja Mohan predicted that the new Bush team would bring 'greater political sensibility to bear upon its nuclear dialogue with India that has been dominated for too long by non-proliferation fundamentalists in Washington'.[9]

Commentators in India found other reasons to applaud the Texan's narrow electoral victory. The impression that Bush would be more ready than Clinton to confront China led some to speculate about a growing 'strategic convergence' between the two countries. Washington might come to view India as a useful counterweight to China. This in turn could produce a US administration that would be 'more sensitive to Indian security concerns, and more willing to accommodate India's own aspirations to be a great power'.[10] And it would ensure there would be no repetition of the joint US-Chinese criticism of India's nuclear program that had so infuriated New Delhi at the time of the 1998 tests.

The new administration's senior appointments further cheered New Delhi. During his Senate confirmation hearings, Colin Powell, Bush's appointee as secretary of state, spoke warmly of the value of solid US-India ties and expressed doubts regarding the efficacy of sanctions. The new US ambassador to New Delhi, Robert Blackwill, was seen as a figure of substance and, better yet, as someone with close ties to the president. Bush's new assistant secretary of state for South Asia had been a senior aide to Senator Sam Brownback, who had authored legislation easing the Glenn amendment sanctions against India and forcefully argued for closer US-India relations as a strategic counterweight to China.

Other top appointees had also voiced support for lifting sanctions and otherwise promoting a more collaborative partnership with New Delhi. The well-known distaste for single-issue bureaus held by the new deputy secretary of state, Richard Armitage, was a sign, New Delhi speculated, that the department's nonproliferation bureau would no longer exercise so much influence in decision-making. Everywhere one turned in Washington, there was talk about maintaining the momentum of the relationship, consolidating the gains of the past several years, and putting flesh on the institutional architecture erected during the two summits of the previous year.

First Encounters

Within days of assuming office, Bush initiated contact with Vajpayee, telephoning to express his condolences following a devastating earthquake in Gujarat and to offer American assistance. (The fact that Bush did not telephone the Chinese president for nearly six months did not escape notice in New Delhi.) The Pentagon sent a six-member response team to assess the extent of the damage and followed up with relief supplies and technical assistance. In February 2001, an American warship participated in an international fleet review in Mumbai. A few months later, the World Bank, with Washington's backing, approved a new loan for an expansion of India's power grid, a move that seemed to indicate an easing of the criteria that since 1998 had restricted the disbursement of aid.

Then there was the Jaswant Singh visit to Washington in April, and Bush's invitation to the Indian diplomat to continue their chat in the Oval Office. The president's 'generous and unprecedented gesture of goodwill' (as *The Hindu* described it) was read as a signal that Bush had a personal interest in the relationship.[11] Bush readily accepted an invitation from the Indian prime minister, delivered through Singh, to visit India. Following a session that afternoon with the US Secretary of Defense, Donald Rumsfeld, Singh reported that the day's meetings had produced 'substantial' achievements, especially in the area of military exchanges and cooperation. Pentagon sources shortly thereafter reported that Rumsfeld had directed his subordinates to look for ways to restore high-level defense contacts with New Delhi. Pentagon insiders spoke with reporters of a 'diplomatic revolution' in military-to-military relations between the two countries.[12]

New Delhi's public response to a major presidential address on ballistic missile defense (BMD) a few weeks later further accelerated the momentum of the relationship. The Indian government skillfully applauded those parts of the speech it could endorse – notably, Bush's call for sharp reductions in the number of nuclear warheads in the Russian and American strategic arsenals, his endorsement of a shift from offensive to defensive technologies, and his offer to consult with other countries on a new international security framework. Less frequently noted was New Delhi's silence on several of the more controversial aspects of Bush's speech, including the specifics of his missile defense plan and his willingness, if need be, to abandon the ABM Treaty. Although thus qualified, the Indian response was nonetheless far more positive than those of most of the world's other major nations, US friends and potential adversaries alike.

New Delhi's apparent endorsement of the president's BMD plans was rewarded during the second week of May when Deputy Secretary of State Armitage stopped in New Delhi to brief Indian officials more thoroughly on Bush's new policies. Indian analysts described the decision to send Armitage as further evidence that the Bush administration viewed India as a major strategic power, a key security interlocutor, and a nation whose opinion mattered, even on issues not directly related to South Asia. The fact that Armitage's itinerary included Tokyo, Seoul, and New Delhi but not Beijing or Islamabad was the occasion of considerable Indian self-congratulation. At last the United States had placed India on the short list of its most valued Asian friends. Washington, it seemed, now gave precedence to India over China on strategic issues.

Armitage's stopover was followed by other senior-level visits in both directions, including a July trip to India by the chairman of the US joint chiefs of staff. Many in the Indian press corps could barely restrain their enthusiasm. Gone were the 'bitter old days' when US 'proliferation absolutists and bleeding-heart liberals' held the relationship hostage to nuclear issues and human rights concerns in Kashmir, one commentator crowed.[13] The press was filled with speculation about 'paradigm shifts' and a strategic rapprochement between India and the United States. Writing in the *Pioneer* at the time of the Armitage visit, one analyst observed that India had become 'strategically America's natural choice of ally in the increasingly inevitable battle with Islamic terror'. More strikingly, he continued: 'The shifting international balance of power will, therefore, give India an unique status and importance that no other US ally has enjoyed in the past'.[14] The British, Canadians, and Australians, among others, must have wondered at that.

Second Thoughts

And yet, a closer look behind these breath-taking developments suggested that a more measured assessment might be in order. While Indians found it gratifying to have the American president ask Jaswant Singh for his assessment of the Asian situation, this might have been nothing more than a gracious host placing the burden of carrying the conversation on his visitor, while allowing the new and perhaps still-not-fully-briefed Bush to avoid talking with specificity about US-India relations or any other subject. New Delhi might also have reflected upon the fact that the American press carried virtually nothing on the Singh visit. In the eyes of US editors, he was simply one more foreigner making his way to the capital of the world's mightiest nation, and not worth notice.

Many Indian analysts savored the idea that hereafter, India rather than China would receive preference, respect, and presidential favor. Here as well, an apparently pleasing interpretation might be found, upon further examination, to hold less happy undertones. Did this mean that once again American policy toward India was little more than the offshoot of US preoccupations with another power? Was New Delhi valued not in its own right, but largely because of tensions in the US-China relationship? If so, this was not all that different from America's unfortunate Cold War insistence on viewing India primarily through the lens of US–Soviet confrontation.

An unguarded statement by Colin Powell ought to have raised warning flags of another sort in New Delhi. Speaking with reporters in July, the secretary of state observed that the administration planned 'to work very hard' with both India and Pakistan 'to make sure that our relations with both countries are strong and thriving and growing'. The American then pledged that the United States would do 'everything we can' to help improve relations between New Delhi and Islamabad and to resolve 'the difficult outstanding issues, whether it is Kashmir or nuclear issues'. 'So you will see us', he concluded, 'deeply engaged in the region and trying to have balanced and strong relations with both countries'.[15]

Thoroughly innocuous as these words were to most Americans, they must have unsettled readers in South Block, who for many years had resisted an American policy of lumping India and Pakistan together in pursuit of a 'balanced' US approach. The easy manner in which Powell expressed a willingness to help on Kashmir and nuclear tensions – issues where New Delhi had no interest in seeing an American involvement, especially not a 'balanced' one – was equally unwelcome.

A closer reading of the Indian response to Bush's missile defense speech might have dampened enthusiasm in Washington as well. The more skeptical noted that India had reasons of its own to encourage Bush's perception of threats arising from rogue nations driven by Islamic fundamentalism. Some commentators wondered if New Delhi's apparent BMD endorsement reflected anything more than an Indian desire to gain access to American nuclear energy technology, especially reactors. These more cautious interpretations were strengthened when Jaswant Singh, visiting Moscow in June, publicly insisted that Indian and Russian views on BMD were identical, and that New Delhi opposed any unilateral abrogation of the ABM treaty. In conveying two starkly contradictory messages on missile defense to the Americans and the Russians, Singh, acute observers concluded, had played the Americans like a virtuoso musician.

Other disquieting developments were visible for those who wished to see them. Notwithstanding Bush's telephoned pledge of assistance to Prime Minister Vajpayee, and grandiose promises from Capitol Hill of a liberal American response, the actual levels of US aid to earthquake-hit Gujarat were quite modest. Worse yet were hints that the administration had actually discouraged a more generous package of aid for fear of complicating congressional adoption of a tax cut, the White House's top domestic priority.

The administration was also slow in moving to lift the Glenn amendment sanctions imposed on India in 1998. The United States would determine the future of sanctions, Washington explained, only after completing a general review of sanctions policy. Not until mid-August did senior Bush officials explicitly state the sanctions would be removed, and even then they spoke of the need to consult first with a Congress currently in recess.[16] Few doubted that a way would ultimately be found to get rid of the sanctions, but the administration's failure to move in this regard with even moderate speed raised eyebrows in New Delhi. And of course the Glenn sanctions represented the least difficult of several types of American restrictions that limited the sale or transfer of high-tech goods to India. Other restrictions dated back to the 1970s, and barred the export of dual-use technology and items that could contribute to India's nuclear or missile programs. This precluded the transfer of civilian nuclear technology as well as cooperation and technical assistance on nuclear safety issues.

By this time, US sanctions had importance for India more for symbolic than for practical reasons. American sanctions, New Delhi insisted, were an anachronistic remnant of an attitude where one country believed it had the moral authority to levy sanctions against another. Sanctions reflected an American assumption that nuclear weapons were permissible for the United States but not for India. What place, Indians asked, did such thinking have in this new friendship between sovereign equals? Worse yet, India, which prided itself on its unblemished record of not assisting other countries to acquire nuclear capabilities, found itself under US nonproliferation sanctions, whereas China, for which there was ample evidence about its nuclear weapons assistance to other nations, was not sanctioned. As one Indian scholar bitingly remarked, 'China gets only words, we get the boot'.

Washington's deliberate pace in moving to lift the Glenn amendment sanctions reflected the policy dilemma confronting the new Bush administration. A statement issued by the State Department in mid-February inadvertently underscored the problem. In calling on Russia to cancel an agreement to ship nuclear fuel to the Tarapur power reactors in India, the department appeared to equate this action with Moscow's far more provocative policy of providing Iran with sensitive nuclear assistance. Secretary of Defense Rumsfeld raised tempers in New Delhi further when he casually lumped India, as a recipient of Russian missile technology, with such pariah states as Iran and North Korea.

In fact, the Bush administration was not nearly as ready as many in India assumed to walk away from the edifice of nonproliferation treaties, international agreements, and US legislation that had grown up over the past generation. Say what they would about 'obsolete' arms control treaties, Bush officials nonetheless were as keen to keep weapons of mass destruction out of the hands of the North Koreas, Irans, and Iraqs of the world as had been the Clinton administration. As they surveyed their options, Bush's new officials discovered a certain utility in at least portions of the existing international nonproliferation regime, even if they did not trumpet this judgment.

Moreover, the 1998 Indian and Pakistani tests, and the failure of US efforts to prevent them, had not lessened the concerns that had led successive American presidents from both political parties to emphasize nonproliferation and restraint in their policies toward the subcontinent. To the contrary, these concerns, amidst heightened Pakistani-Indian tensions, were as pressing as ever. This too stayed those who might otherwise have been prepared to de-emphasize or even abandon US nonproliferation efforts in the region.

Proponents in the Bush administration of a fresh American approach to South Asia ran up against the same conundrum that had bedeviled their predecessors: How to recognize the reality of India's overt nuclear weapons status without undermining US hopes of blocking the further spread of these weapons? Would the United States undercut its hopes of keeping nuclear weapons out of the hands of Saddam Hussein by frankly acknowledging that the international nonproliferation regime did not envision, and made no provisions for, nuclear-armed India and Pakistan? The inability to demonstrate that a more open acceptance of India's nuclear weapons status would not have adverse proliferation consequences in the Middle East or elsewhere around the world constituted the single greatest difficulty confronting India's friends in Washington, and largely explained why the administration did not move more quickly to lift the Glenn sanctions.

In a perverse way, then, the greatest threat to a healthy US-India relationship as the new Bush team settled in may have been its successes of the past few years, and the overblown expectations that had been generated. When discussing the relationship, there was a tendency in some quarters, both American and Indian, toward cheerleading or boosterism. One frequently encountered exaggerated claims for the relationship, and an automatic assumption that American and Indian interests mesh.

Vajpayee's use of the phrase 'natural allies' to describe the US-India partnership was a case in point. As an expression of optimism about the future, perhaps it was a felicitous passage. But for most of the past half century, Dennis Kux's 'estranged democracies' constituted a far more apt and accurate description. In comparison to American ties with Europe and Japan, US-India relations contained little of the richness, variety, or ease of communication common to these more established US partnerships.

Partners in Arms

The September 11 attacks and the ensuing war against international terrorism appeared to open up a new and more meaningful venue for Indo-American collaboration. New Delhi's speedy offer of unprecedented intelligence and military cooperation was met with gratitude and tangible marks of appreciation from Washington. The long-delayed decision to lift the remainder of the 1998 nuclear-related sanctions was announced.

The pace of high-level visits in both directions accelerated. Jaswant Singh and Vajpayee's national security adviser Brajesh Mishra made separate trips to Washington in the first weeks after the attacks. Colin Powell and Donald Rumsfeld each journeyed to New Delhi for consultations and coordination; Rumsfeld's visit represented the first to New Delhi by an American secretary of defense since 1995. Bush telephoned the prime minister to alert him that the US bombing campaign against Afghanistan was about to commence. And in mid-November, Vajpayee himself visited Washington, where he had a full round of meetings with the president and senior administration and congressional officials.

As Ambassador Blackwill rightly pointed out, the frequency, intensity, and transparency of Indo-American contacts had all increased dramatically.

Absent the tragic events of September 11, Blackwill observed, it would have taken years for the two countries to reach that level of cooperation.[17] No wonder many concluded that the efforts over the previous few years to create a more robust US-India partnership had borne fruit of the richest variety.

Yet within weeks of the September 11 attacks, cracks in the facade of Indo-American solidarity had begun to appear. Many Indians were angered when it became apparent that Washington, anxious to enlist allies in the war against terrorism, sought to resurrect something of its Cold War partnership with Pakistan. Once highly critical of the military regime run by General Pervez Musharraf, Washington now seemed intent upon welcoming Musharraf as a full-fledged and highly esteemed partner in the international coalition against terrorism. The Bush administration lifted US sanctions against Islamabad, pledged to provide generous assistance and to help Pakistan renegotiate its debt obligations, and in countless other ways gave the Musharraf government a legitimacy and a respectability it had never before enjoyed. 'To Indians', observed the *Hindustan Times*, 'this is like revisiting a nightmare'.[18]

Tempers in New Delhi rose further following the 1 October attack on the state assembly building in the Kashmiri capital, Srinagar, which killed 38 people. Washington displayed marked reluctance to accept India's contention that the terrorism emanating from Afghanistan was inextricably linked to the violence in Kashmir. Bush had promised an all-out fight against international terrorism and the states that harbor terrorists, but he appeared both deaf and blind to Pakistani-backed terrorism in Kashmir. At a minimum, India believed, the Bush administration should insist that Islamabad shut down the training camps, logistical support, and other assistance it offered the Kashmiri insurgents. Some Indians went further, and argued that if Bush's declarations meant anything, he would have no choice but to move against Pakistani-based organizations implicated in the violence in the Kashmir Valley, and perhaps even to label Pakistan itself a state sponsor of terrorism.

Rather than accepting India's assertion that Pakistan was responsible for the Srinigar assault, however, Bush dispatched Colin Powell to the region to tell both countries to 'cool it', an action, New Delhi believed, that equated the victim and the criminal. The United States, many Indians concluded, was guilty of a double standard – calling for full-throttled war against those perpetrating violence on American shores, while ignoring terror directed against India. Strategic analyst Brahma Chellaney spoke for many of his countrymen when he complained that by helping Musharraf solidify his hold on power, the United States was 'building up a fiendish general whose concrete record of covert and terrorist operations against India parallels the mythologised record of... Osama bin Laden's terrorist exploits'.[19] 'The time for diplomatic niceties is over', an Indian diplomat darkly observed on the eve of Powell's arrival in New Delhi. India, noted a New Delhi correspondent, 'has reached the end of its tether'.[20]

But worse was to come. On 13 December, an even more daring attack, this time on the parliament complex in the middle of New Delhi, threw the region into a full-blown crisis. Once again the Vajpayee government had no doubt that Pakistan was responsible for the outrage. In the succeeding weeks tensions escalated as Indian public opinion demanded an accounting. Air, train, and bus service between India and Pakistan was terminated. India withdrew its high commissioner in Islamabad for the first time since the 1971 Indo-Pakistani war. The armed forces of both countries went on heightened alert and took up advanced positions along the border. Initial American calls for restraint and suggestions for a joint Indo-Pakistani inquiry into the incident were disdainfully swept aside by New Delhi. The smell of war hung in the air.

Now genuinely alarmed that events were about to spiral out of control, Washington moved forcefully to dampen tensions and to show New Delhi that the United States took seriously its accusations about Pakistan's complicity in the Srinigar and New Delhi attacks. The administration – remarkably belatedly, in Indian eyes – placed the two Pakistan-based groups India deemed responsible for the Srinigar and New Delhi attacks on the US list of terrorist organizations. While not publicly accepting India's claim that the Pakistani government itself was implicated in terrorist activities, Washington's words and actions clearly implied that Islamabad could and must do more to crack down on terrorism.

Over a period of several weeks Colin Powell worked the telephones assiduously, in what may represent the most intensive involvement ever on a South Asian issue by an American secretary of state. Bush telephoned Vajpayee as well, urging patience while emphasizing that his administration had no intention of ignoring Indian concerns. L. K. Advani, India's powerful home minister, and George Fernandes, the defense minister, visited Washington in consecutive weeks in January. And Powell in mid-January made his second trip to the region in three months.

In other ways as well, the experience of fighting a common enemy drew the two countries together, even as the United States politely declined New Delhi's offer of bases for operations in Afghanistan. Washington provided monitoring equipment and sensors to assist the Indian army in preventing infiltration across the line of control in Kashmir. In early December, the

Indo-American Defense Policy Group met to discuss joint military training and exercises, cooperation in search and rescue, peacekeeping, and disaster relief efforts, and Indian participation in missile defense exercises.

Also on the agenda were arms sales, opening up the possibility of Indian purchases of major weapons platforms of a sort never before permitted. Following the mid-December attack on parliament, the two stepped up their intelligence sharing, with the Americans handing over sensitive information relating to Pakistan's complicity in the assault. Remarking on how the two countries had stood shoulder-to-shoulder in the fight against terrorism, and deliberately echoing Vajpayee's formulation, Powell told a New Delhi press conference that India and the United States were 'natural allies, two great democracies who believe in a common set of values'. A few weeks later, Bush underscored the point. 'My administration', he pledged, 'is committed to developing a fundamentally different relationship with India.'[21]

The Security Dimension

The community of interests seemingly highlighted by the September 11 attacks reinforced a perception already common in both countries of a broader political and strategic 'complementarity' of interests pulling India and the United States together. There is, the *Telegraph* had editorialized earlier that spring, a 'growing strategic convergence' between the two countries.[22] India is now ready to be 'a strategic partner of the highest caliber' for the United States, a Washington think-tank analyst observed.[23]

Briefing reporters in mid-July, the Bush administration's newly-confirmed assistant secretary of state for South Asian affairs repeatedly referred to the 'strategic ties' Washington sought to build with India.[24] The United States wished 'to engage India in a strategic dialogue that encompasses the full range of global issues', the US trade representative had added. The administration 'appreciates that India's influence clearly extends far beyond South Asia'.[25]

Yet the closer one peers, the less substantial one finds those 'strategic' linkages and convergences allegedly drawing the United States and India together. True, officials in both capitals today are far more aware of their common interests and shared perspectives, and far more open in talking about them, than their predecessors of a decade or a generation ago. But the process of translating these similar concerns into joint or coordinated policies has barely begun. Moreover, the two countries continue to differ on many of the very issues that are cited as furnishing a basis for collaboration.

In the Middle East, for instance, the two have very different ideas on policy toward both Iran and Iraq. During a four-day visit to Tehran in April

2001, Vajpayee signaled the cordiality of Indian-Iranian ties by formalizing a new strategic pact obligating the two countries to working closely together in opposition to the Taliban and other forces that could destabilize west and central Asia. Vajpayee is reportedly reviewing new arms sales to Tehran, which would complement training New Delhi is already providing Iranian naval personnel and no doubt unsettle many in the Bush administration. On Iraq, a similar gap between Indian and American positions exists. New Delhi has little sympathy for the American insistence on maintaining sanctions against Baghdad, deplores US characterization of Iraq as a 'rogue state', and is eager to pursue business opportunities in, and secure a steady supply of oil from, Iraq.

Southeast Asia, another region described as a venue for US-Indian cooperation, is hardly more promising. New Delhi, its 'Look East policy' notwithstanding, has few assets and little ability to influence events in the region. Aside from occasional port calls and high-level visits, its presence in Southeast Asia is minimal, and the mechanisms for Indo-American collaboration not apparent. While the Indian government seeks a more cordial relationship with the military junta in Burma, Washington holds the regime at arms length. It is not by accident that the United States has been decidedly unenthusiastic about New Delhi's aspirations for membership in the Asia-Pacific Economic Cooperation (APEC) forum.

Moreover, it is difficult to imagine a meaningful strategic partnership where one partner maintains sanctions against the other. In the weeks after September 11, Bush lifted the remaining sanctions that had been imposed following India's nuclear tests in 1998, but other restrictions pertaining to nuclear and missile technology transfers remain in force. These will probably be removed in due course, but until then, New Delhi will be blocked from acquiring radars, antimissile defense systems, and other items it badly wants. Beyond that, the continued existence of sanctions of any sort will serve as a constant reminder to many Indians that the United States does not yet regard them as full-fledged partners and sovereign equals.

It is true that Washington and New Delhi have discussed increased military cooperation in non-controversial fields such as peacekeeping, search and rescue, disaster response and humanitarian assistance, and environmental security. But joint action in these areas of peripheral or secondary importance does not indicate a genuine strategic partnership, any more than cooperation on HIV/AIDS, white collar crime, or women- and child-trafficking. To the contrary, an emphasis on these forms of cooperation as a substitute for convergence on issues more directly associated with traditional political and security concerns may well indicate an immature partnership still searching for a raison d'être.

An Anti-China Consortium?

There remains the important matter of China. Indians have neither forgotten nor forgiven China's close ties with Pakistan, links that up to the present day give Pakistan a military capability far greater than anything Islamabad could achieve by itself. Reports in early 2001 of new transfers of Chinese ballistic missile technology to Pakistan – notwithstanding Chinese pledges to eschew all such transfers – underscored Beijing's continued challenge to India's basic security interests. Recollections of India's humiliating defeat in its 1962 conflict with China reinforce current strategic concerns, while China's apparent indifference to Indian desires to resolve their decades-old border disputes fosters additional suspicions about Chinese intentions. Confronting an unfriendly neighbor along its northern border, some in India argue, New Delhi would do well to seek a closer strategic relationship with the United States.

This judgment about the usefulness of a US-India strategic partnership as a hedge should relations with Beijing sour finds adherents in Washington as well. Some Americans – in and outside government – appear eager to enlist New Delhi in an anti-China grouping of some sort. A number of prominent members of Congress, from both political parties, have publicly called for a closer security relationship with India for precisely this reason. Former Secretary of the Navy James Webb, who enjoys close ties to many senior officials in the Bush administration, has written that the president should more vigorously cultivate ties with New Delhi since India is 'a natural and historic counterpoint to Chinese expansionism'.[26] Webb may be more forthright in expressing his opinions than some in Washington, but those opinions are by no means unusual.

Yet, New Delhi would make a mistake to base its policy on the assumption that the United States is prepared to join forces with India in a partnership aimed against China. For one thing, while some in Washington believe that China is destined to become an adversary, this is not the majority opinion, either within the Bush administration or among Americans generally. Washington, for all the talk during the presidential campaign about 'strategic competition' with China, is hardly eager for a more adversarial relationship with Beijing. Witness the annual votes in Congress on China's trade status, or the speed with which the Bush administration moved to repair relations with Beijing following the April 2001 standoff over the detention of an American aircrew.

Absent irrefutable evidence of Chinese antagonism, the United States is likely to be very cautious about creating groupings overtly anti-Chinese in nature. Even should Washington eventually decide that it has no choice but to assemble an anti-China coalition, it is not entirely clear that India would be a logical partner. Mid-level US military officers familiar with Indian capabilities express bewilderment at the Pentagon's eagerness to accelerate military-to-military contacts. As an ally, they suggest, New Delhi might represent a strategic liability as much as an asset.

Nor would most Indians be eager to join with the United States in an anti-China consortium in which they would inevitably be the junior partner. Of course India's views on China in the coming years will be heavily influenced by China's relations with Pakistan, and more specifically, whether Beijing persists in assisting Islamabad in its nuclear and missile programs. If China continues such assistance, the idea of a closer partnership with Washington will gain new adherents in New Delhi. But if Beijing pursues a moderately prudent and restrained course in its assistance programs for Pakistan, India will have little incentive to join a US-led grouping directed against China. New Delhi rightly recognizes that aligning with the United States in a combination aimed at China would only encourage Beijing to step up its transfers of threatening technology to Islamabad, or to take other measures that would create difficulties for India, such as siding with India's neighbors, including Bangladesh and Burma, who have disputes with New Delhi, or even supporting secessionist groups in India's northeast.

Moreover, the improvement in US-India ties over the past several years appears to have prodded Beijing to repair its own relationship with New Delhi. The breach in Sino-Indian relations that followed the 1998 nuclear tests has been largely mended. Barely a year after New Delhi publicly justified its tests by pointing to a threat from China, the two countries announced the establishment of a 'strategic dialogue'.

Beijing has also significantly modified its traditional support for Islamabad on Kashmir. If China continues to display at least a modest level of sensitivity to Indian concerns, this too will reduce India's compulsion to join with the Americans in a consortium directed against the Chinese. To the contrary, foreign entanglements of this sort would strike many Indians as a foolish diversion of resources from more pressing domestic concerns. As a senior Indian diplomat recently put it, 'our main priority right now is to develop ourselves, and to stay clear of international entanglements.'

Doubts about the United States will also limit whatever attractions the idea of a US-India bloc might otherwise have. New Delhi is not at all certain that its geostrategic interests are the same as America's, no matter the fine talk about convergent views. The most likely source of Sino-American conflict over the next few years, for instance, is Taiwan. But Taiwan is hardly a core concern for India. Indeed, it is difficult to imagine any circumstances where New Delhi would have a vital interest in a conflict originating in the Taiwan Strait.

In addition, many Indians harbor doubts about the long-term staying power of the United States. Neither old-style Nehruvians nor steely-eyed realists are convinced that Washington would be a dependable ally. And the last thing India would want, in this view, is to adopt an advanced position vis-à-vis China, only to have the Americans lose interest or change their minds.

In short, although voices calling for closer strategic ties directed against a rising China can be heard in both India and the United States, calmer heads counseling restraint are likely to prevail. There is no 'India card' that Washington might try to play in its competition with Beijing. Moreover, New Delhi in the coming years will probably find it much more useful to use an 'American card' to foster a more cooperative attitude from China than a 'China card' to promote closer strategic ties with Washington.

Economic Linkages

For much of the past decade, economic ties were frequently lauded as the force pulling the United States and India together; they would provide the 'ballast' for the relationship, in the conventional formulation. The economic liberalization New Delhi initiated in 1991 persuaded many in the American business community that India was the next 'emerging market'. Indeed, President Clinton's Commerce Department awarded India this designation, and until recently the department had a larger presence in India than anywhere else in the world.

The success of India's information technology sector, and the high percentage of Indians and Indian-Americans in California's Silicon Valley and other US high-tech centers, lent further credence to the belief that India represented a new and largely untapped reservoir of opportunity. Trade and investment, the Indian ambassador in Washington observed in mid-2001, had emerged as 'the prime mover' in the bilateral relationship.[27]

Alas, harsh realities have yet to catch up to the enticing expectations. Today, ten years after the inauguration of India's reform program, the country remains a bit player in the overall American economic picture. While the United States is India's largest trade partner and source of foreign investment, two-way trade between the two countries still represents less than one per cent of America's total overseas commerce. Trade between India and the United States in 2000 totaled $14.4 billion, that between China and the United States $116.2 billion.[28]

This disparity is all the more striking given India's inherent advantages over China, including a developed legal system and the prevalence of the English language. Belgium buys nearly three and one-half times as much from American producers as does India, with a hundred times the population. Thailand on a per capita basis purchases 23 times as much[29] from the United States as does India, Malaysia 111 times as much. The investment picture is only marginally less bleak. While US direct investment in India has grown over the past decade, the city of Shanghai still draws more American investment than all of India. Worse yet, many of the US firms that flocked to India in the mid-1990s – by some accounts, a majority – have since packed their bags and returned home to await a more propitious business climate.

For many American business people, the difficulties experienced in Maharashtra by the US energy giant Enron have become a metaphor for the frustrations of doing business in India. The relative merits of the grievances of the Texas-based corporation and the Maharashtra State Electricity Board have by now become almost irrelevant. Instead, Enron has become a cautionary story for American investors and corporate chieftains. Influenced by Enron's travails, many US companies appear to have concluded that doing business in India is just not worth the aggravation.

For all the hoopla about India's 'opening up' its economy to the outside world, New Delhi's pace of reform has been very measured. According to the widely-noted *2001 Index of Economic Freedom*, India has one of the world's least free economies, ranking 133rd out of the 155 countries surveyed.[30] Despite substantial tariff reductions, for instance, India still possesses some of the highest tariff barriers in the world. US exports to India during the 1990s grew by a paltry $1.2 billion – despite the celebrated 'opening' of India's economy.[31]

Until India makes progress in the so-called 'second wave' of liberalization – including privatization, deregulation, freeing up capital flows, reducing subsidies, and reforming labor laws – the American business community is unlikely to find India an attractive venue for expansion. Yet real doubts persist whether the current government in New Delhi, or any likely successor, has either the will or the political muscle to push the reform agenda forward.

Finally, there exists a further difficulty in expecting these very modest levels of economic activity to serve as the ballast for a more substantial relationship between Washington and New Delhi. The fact of the matter is that the two countries have fundamental differences on many of the day's most important economic questions – the North-South divide, for instance, or the priorities of the World Trade Organization. US Trade Representative Robert Zoellick publicly singled out India as an especially 'troublesome' country in building a consensus for new international trade negotiations.[32] At the Doha trade summit in late 2001, India and the United States found themselves on opposing sides of the question on many of the most contentious issues. Rather than bringing the two countries together, economic issues threaten to pull them apart.

A Community of Democracies?

Nor – for all the talk about 'the world's two largest democracies' – do shared values and a common commitment to political pluralism guarantee a complementarity of interests or purposes. The two countries appear to have different ideas, for instance, on what their shared allegiance to democracy implies for policy. In the United Nations General Assembly, they come down on opposite sides of important resolutions as often as not. At the Community of Democracies summit in Warsaw in July 2000, Washington lobbied to show a videotaped message from Burma's opposition leader Aung San Suu Kyi. New Delhi, however, which seeks to cultivate better ties with Burma's military junta, opposed this affront to Rangoon's sensibilities. In truth, the 'democracy linkage' is perhaps a necessary, but certainly not a sufficient, ingredient for the forging of a long-term stable partnership between the United States and India. Shared democratic values did not keep the two from quarreling in the past, nor will they guarantee a convergence of interests in the future.

In truth, many Indians have yet to decide just what sort of relationship they want with the United States. For all the celebratory words emanating from New Delhi concerning the vastly improved tone in US-India relations, India remains conflicted and unsure about its new partner.

How else to explain the pronounced warmth in ties between India and Russia, which goes far beyond anything demanded by old bonds of friendship? Indo-Russian relations possess a cordiality out of all proportion to the material inducements Moscow offers India, and are pursued by New Delhi even at the risk of offending a Washington still inclined to suspect Russian intentions. When Russian President Vladimir Putin visited India in late 2000, the two countries announced the creation of a new 'strategic partnership'.

While insisting that they did not seek to revive their Cold War alliance, Vajpayee and Putin called for a 'multipolar global structure', which could only be interpreted as a rejection of the current international order where the United States is unrivaled in economic clout and military might. On Vajpayee's return visit to Moscow in November 2001, the two sides reaffirmed their renewed friendship and agreed on new Russian arms sales to New Delhi.

Washington has no need to fear, let alone condemn, this rejuvenated Russo-Indian relationship. Even so, it seems obvious that one of the principal motivations driving New Delhi is an uneasiness over too close an embrace by the world's sole superpower. An excessive reliance on the United States, Indian analysts have warned, would give Washington unwelcome leverage over India. The Indian government no doubt sees a revived relationship with Moscow as giving it maneuvering room so as to escape Washington's smothering clutches.

The situation is further complicated by the fact that not all Indians have moved beyond an attitude toward the United States, common until recently, that identified America and Americans as the source of most of the world's problems. As one American observer has acerbically remarked, India's political and intellectual élites have historically combined 'the most insular tendencies of Fabian socialism, tiermondisme and a British public school-bred snobbery into an especially intense variety of anti-Americanism.'[33] Many Indians are still quite capable of seeing a hidden American hand, a sinister American conspiracy, behind events. And what constitutes 'leadership' in the eyes of many Americans all too often appears more like 'hegemony' in India. These unfavorable attitudes and stereotypes possess nowhere near the strength they once had, but they persist and inevitably color the way Indians of a certain generation and background view relations with Washington.[34]

So it is only prudent that the United States avoid getting too carried away with Vajpayee's evocation of a 'natural' alliance linking Washington and New Delhi. To characterize the formulation 'natural allies' as nothing more than a rhetorical flourish, designed to please an American audience, goes too far. Nonetheless, Indian sources suggest that the phrase first attracted the prime minister's notice when Fidel Castro employed it during a meeting of the Nonaligned Movement (NAM) to describe the relationship between the NAM and the Soviet Union. Vajpayee, then India's foreign minister, had attended the meeting and remembered the phrase, although by the time he recycled it to describe the US-India relationship, he may no longer have recalled its genesis. Most Americans, nonetheless, would not find its paternity reassuring.

Or take something seemingly as straightforward as Vajpayee's speech before a joint session of Congress during his September 2000 Washington visit. Many would see the occasion of this address – an honor not extended more than every year or two – as another indication of the vibrancy of Indo-American relations. Unfortunately, the more prosaic reality is that US domestic politics and calculations of electoral advantage probably played as large a role as affection for India or belief in the importance of ties with New Delhi in the decision by House Speaker Dennis Hastert to invite Vajpayee to address the joint session.

Hastert's invitation to the prime minister did, however, reflect a newfound appreciation among US politicians of the value of courting the Indian-American community. This community, now nearly 1.7 million strong, is frequently cited as a reason for optimism about the future of US-India relations. Such faith in the growing economic and political clout of the community is not misplaced. Indian-Americans command a respectful attention from US politicians that would have been unimaginable as recently as a decade ago.[35]

But here, once more, aspirations tend to outrun realities. For one thing, the Indian-American community has yet to develop a political maturity commensurate with its economic and educational attainments. The community is riven by personality conflicts and competing organizations, each jockeying for access and influence and rarely working in a coordinated fashion.[36] Indian-Americans need to develop a greater sophistication both in recognizing their friends and in the way in which they interact with those friends.

For instance, some community activists have berated several of their closest allies on Capitol Hill for including Pakistan in a South Asian fact-finding trip. The demand that supporters abandon even a hint of independent judgment is certain to create resentment among India's congressional friends. Moreover, the community has yet to learn how to demand accountability from those elected officials who claim to speak for its interests. Several members of the US Congress, for example, who at the time of the Gujarat earthquake early in 2001 loudly advertised their support for a generous American response to the disaster, subsequently voted against a US aid package. Until the community better understands how to translate its economic muscle into actual and not just rhetorical political support, it will not exercise the influence on behalf of closer US-India ties many assume it already has.

Another way to gauge the current state of Indo-American relations, and to determine where they might be strengthened, is to compare this relationship with other US bilateral relationships that have been deemed important, even 'special'. Here one thinks, among others, of Washington's ties to the United Kingdom and to Israel. And judged by this standard, one again cannot help but be impressed by the limited nature of US-India ties.

What, historically, has made a relationship 'special' for the United States? In virtually every instance, agreement upon a strategic agenda or vision has existed. In most cases, a common security threat has furnished the glue in America's 'special relationships'. The perception of a shared threat has then promoted close collaboration in the strategic and defense spheres, including integrated planning, joint training and operations, and the provision of sophisticated US military technology. Several (though not all) of Washington's closest partnerships have extended this technology sharing into the missile and nuclear fields.

Intelligence cooperation has been another distinguishing characteristic of America's most intimate friendships. Special relationships between countries or governments are usually marked as well by warm personal ties, starting at the top but running throughout the bureaucracy. These close personal links facilitate the development of informal, back-channel avenues of communication and ensure a continual back-and-forth that characterizes and sustains the special quality of these bilateral partnerships. Finally, special relationships usually exist not only at official levels, but also at the popular level. Absent widespread emotional ties, feelings of kinship (literal or figurative), or a sense of common enterprise, no relationship between two nations will long be viewed as special.

It is not at all clear that any of these characteristics are to be found in US-India relations at present, or can be expected to develop beyond a fairly rudimentary state in the near future. The attention that high-level visits from American officials receive in India suggests they lack the routine character one would expect in a special relationship. The inattention similar visits from senior Indian officials receive in Washington suggests the same thing.[37] And notwithstanding the dramatic change in the American conception of India and Indians – as high-tech entrepreneurs have shoved aside earlier images of destitute beggars – India has a long way to go before it achieves a standing in the American mindset comparable to that held by Britain in the 1940s or 1950s, or that enjoyed by Israel among influential segments of American society today.

The Road Ahead

In a whole host of ways, this is a healthier, more collaborative and mutually-beneficial relationship than Washington and New Delhi have seen in many years, if ever. An important shift has taken place in American thinking about India and its place on the world map. For a growing number of Americans, including many senior officials, India is no longer merely a South Asian country, but one with a reach and a role extending well beyond the subcontinent. For most of the past half century, Washington policymakers linked India and Pakistan as two more or less equals. Now that equation is seldom made. Compared with the past, there exists today, in both the United States and India, a far larger number of individuals and interests with a clear-cut stake in a flourishing bilateral relationship.

Yet, for all the celebratory talk about a new partnership between Washington and New Delhi, much hard work remains to be done before this relationship meets the expectations of its most enthusiastic proponents. A note of caution would appear in order in the face of the uncritical enthusiasm that passes for strategic analysis in some circles, American and Indian, at the moment. Certainly we should applaud the healthy new tone to Indo-American relations that recent years have fostered. But unrestrained giddiness about 'paradigm shifts' or a strategic rapprochement between India and the United States is premature.

To the contrary, substantive differences over the nature and goals of Indo-American partnership are likely to complicate future relations between the world's two largest democracies. A short list of issues where Washington and New Delhi will find it difficult to collaborate would include Pakistan, China, Iran, Iraq, the World Trade Organization, and the future of the global nonproliferation regime. India will continue to prefer a multipolar world order, whereas the Bush administration, even more than Clinton's, is likely to assert US dominance and insist on Washington's right to act unilaterally.

Nor is New Delhi going to be satisfied with what it will inevitably interpret as an American failure to accord India its due. The Bush administration is not likely to give India the free hand in South Asia it desires, or openly acknowledge Indian hegemony in the region. It will not grant New Delhi the formal, legal status of a nuclear weapons state, even if it accepts the *de facto* existence of an Indian nuclear arsenal.

It will oppose Indian actions, such as missile development and deployment, that Washington sees as a threat to the stability of the subcontinent, even as it accepts few limitations on its own right to act as its security needs dictate. It will not support India's bid to become a permanent member of the UN Security Council, especially if New Delhi demands admittance on the same terms as the original five members – that is, with a veto. And it will continue to lavish far more attention and energy on China than on India. This of course will reflect the troubled nature of the Sino-American relationship. But it will also elbow India off the personal radar screens of US officials and feed anxieties in New Delhi that India is being slighted, ignored, or taken for granted.

To raise doubts about the depth of current relations is not to decry the very real and significant changes in the tenor of the relationship in recent years. Nor is it to challenge the value attributed to a vigorous Indo-American partnership by influential people in each of the two countries. It is merely to suggest that for all the gains that have occurred, US-India ties will require constant attention lest the two nations lapse back into old habits and suspicions that have made this relationship a difficult one for so long. Grandiose expectations and overblown rhetoric do not help.

Washington is now ready to embrace India. But the United States, like all countries, will determine its policies according to calculations of interest. It is up to New Delhi to demonstrate to the Americans that it is in their interest to institutionalize a new and closer partnership with India. Indian actions, at home as much as abroad, will have a large role in determining the future of this relationship. Building a vibrant economy, accelerating reform, solidifying democratic institutions and values, investing in its human and capital infrastructure, improving relations with its neighbors, meeting the needs and aspirations of its people: If India takes care of these matters, it will be a success – and an irresistible partner to the world's sole remaining superpower.

NOTES

This essay, completed in mid-January 2002, covers developments through 2001.

1. *Far Eastern Economic Review*, 3 May 2001, p.66.
2. William B. Saxbe with Peter D. Franklin, *I've Seen the Elephant: An Autobiography* (Kent, OH: Kent State University Press 2000) p.209.
3. *Washington Post*, 17 Sept. 2001.
4. Dennis Kux, *India and the United States: Estranged Democracies* (Washington DC: National Defense University Press 1992); Andrew J. Rotter, *Comrades at Odds: The United States and India, 1947–1964* (Ithaca, NY: Cornell University Press 2000); H. W. Brands, *India and the United States: The Cold Peace* (Boston: Twayne 1990).
5. Sec. 102 (b) of the Arms Export Control Act.
6. Commentator C. Raja Mohan, writing in *The Hindu*, 25 March 2001.
7. Joint Statement by Prime Minister Vajpayee and President Clinton, 15 Sept. 2000.
8. Satu P. Lamaye, 'Stuck in a Nuclear Narrative', Pacific Forum CSIS Comparative Connections, www.csis.org/pacfor/cc/0101Qoa.html.
9. Or as the American ambassador in New Delhi would later say, the United States would no longer be 'a nagging nanny'. *Telegraph* editorial, 6 April 2001; Mohan in *The Hindu*, 25 March 2001; 'The Future of US-India Relations', speech by US Ambassador Robert D. Blackwill, 6 Sept. 2001, Mumbai.
10. *Telegraph* editorial, 6 April 2001.
11. *The Hindu*, 10 April 2001.
12. *Defense News*, 23 April 2001, p.3; Mark W. Frazier, 'Problems and Prospects for India-China Relations', p.10, manuscript in the author's possession.
13. *The Hindu*, 5 May 2001.
14. *The Pioneer*, 8 May 2001.

15. www.state.gov/secretary/rm/2001/index.cfm?docid=4166.
16. *Washington Post*, 12 Aug. 2001.
17. *India Abroad*, 5 Oct. 2001.
18. *Hindustan Times*, 5 Oct. 2001.
19. www.rediff.com/news/2001/oct/15brahma.htm.
20. www.rediff.com/us/2001/oct/16ny2.htm.
21. Powell in *New York Times*, 17 Oct. 2001; Bush in ibid. 10 Nov. 2001.
22. *Telegraph* editorial, 6 April 2001.
23. Victor M. Gobarev, 'India as a World Power: Changing Washington's Myopic Policy', *CATO Institute Policy Analysis* No.381, 11 Sept. 2000.
24. *Times of India*, 21 July 2001.
25. *New York Times*, 27 Aug. 2001.
26. *Wall Street Journal*, 13 April 2001. See Mohammed Ayoob, 'Rocky Road to Asian Peace', *Washington Times*, 8 Nov. 2001, for another example.
27. Remarks by Ambassador Lalit Mansingh, 20 June 2001, Washington.
28. US Census Bureau figures, in www.census.gov/foreign-trade/balance/c5330.html and www.census.gov/foreign-trade/balance/c5700.html.
29. International Monetary Fund, *Direction of Trade Statistics Yearbook, 2000* (Washington DC: IMF 2000) pp.474–75. These trade figures are from 1999. Statistics from 1997, before the Asian financial crisis stifled trade flows in Southeast Asia, would reveal an even more lop-sided picture.
30. Larry M. Wortzel and Dana R. Dillon, 'Improving Relations with India Without Compromising US Security', Heritage Foundation Backgrounder No.1402, 11 Dec., 2000.
31. US Census Bureau figures, in www.census.gov/foreign-trade/balance/c5330.html.
32. *Far Eastern Economic Review*, 11 Oct. 2001, p.37.
33. *Asian Wall Street Journal*, 22 Aug. 2001.
34. George Fernandes, Indian defense minister, recently singled out radical Noam Chomsky as an American whose views he particularly admired, an admission that must surely have raised eyebrows in the Pentagon. Fernandes' assumption of the defense portfolio from the unabashedly pro-American Jaswant Singh in the weeks after September 11 prompted new questions about the durability of the enhanced defense ties between the two countries. See *India Abroad*, 9 Nov. 2001, for the Chomsky reference. For a recent look at how culturally-induced images influenced US-India relations in an earlier era, see Rotter, *Comrades at Odds* (note 4).
35. For background on the growing political clout of the Indian-American community, see Robert M. Hathaway, 'Unfinished Passage: India, Indian Americans, and the US Congress', *Washington Quarterly* 24 (Spring 2001) pp.21–34.
36. For one such example, see www.rediff.com/news/2001/nov/06vaj1.htm.
37. See, for instance, the anguished comments by one Indian analyst about the absence of US press coverage of Vajpayee's November 2001 visit to Washington. www.rediff.com/news/2001/nov/13flip.htm.

3

India, Pakistan and Kashmir

STEPHEN PHILIP COHEN

India has for several years been regarded as an emerging or rising state.[1] After decades of unfulfilled promise, it now seems to be inching ahead, with more rapid economic growth, new attention from the major powers, and the development of a modest nuclear arsenal. Adding these developments to India's traditional strengths – a unique and persistent democracy and an influential culture – it is no wonder that many have predicted the emergence of India as a major Asian power, or even a world-class state. However, this remains a problematic development as long as India's comprehensive and debilitating rivalry with Pakistan continues, including that dimension of the rivalry that encompasses the 50-year-old Kashmir dispute.

Further, the India–Pakistan conflict is now especially alarming because it has implications for the international system itself. The region is the site and the source of some of the world's major terrorist groups. Aside from Al-Qaeda, these include a number of groups based in or tolerated by Pakistan, and India itself has tolerated or encouraged various terrorist groups operating in nearby states, and has its own internal terrorist problem quite apart from Kashmir. India and Pakistan have fought three wars in Kashmir and their conflict now contains the seeds of a nuclear holocaust. This essay attempts a deeper probe of the India–Pakistan relationship, including the difficulties that India faces in managing, let alone resolving, the Kashmir dispute.

A PAIRED-MINORITY CONFLICT

The origins of the India–Pakistan conflict have been traced to many sources: the failure of the British to manage a peaceful and politically acceptable

Partition; the deeply rooted political rivalries between the subcontinent's major religious communities – Hindus, Sikhs, and Muslims; the struggle for control over Kashmir; Kashmir's importance to the national identities of both states, and the greed or personal shortsightedness of leaders on both sides of the border, in particular, Nehru's romance with Kashmir and his Brahminical arrogance (the Pakistani interpretation), or Mohammed Ali Jinnah's vanity, shortsightedness, and religious zeal (the Indian interpretation). All of these and other factors play a role, but the conflict is greater than the sum of its parts.

The world's most intractable disputes are paired minority conflicts.[2] Such conflicts are rooted in perceptions held by important groups on both sides – even those that are not a numerical minority, and which may even be a majority – that they are the threatened, weaker party, under attack from the other side. Paired minority conflicts are most often found within states, although many of these, such as the bitter Sinhala-Tamil conflict in Sri Lanka, have international implications. Others occur between states, including that between Israel and some of its Arab neighbors.

Another state-level paired minority conflict is that of Iraq and Iran, where Iraq fears the larger (and ideologically threatening) Iran, which in turn sees Iraq as the spear point of a hostile Arab world. South Africa and Northern Ireland are two other sites of such conflicts, and in South Asia, Sri Lanka has a paired minority conflict between its minority Tamil population and the Sinhalese. The former believe they are under a comprehensive threat from the more numerous Sinhalese, while the latter believe *themselves* to be the threatened minority, given the fact that there are sixty million Tamils across the Palk Straits. The Tigers argue that Tamils can never be secure unless there is a Tamil homeland on the island.

These conflicts seem to draw their energy from an inexhaustible supply of distrust. It is difficult for one side to compromise even on trivial issues, since doing so might confirm one's own weakness and invite further demands. Furthermore, leaders entrapped in such conflicts are resistant to make concessions when they have the advantage, believing that as the stronger side they can bend the other party to its will. As if they were on a teeter-totter, the two sides take turns in playing the role of advantaged/disadvantaged. They may briefly achieve equality, but their state of dynamic imbalance inhibits the prospect of long-term negotiations and tends to abort any effort to have an institutionalized peace process.

These paired minority conflicts are also morally energized. Politics takes place where the search for justice overlaps with the pursuit of power. In South Asia, goaded by a sense of injustice, conflict is legitimized because it seems to be the only way to protect the threatened group. Additionally, the group sees itself as threatened because it is morally or materially *superior*. Even past defeats and current weaknesses are 'explained' by one's own virtues, which invite the envy of others.

Psychological paired minority conflicts are characterized by distrust of those who advocate compromise, whether outsiders or citizens of one's own state. The former may be fickle; they may shift their support to the other side for one reason or another.

Time is a critical component of these conflicts. One or both parties may be looking ahead to a moment when they can achieve some special advantage or when the other side will collapse. Do long-term demographic trends, real or imagined, appear to be threatening? Is your country, or your group, acquiring some special advantage in terms of technology, alliances, or economics that will change your relative position of power in the future? In brief, does the calendar work for or against you? If either side believes that time is on its side, and waiting will improve its position – or damage that of the other side – then 'step by step' efforts to reduce suspicion or promote confidence are doomed to fail.

INDIAN INSECURITY

One of the most important puzzles of India-Pakistan relations is not why the smaller Pakistan feels encircled and threatened, but why the larger India does. It would seem that India, seven times more populous than Pakistan and five times its size, and which defeated Pakistan in 1971, would feel more secure. This has not been the case and Pakistan remains deeply embedded in Indian thinking. There are historical, strategic, ideological, and domestic reasons why Pakistan remains the central obsession of much of the Indian strategic community, just as India remains Pakistan's.

Generations and Chosen Griefs

The first generation of leaders in both states – the founding fathers, Mahatma Gandhi, Sardar Patel, Mohammed Ali Jinnah, and Jawaharlal Nehru – were devoted to achieving independence and building new states and nations. With the exception of Gandhi, they did not believe that partition would lead to conflict between India and Pakistan. On the Indian side, many expected Pakistan to collapse, but did not see the need to hasten that collapse by provoking a conflict with Pakistan. On the Pakistani side, once Independence was achieved, Jinnah hoped that the two countries would have good relations. In several important speeches delivered after

Independence Jinnah played down his earlier emphasis on Hindus and Muslims constituting 'two nations'. He set forth the vision of a predominately Muslim but still-tolerant and multi-religious Pakistan counterpoised against a predominantly Hindu India – in effect two secular states, in which religion was a private, not a public matter.[3] Implicit in this arrangement was that the presence of significant minorities in each would serve as hostage to good relations.

A second generation of Indian and Pakistani leaders was unprepared to solve the problems created by partition. Nothing in their experience had led them to place reconciliation ahead of their own political advantage and the temptation to 'just say no'. They did reach several agreements that cleaned up the debris of partition, and there were trade and transit treaties, hotlines, and other confidence-building measures (CBMs) installed as early as the 1950s.

However, two great post-partition traumas aborted the process of normalization. For India, it was the humiliating defeat by China in 1962, and for Pakistan, the vivisection of their country by Indian hands in 1971. The ten-year difference is important: the present generation of Indian leaders are further away from their national humiliation than are their Pakistani counterparts, even though the rise of China as a major economic power rekindled anti-Chinese fears in New Delhi.

In each case, the other side denies the seriousness of the other's grievances, and doubts the sincerity of the other side's claim.[4] In 1962, Ayub Khan stated his skepticism that there was a real India–China conflict, and Pakistanis still belittle Indian obsessions with Beijing. Indians seem to assume that Pakistanis have more or less forgotten the events of 1971 and cannot understand why Pakistani officials remain suspicious when New Delhi professes its good intentions.

Further, these two conflicts had profound domestic consequences, not a small matter in a democracy. No Indian politicians have been able to admit publicly that the Indian case *vis-à-vis* China is flawed.[5] None have dared suggest, as V.K. Krishna Menon once did, that the two states exchange territory. As for Pakistan, there have been few scholars or journalists – and no politicians – bold enough to suggest that Islamabad settle for anything short of 'self-determination', or a plebiscite, leading to accession, lest they be attacked for being pro-Indian and anti-Islamic.

Finally, each trauma led directly to the consideration of nuclear weapons and the further militarization of the respective countries. In India's case, the lesson of 1962 was that only military power counts and that Nehru's faith in a diplomacy that was not backed up by firepower was disastrously naïve.

The linkage between the trauma of 1971 and the nuclear option is even tighter in Pakistan – and, for Zulfiqar Ali Bhutto, a nuclear weapon had the added attraction of enabling him to reduce the power of the army. Ironically, Pakistan has wound up with both a nuclear program and a politically powerful army.

Traditions: New and Invented

While many Hindu and Islamic traditions suggest ways of reducing differences and ameliorating conflict, each also has elements that contribute to the idea of what Elias Canetti terms a war-crowd. Indians and Pakistanis draw selectively from these traditions and point to those aspects of each other's traditions that seem to 'prove' that the other intends to conquer and dominate. For example, Pakistanis like to cite the *Arthashastra* as 'proof' of an Indian/Hindu approach to statecraft that emphasizes subversion, espionage, and deceit.[6] For their part, Indian strategists, especially on the Hindu nationalist end of the spectrum, emphasize those aspects of Islamic teachings that portray a world divided between believers and unbelievers, and set forth the obligation of the former to convert the latter.

While Pakistani ideologues see the spread of Islam to South Asia as having purged and reformed the unbelievers, their Indian counterparts read this history as reinforcing the notion of a comprehensive civilizational and cultural threat to India. When the Muslims arrived, India was temporarily weaker, but morally greater. India's riches and treasures attracted outside predators who, despite their momentary technical or military superiority, lacked the deeper moral qualities of an old and established civilization. The first predators were the Islamic invaders; these in turn betrayed India and failed to protect it from the subsequent wave of Western conquerors. In the history of Islam and Christianity in India, Hindus were the odd men out.

Indians also see Pakistan as an important example of neo-imperialism. The Indian view is that that when neighbors (that is, Pakistan) are allied to powerful intruders (such as Britain, the United States, or China), their domestic politics *and* their foreign policies are distorted.[7] The US-Pakistan alliance is widely believed to have militarized Pakistani politics and foreign policy through the connection between the Pakistan army and the United States, making it impossible for Delhi to come to an accommodation with Islamabad over Kashmir.

Most Indians also believe that Pakistan compounded the error by allowing its territory to be used for Cold War alliance objectives, introducing a superpower into the region. The American tie is also seen as encouraging Pakistan to challenge the rightfully dominant regional power by providing the advanced weapons that enabled Pakistan to attack India in 1965. The preferred Indian solution to such a distortion of the natural regional power structure is the international recognition of benign, accommodating, liberal regional dominant powers – not the meddling in one region by either a global hegemon or adjacent regional powers.

Pakistan is seen as an essential element in a shifting alliance between the West, Islam, China, and other hostile states directed against New Delhi. In recent years the emphasis has expanded to include the sea of extremist Islamic forces led by Pakistan, with China as a silent partner. Samuel P. Huntington's thesis of a grand alliance between Islamic and 'Confucian' civilization was greeted warmly by that portion of the Indian strategic community that had long since made the connection. The ring of states around India provides a ready-made image of encirclement, of threat from all quarters. India has threats from the north, the east, the west, and over the horizon, as naval theoreticians eagerly point out the threat from the sea, from whence both the Arabs and the Europeans came, and – 30 years ago – the aircraft carrier *USS Enterprise* sent by President Nixon to intimidate New Delhi.

Why is India threatened by some combination of Pakistan, Islam, China, and the West? It is because Indians believe that outsiders are jealous of India, and try to cut it down to size. This sense of weakness, of vulnerability, is contrasted with India's 'proper' status as a great power, stemming from its unique civilization and history. It is India's very diversity, long regarded as a virtue, which offers a tempting target for Pakistan, the Islamic world, and others. Even India's minorities (tribals, Sikhs, Christians, and Muslims) are seen, especially by the Hindu Right, as a potential fifth column, awaiting foreign exploitation.

Pakistan as an Incomplete State

Finally, the very nature of the Pakistani state presents a threat to India. In a survey of India's security problems written in 1983, U.S. Bajpai, a distinguished retired diplomat, offered not so much an analysis of the 'Pakistan factor' as an indictment of Pakistan's many shortcomings.[8] Pakistan's limited cultural and civilizational inheritance, its military dictatorship, its theocratic identity, its unworkable unitary system of government (as opposed to India's flexible federalism), the imposition of Urdu on an unwilling population, the alienation of Pakistan's rulers from their people, Islamabad's support of 'reactionary' regimes in West Asia (India identified its interests with the 'progressive' segments of Arab nationalism, such as Saddam's Iraq), its dependency on foreign aid, and the failure to develop a strong economic base were Pakistan's embarrassment. This perspective has enjoyed a renaissance in the ten years after Pakistan began open support for the separatist and terrorist movements that emerged in Indian-administered Kashmir.[9]

Why should India fear such a state? Pakistan is a threat because it still makes the claim that Partition was imperfectly carried out, because some Pakistanis harbor revanchist notions towards India's Muslim population, and because it falsely accuses India of wanting to undo Pakistan itself. Thus, Pakistan still makes a claim on Kashmir, and has deeper designs against the integrity and unity of India itself.[10] Because Pakistan continues to adhere to the theory which brought it into existence – the notion that the subcontinent was divided between two nations, one Hindu, one Muslim – and because it purports to speak on behalf of Indian Muslims, Pakistan's very identity is 'a threat to India's integrity.'[11] More recently, Pakistan has served as the base for Islamic 'jihadists' who not only seek the liberation of Kashmir, but the liberation of all of India's Muslims.

PAKISTAN VIEWS INDIA

If Indian strategists regard Pakistan as a major threat to Indian security, then Pakistani leaders, especially the powerful military, regard their country as even more threatened. Yet, some even see Pakistan as better able to withstand the challenge than the much larger and more powerful India.[12] Pakistan's leaders have a profound distrust of New Delhi, and the latter's reassurances that India 'accepts' the existence of Pakistan are not taken seriously.

The dominant explanation of regional conflict held by Pakistan's strategic community is that from the first day of independence there has been a concerted Indian attempt to crush their state. This original trauma was refreshed and deepened by the loss of East Pakistan in 1971. Many Pakistanis now see their state as threatened by an increasingly Hindu and extremist India, motivated by a desire for religious revenge and a missionary-like zeal to extend its influence to the furthest reaches of South Asia and neighboring areas. There is also a strand of Pakistani thinking that draws upon the army's tradition of geopolitics, rather than the two-nation theory or ideological explanations to explain conflict between India and Pakistan.[13]

Like Israel, Pakistan was founded by a people who felt a sense of persecution when living as a minority, and even though they possess their own states (which are also based on religious identity), both remain under threat from powerful enemies. In both cases, an original partition demonstrated the hostility of neighbors, and subsequent wars showed that these neighbors remained hostile. Pakistan and Israel have also followed parallel strategic policies. Both sought entangling alliances with various outside powers (at various times, Britain, France, China, and the United States), and both ultimately concluded that outsiders could not be trusted in a moment of extreme crisis, leading them to develop nuclear weapons.

Further complicating India-Pakistan relations, the 1971 defeat was of central importance to the Pakistan army, which has governed Pakistan for more than half of its existence. Thus, to achieve a normal relationship with Pakistan, India must not only influence the former's public opinion; it must also change the institutionalized distrust of India found in the army. The prospects of this are very slim.

Finally, Pakistani hostility to India has roots other than the tortured relationship between the two countries. Indians assert that Pakistan needs the India threat to maintain its own unity. There is an element of truth in this argument – distrust of India, and the Kashmir conflict, do serve as a national rallying cry for Pakistanis, and thus as a device to smooth over differences between the dominant province, Punjab, and the smaller provinces of Baluchistan, Sind, and the Northwest Frontier. India-as-an-enemy is also useful to distract the Pakistani public from other concerns, such as social inequality, sectarian (Sunni-Shi'ia) conflict, and the distinct absence of social progress in many sectors of Pakistani society. These factors do partially explain Pakistan's fear of India – but there remains a real conflict between the two states, Kashmir.

STRATAGEMS IN A PAIRED-MINORITY CONFLICT

States or groups that see themselves as threatened minorities have at least five strategies to cope with the situation. In the abstract, these include fleeing the relationship, either physically or psychologically; assimilation (joining the dominant power); accommodation (living as a weaker state by yielding, compromising with the dominant power); changing the perceptions of the enemy state (by people-to-people diplomacy, persuasion or bribery); using outsiders to redress the balance of power; and finally, changing the balance of power by war or other means (such as increasing one's economy or population faster than the other side). Over the past fifty years India and Pakistan have contemplated each of these strategies.

Fleeing the Relationship

India and Pakistan, created as a 'Homeland' for Indian Muslims, have tried to flee their relationship several times. The first instance was literally a physical escape; the others symbolic, psychological, and strategic flight. The key West Pakistani leaders were from Uttar Pradesh, Delhi, and Bombay, the key East Pakistani leaders were Bengali Muslims. While Pakistan was deemed to be homeland for Indian Muslims, most of its founders were fairly secular politicians worried about being outnumbered in democratic India where Hindus would have a controlling majority. They had no interest in creating a theocratic state, but favored a tolerant Muslim majority state where Hindus, Sikhs, and Christians would live as contented minorities.[14] Indeed, some Islamist groups such as the Jamaat-i-Islami originally opposed Pakistan on the grounds that Islam could not be contained within a single state.

Intermittently, India has pursued a policy of psychologically escaping the relationship with Pakistan by simply refusing to engage in serious negotiations with it, in the hope that time would eventually lead to the maturation of Pakistan. Eventually, Islamabad would have to realize that Pakistan could not hope to compete with the larger and more powerful India, until that moment came, then India would be best advised to ignore Pakistan.

Demonization is a variation on fleeing a relationship. If the leaders of the other country are evil, misguided, or corrupt, then there is no need to talk to them. Indeed, dialogue with such a country, or its leaders, is immoral and dangerous. For many Indians Mohammed Ali Jinnah, the founder of Pakistan, has long personified the evil leader who was triply misguided. Jinnah challenged India's civilizational unity by his two-nation theory, he began the militarization of Pakistan by seeking arms from the West, and he was aloof, cold, and undemocratic, jealous of Indian rivals, whipping up hatred and fear of India.[15] His successors, largely military officers, are thought not to have even Jinnah's leadership qualities and lack the moral authority to place their country on a solid footing.

Many Hindu Indians believe that Pakistanis are insecure because most were converts to Islam from Hinduism, and their new faith creates additional problems for India because Islam is seen as a religion that is notably illiberal.[16] A former Director of Military Intelligence of the Indian army has written at length on how the 'psychological' origins of the India-Pakistan dispute are entirely the responsibility of Pakistan's leaders: they carved Pakistan out of India, their hatred of India has permitted them to become 'the plaything of external forces', and they are content to be dominated by the military. Concluding, General Kathpalia sums up: 'There is no doubt that the troubles of India and Pakistan are basically of the making of the leadership. In the last 41 years the leadership of one country has consistently fanned popular hatred and suspicion and pursued it as an instrument of policy'.[17] Today, Indian diplomats despair of negotiating with Pakistan, a chronically weak state under the control of the most anti-Indian elements, such as the military, the intelligence services, and the Maulvis.

Pakistan's image of the Indian leadership is no less hostile. An important component of Pakistan's founding ideology was that Muslims could not trust the 'crafty' Hindus, who still suffered from an inferiority complex.[18] While Gandhi and Jinnah were once respected rivals, their successors in both states lacked even professional respect for each other.

Assimilation

The opposite of fleeing a relationship is assimilation, and one of the fundamental differences between India and Pakistan is the expectation by some Indians that Pakistan might rejoin India. Assimilation has never been contemplated by Pakistan's leaders, although there are important linguistic and ethnic minorities who would have accepted a place in the Indian Union. In the last elections before independence, the dominant political party in the Punjab was the Unionist Party, an alliance of Hindus, Muslims and Sikhs, and both the Northwest Frontier Province and Sind had Congress governments. As for India, most of its leaders assumed that the Pakistan experiment would fail and Pakistan would come back to the fold.

Indians no longer talk of the reintegration of Pakistan into India, but there are widespread (if generally private) discussions of how India might establish friendly relations with successor states to present-day Pakistan. Many Indians regard Bangladesh as an acceptable neighbor, and believe that they could develop a similar relationship with a Sindhu Desh, Baluchistan, Northwest Frontier, and even a militarily diminished West Punjab. Bangladeshis may not like or love India, but they fear and respect Indian power, and would not dream of challenging New Delhi the way that Pakistan has.

Accommodation

If Pakistan cannot rejoin India, many Indians expect it to eventually accommodate Indian power. Such a Pakistan would not challenge India militarily or in internal fora, it would tone down its Islamic identity, and it would settle the Kashmir dispute by making major concessions to New

Delhi. It would also acknowledge India's regional economic dominance, and would not impose restrictions on the import of Indian films and other cultural artifacts.

However, Pakistani strategists view the accommodating strategies of Nepal, Sri Lanka, Bhutan, and even Bangladesh as precisely the wrong model for Islamabad. These states have lost their freedom of action, they have been penetrated by Indian culture, and New Delhi has undue influence on their domestic politics, even intervening by force, where necessary. The absorption of Sikkim is often cited by Pakistani strategists, as is the Indian intervention in Sri Lanka and its military presence in Bhutan.

The view of many Pakistanis is that because Pakistan is larger and more powerful than any of these states it does not need to accommodate India. This resistance to accommodation or compromise with India is especially powerful in the Pakistan armed forces. Pakistan, its officers argue, may be smaller but it is not weaker. It is united by religion and a more martial spirit than India, and need not lower its demands of India, especially on Kashmir.

Altering Perceptions

From time to time, there have been attempts to change perceptions of Indians or Pakistanis. A number of outside countries, foundations, and private individuals have supported efforts to change the perceptions of Indians and Pakistanis, to promote better understanding between the two. Over the past ten years, there have been at least 100 programs to bring together students, journalists, politicians, strategists, artists, intellectuals and retired generals from both countries. Much of the goodwill created by such efforts was washed away by the hawkish television coverage of the Kargil war and the Indian Airlines hijacking in 1999.[19]

Most of the India-Pakistan dialogues, intended to promote understanding, wind up rehearsing old arguments, often for the sake of non-South Asian participants present. History is used – and abused – to emphasize the legitimacy of one's own side, and the malign or misguided qualities of the other. Such dialogues take the form of a duel between long-time adversaries, each knowing the moves of the other and the proper riposte to every assertion or claim. Any discussion of the way in which India can work out its differences with smaller neighbors is likely, sooner or later, to lead to certain issues (nuclear proliferation, trade, water, and so forth), or to the responsibility of outside powers for regional disputes.[20] Meetings between Indians and Pakistanis rarely last long enough to systematically discuss the differences between the two sides and how those differences might be ameliorated or accommodated.

The Indian and Pakistani governments have also tried to influence deeper perceptions across the border. Several Indian governments have undertaken major initiatives in an attempt to win over Pakistani opinion. This was especially the case of non-Congress governments, beginning in 1979 with the prime minister, Morarji Desai and his foreign minister, Atal Behari Vajpayee. Subsequently, major initiatives were taken by Inder Kumar Gujral, both when he was foreign minister and then prime minister; Vajpayee undertook yet another goodwill mission when he traveled to Lahore in the spring of 1999 to meet with Prime Minister Nawaz Sharif in Lahore.

These recent efforts seem to have failed dramatically, with the Lahore meeting discredited by the subsequent Kargil war, and the Nawaz linkage destroyed by the army coup of October 1999. The Indian proponents of a conciliatory line towards Pakistan came under strong attack from both the opposition parties and more hawkish elements of the BJP itself. On Pakistan's part, President Zia's 'cricket diplomacy' of the late 1980s raised the prospect of a more forthcoming Pakistani policy.[21] Nevertheless, Pakistan's two democratically elected prime ministers, Benazir Bhutto and Nawaz Sharif both assumed a very hawkish policy towards India, especially after the 1989 uprising in Kashmir.

Several non-regional states and organizations have tried to promote India-Pakistan cooperation or dialogue. In the 1950s and 1960s, the United States wanted to broker a détente between the two states so that they might join in a common alliance against threats from the Soviet Union and Communist China. Considerable diplomatic energy was expended on these efforts but the only result was to provide each with enhanced diplomatic leverage against the other, sometimes with ironic results.

In 1949 Nehru had offered Pakistan a 'no war' pact, but Pakistan did not respond. Then, in 1958, Ayub Khan offered India a 'joint defense' agreement provided the Kashmir dispute was solved, after which Nehru again reiterated India's offer of a no-war pact. Several years later, with the US-Pakistan alliance revived after the Soviet occupation of Afghanistan, President Zia-ul-Haq offered Delhi a 'no-war' proposal, flabbergasting the Indians. Of course, neither proposal was serious, their purpose being to impress outside powers of Indian (or Pakistani) sincerity.

Much the same can be said of recent proposals for the institution of confidence building measures (hotlines, summits, dialogues, and various technical verification proposals) between the two countries. Outsiders regard such measures as no-risk high-gain arrangements. However, in the India–Pakistan case cooperation is seen as low-gain and high-risk. If cooperation fails, losses will be public and politically damaging; there might also be a multiplier effect in that the risk of conflict might increase if an active attempt at cooperation fails and if the costs of conflict are very high.

In South Asia the regional organization, the South Asian Association for Regional Cooperation (SAARC), has provided a venue for meetings between Indian and Pakistani leaders and sponsors some cooperative projects on regional issues.[22] However, SAARC cannot deal with bilateral issues, and the smaller members are vulnerable to Indian pressure concerning the focus of SAARC initiatives. India has twice been able to force a postponement of its annual meetings when it was displeased with developments in Pakistan.

Seeking Outside Allies

Seeking outside allies against each other has been India's and Pakistan's most consistent policies for over fifty years, and one of the most important ways in which they have constructed their relationship. Sometimes these allies have been willing, usually they have been reluctant. Pakistan has enlisted several Arab states, Iran, the United States, China, and North Korea in its attempt to balance Indian power. Washington usually felt uncomfortable in this role, resisting Pakistan's efforts to extend the security umbrella to include an attack by India. The Reagan administration drew the line at calling India a communist state, which would have invoked the 1959 agreement to take measures to defend Pakistan against communist aggression.

The Chinese have been less restrained, and while there is no known treaty which binds Pakistan and China together, Beijing has provided more military assistance to Pakistan than it has to any other state. Beijing saw its support for Pakistan as serving double-duty, since a stronger Pakistan could counter the Soviet Union and resist Indian pressure. Yet, China has moderated its support for Pakistan's claims to Kashmir, and gradually normalized its relationship with India. In turn, New Delhi saw an opportunity after 1988 to weaken the Beijing-Islamabad tie by moving closer to China, and has been circumspect in its criticism of Chinese policies in Tibet and elsewhere.

On India's part, the Soviet Union was seen as a major ally in its competition with Pakistan. The Soviets provided a veto in the United Nations, massive arms supplies, and general sympathy for New Delhi. However, this support was not directed so much against Pakistan as it was against China; when the Gorbachev government began to normalize relations with Beijing, its support for India gradually declined.

It can be expected that these permutations will continue indefinitely, with India and Pakistan seeking outside support against the other. This has been the dominant feature of Indian diplomacy for decades, and it is unlikely to change soon.

Changing the Balance of Power

Both India and Pakistan have also attempted to use their armed forces to change the regional balance of power. The closest the two have come to a decisive turning point was in 1971, when the Indian army achieved the surrender of the Pakistan army in East Pakistan. However, rather than pressing on to a decisive victory in the West – which would have been very costly and might have brought other states into the contest – India settled for a negotiated peace and the Simla agreement. Both the United States and China provided verbal support for Pakistan in 1970–71, but neither seemed prepared to take any direct action that would have prevented India from defeating the Pakistanis in East Pakistan.[23] A second opportunity came in 1987 during the Brasstacks crisis, when India had conventional superiority and Pakistan had not yet acquired a nuclear weapon.[24]

By 1990 both India and Pakistan had covertly exercised their nuclear options, and seem to have concluded that the risk of escalation had reached a point where the fundamental balance between the two could not be achieved by force of arms. This did not prevent the discreet use of force, and Pakistan adopted a strategy of hitting at India through the support of separatist and terrorist forces, and in 1999, a low-level war in Kargil. This now raises the prospect of escalation to nuclear war, but so far there has been no Indian or Pakistani advocacy of a *decisive* nuclear war.

KASHMIR

Kashmir is both a cause and the consequence of the India-Pakistan conundrum. It is primarily a dispute about justice and people, although its strategic and territorial dimensions are complicated enough.[25] As in many other intractable paired-minority conflicts, it is hard to tell where domestic politics ends and foreign policy begins.

There are two Kashmirs. Besides the physical territory, another Kashmir is found in the minds of politicians, strategists, soldiers and ideologues. This is a place where national and sub-national identities are ranged against each other.[26] The conflict in this Kashmir is as much a clash between identities, imagination, and history, as it is a conflict over territory, resources and peoples. Competing histories, strategies, and policies spring from these different images of self and other.

Pakistanis have long argued that the Kashmir problem stems from India's denial of justice to the Kashmiri people (by not allowing them to join Pakistan), and by not accepting Pakistan's own legitimacy. Once New Delhi were to pursue a just policy, then a peaceful solution to the Kashmir problem could be found.[27] For the Pakistanis, Kashmir remains the 'unfinished business' of the 1947 partition. Pakistan, the self-professed homeland for an oppressed and threatened Muslim minority in the subcontinent, finds it difficult to leave a Muslim majority region to a Hindu-majority state.

Indians, however, argue that Pakistan, a state defined and driven by its religion, is given to irredentist aspirations in Kashmir because it is unwilling to accept the fact of a secular India. India, a nominally secular state, finds it difficult to turn over a Muslim majority region to a Muslim neighbor *just because* it is Muslim. The presence of this minority belies the need for Pakistan to exist at all (giving rise to the Pakistani assertion that Indians have never reconciled themselves to Pakistan).[28]

Indians also point to Bangladesh as proof that Jinnah's call for a separate religion-based homeland for the subcontinent's Muslims was untenable. In contrast, India's secularism, strengthened by the presence of a Muslim-majority state of Kashmir within India, proves that religion alone does not make a nation. Indians maintain that Kashmir cannot be resolved until Pakistanis alter their views on secularism. Of course, this would also mean a change in the identity of Pakistan, a contentious subject in both states.

These same themes of dominance, hegemony, and identity are replicated within the state itself. The minority Buddhist Ladakhis would prefer to be governed directly from New Delhi, and (like their Shi'ia neighbors) fear being ruled from a Sunni Muslim-dominated government in Srinagar. In Jammu, much of the majority Hindu population has long been discontented with the special status lavished upon the Valley by the Union government in New Delhi. Finally, the small Kashmiri Pandit Brahmin community in the Valley is especially fearful. It has lost its privileged position within the administration of the state and much of its dominance in academia and the professions. After the onset of militant Islamic protests, most of the Pandit community fled the Valley for Jammu and several Indian cities (especially New Delhi), where they live in wretched exile. Some of their representatives have demanded *Panun Kashmir*, a homeland for the tiny Brahmin community within Kashmir.

There are other 'causes' of the Kashmir problem. The original problem, caused by a failed partition, was followed by a process by which Indian and

Pakistani leaders turned Kashmir into a badge of their respective national identities. For Pakistan, which defined itself as a homeland for Indian Muslims, the existence of a Muslim majority area under 'Hindu' Indian rule was grating. After all, the purpose of Pakistan was to free Muslims from the tyranny of majority rule (and hence, of rule by the majority Hindu population). For Indians, their country had to include such predominantly Muslim regions to demonstrate the secular nature of the new Indian state; since neither India nor Pakistan, so-defined, could be complete without Kashmir, raising the stakes for both.

Kashmir also came to play a role in the respective domestic politics of both states. In Pakistan Kashmir was a helpful diversion from the daunting task of nation building and there are powerful Kashmiri-dominated constituencies in several Pakistani cities. In India the small, but influential Kashmiri Hindu community was over-represented in the higher reaches of the Indian government, not least in the presence of the Nehru family, a Kashmiri Pandit clan that had migrated to Uttar Pradesh from the Valley.

Further, Kashmir acquired an unexpected military dimension. Not only has the 'line of control' (the former cease-fire line) become a strategic extension of the international border to the south, China holds substantial territory (in Ladakh) claimed by India. From 1984 onward advances in training and high altitude warfare have turned the most inaccessible part of Kashmir – the Siachen Glacier – into a battleground.[29] The recent limited war in Kargil raised the stakes considerably, as it was the first time that offensive airpower has been used between Indian and Pakistani forces since 1971.

Kashmir was also tied to the Cold War. Washington and Moscow armed India and Pakistan (often both at the same time), they supported one side or the other in various international fora and the Soviets wielded the veto threat on behalf of India in the UN Security Council. However, the superpowers reached an understanding that they would not let the Kashmir conflict (or India-Pakistan tensions) affect their core strategic relationship.[30] Ironically, the process by which the Cold War ended had an impact on Kashmir itself because the forces of democracy and nationalism that destroyed the Soviet Union and freed Eastern Europe were at work in Kashmir.[31]

Finally, Kashmir has been the scene of a of a national self-determination movement among Kashmiri Muslims. Encouraged by neither India nor Pakistan, this burst into view in late 1989 after a spell of particularly bad Indian governance in the state. Angry and resentful at their treatment by New Delhi, and not attracted to even a democratic Pakistan, younger Kashmiris looked to Palestine, Afghanistan, Iran, the Middle East, and

Eastern Europe for models, and to émigrés in America, Britain, and Canada for support.

This emergence of a movement for self-rule by a younger generation of Kashmiris was the result of decades of mismanagement, but more specifically the manipulation of Kashmiri politics in the 1980s first by Indira Gandhi and then by Rajiv Gandhi. It coincided with the slow and imperfect growth of political mobilization of the valley Kashmiris.[32] Kashmiris were mobilized too late, too quickly and, imperfectly.[33] 'Kashmiriyat' (the refined amalgam of Hindu-Muslim culture that characterizes the Valley and surrounding areas) remains; it has been a rallying point for some separatists, but must now compete with more virulent forms of militant Islamic doctrine, a form of Islam that had been alien to the Kashmiri population before the 1980s.

Undoubtedly Pakistani support was provided – it was never hidden – and Pakistanis speak proudly of their assistance to the Kashmiris and their right to help the latter free themselves from an oppressive Indian state. However, Pakistan's role was not the decisive factor in starting the uprising, although it has been a critical factor in sustaining it.

Since the uprising of 1989, the situation in Kashmir has become a bloody stalemate. India continues to apply a mixture of pressure and inducement, organizing its own counter-terrorist squads made up of ex-terrorists and sent by them against the Pakistan-sponsored 'freedom fighters'. Numerous bomb blasts in major Indian and Pakistani cities, several unexplained railway wrecks, the occasional air hijacking, and miscellaneous acts of sabotage seem to be evidence of organized attempts to exploit local grievances and extract revenge. While Indian officials claim a decline in 'militancy', international human rights groups and independent observers report little change, and within Kashmir the death toll mounts. Most of the Kashmiri population remains alienated, whether they are the Pandits (many of whom have fled their homes), or the Valley Muslims, bitterly divided and increasingly terrorized by radical Islamic groups.

Resolution: A Record of Failure

The failure of diplomacy to address, let alone resolve the Kashmir dispute is remarkable, given the amount of attention paid to it. After the 1948 and 1965 India–Pakistan wars, and the India–China war of 1962, there were concerted efforts to resolve Kashmir. In 1948, the United Nations became deeply involved; Kashmir is the oldest conflict inscribed in the body of UN resolutions and is certainly one of the most serious.[34] After the 1962 India–China war there were intensive but fruitless American and British efforts to bridge the gap between Delhi and Islamabad. The end of the 1965 war saw the Soviet Union as a regional peacemaker. The Soviets did manage to promote a general peace treaty at Tashkent, but this could not prevent a civil and international war in 1970–71 over East Pakistan/Bangladesh.

The most consistent feature of great power influence on the Kashmir problem has been its ineffectiveness. Beyond their regional Cold War patronage, both the United States and the Soviet Union have played significant, often parallel and cooperative roles in the subcontinent.[35] Over the years the United States had considerable influence with both India and Pakistan; at one point the Soviet Union, generally regarded as pro-Indian, moved closer to Pakistan, even providing military assistance to Islamabad and brokering the 1966 Tashkent agreement. Yet neither superpower seemed to be able to make a difference. This suggests that any outside power should step carefully if it seeks to end or even moderate this conflict.

Kashmir was important only insofar as it concerned their respective regional partners, yet both resisted being dragged into the Kashmir issue by those same partners. While Indians and Pakistanis often based their regional calculation on the assistance of outside support for their position on Kashmir, this support has been limited and constrained. For years the Soviets provided India with an automatic veto in the United Nations on Kashmir-related resolutions, and otherwise backed New Delhi diplomatically.

The Pakistanis became more dependent on the United States for political and military support, but could never get the United States to commit itself to firm security assurances against India, precisely because Washington was afraid of being sucked into a Kashmir conflict. Both Washington and Moscow made several inconclusive efforts to mediate the dispute or bring about its peaceful resolution, but were wary of anything more. It took the 1990 crisis with its nuclear dimension to bring the United States back to the region, and then only briefly.

After India defeated Pakistan in 1971, India kept outsiders at a distance as it sought to reach a bilateral understanding with Pakistan. Mrs Gandhi and Zulfiqar Ali Bhutto met in the Indian hill station of Simla in late June and early July 1972.[36] There, after a long and complicated negotiation, they committed their countries to a bilateral settlement of all outstanding disputes. Presumably, this included Kashmir (which was mentioned only in the last paragraph of the text). The Simla Agreement did not rule out mediation or multilateral diplomacy, if both sides agreed.

Divergent interpretations of Simla added another layer of India-Pakistan distrust. While there is a formal text, there may have been verbal agreements between the two leaders that have never been made public.

According to most Indian accounts, Zulfiqar Ali Bhutto told Mrs. Gandhi that he was willing to settle the Kashmir dispute along the Line of Control, but a final agreement had to be delayed because he was still weak politically. Pakistani accounts claim that Bhutto did no such thing, and that in any case the written agreement is what matters. For India, Simla had supplanted the UN resolutions as a point of reference for resolving the Kashmir dispute. After all, Indian leaders reasoned, the two parties had pledged to work directly with one another, implicitly abandoning extra-regional diplomacy. For Pakistan, Simla supplemented but did not replace the operative UN resolutions on Kashmir.

After the Simla Agreement, the Kashmir dispute seemed to subside. The Indian government began to view the LOC as a more or less permanent border, but both sides continued to nibble away at it when an opportunity arose – most spectacularly in the case of India's move to occupy much of the Siachen Glacier.[37] For Pakistani diplomats the Simla Agreement neither replaced the UN resolutions nor did the conversion of the cease-fire line into a LOC produce a permanent *international* border. Guided by these varied interpretations both sides continued to press their respective claims whenever the opportunity arose, but for 17 years Kashmir was widely regarded outside the region as either solved or on the way to resolution. Other regional issues displaced Kashmir: the 1974 Indian nuclear test, Pakistan's covert nuclear weapons program, and the Soviet invasion of Afghanistan in December 1979. Between 1972 and 1994 India and Pakistan held 45 bilateral meetings, of which only one was fully devoted to Kashmir.[38]

Towards a Solution?

Over the years many solutions have been proposed for the Kashmir problem.[39] These included partition along the Line of Control, 'soft borders' between the two parts of Kashmir (pending a solution to the entire problem), a region-by-region plebiscite of Kashmiris, referendum, UN trusteeship, the 'Trieste' and 'Andorra' models (whereby the same territory is shared by two states, or a nominally sovereign territory in fact is controlled jointly by two states), revolutionary warfare, depopulation of Muslim Kashmiris and re-population by Hindus from India, patience, good government, a revival of 'human values', and doing nothing.[40] The dispute has not been resolved because of at least three factors.

First, over the long run, the existence of the Cold War led both Americans and the Soviets to see this regional dispute not for what it was but as part of the systemic East-West struggle.

Second, both states have been inflexible over the years. India's strategy has been to gradually erode Kashmir's special status under Article 370 of the Constitution of India, which grants the state a special status in the Indian Union. It also pretended that the problem was 'solved' by the Simla Agreement. This dual strategy of no-change within Kashmir, and no-discussion of it with Pakistan failed to prepare New Delhi for the events of the late 1980s. India rejected the political option, it rejected a strategy of accommodating Kashmiri demands, it excluded Pakistan from its Kashmir policy, and it has stubbornly opposed outside efforts to mediate the dispute. Yet, New Delhi lacks the resources, the will or a strategy to deal with the Kashmir problem unilaterally. Pakistan, on the other hand, has often resorted to force in attempting to wrest Kashmir from India, further alienating the Kashmiris themselves in 1947–48 and in 1965, and providing the Indian government with the perfect excuse to avoid negotiations.

Third, it must be said that the Kashmiris, while patently victims, have not been reluctant to exploit the situation. A significant number of Kashmiris have always sought independence from India *and* Pakistan. The two states disagree as to *which* should control Kashmir and the mechanism for determining Kashmiri sentiment, but they are unified in their opposition to an independent state. Thus the seemingly well-intentioned proposal, heard frequently from Americans and other outsiders, that Kashmiris be 'consulted' or have a voice in determining their own fate is threatening to both Islamabad and Delhi.

Like proposals to resolve other complex disputes, such as those in the Middle East or China-Taiwan and the two Koreas, 'solutions' to the Kashmir problem must operate at many levels. The examples of the Middle East, South Africa, and Ireland, indicate that seemingly intractable disputes can be resolved, or ameliorated, by patience, outside encouragement, and, above all, a strategy that will address the many dimensions of these complex disputes. If a strategy for Kashmir had begun in the early or mid-1980s, then some of the crises that arose later in that decade might have been averted, and it would not now be seen as one of the world's nuclear flash-points.

Any comprehensive solution to the Kashmir problem would involve many concessions, and changes in relations between India and Pakistan (and within each state) It would require a change in India's federal system; it might require changes within Kashmir between its constituent parts; it would necessitate a re-examination of the military balance between India and Pakistan and provisions that would prevent the two states from again turning to arms in Kashmir. Above all, it would require major concessions on the part of Pakistan – and India might have to accept a Pakistani *locus standi* in Kashmir itself.

There also would have to be incentives for Pakistan to cooperate in such ameliorative measures, since its basic strategy is to draw outsiders into the region and to pressure India. In brief, India has to demonstrate to Pakistan that it would be willing to make significant concessions, but also pledge that if Pakistan ceased its support for Kashmiri separatists Delhi would not change its mind once the situation in the Valley had become more normal.

Doing nothing is likely to be the default option for Kashmir. At best, there might be an arrangement that would ensure that the state does not trigger a larger war between the two countries. However, this does little to address Kashmiri grievances or the widespread human rights violations in the state, nor does it address the deeper conflict between India and Pakistan.

Both India and Pakistan regularly pass through a point where both sides momentarily agree that the time may be right for talks. Just as regularly, one or the other side decides that the risk of moving forward is too great. Often, they believe that time will be on their side, and delay will weaken the case of the other side or strengthen its own. To some degree, both sides also believe that the other will not compromise unless confronted by overwhelming force. The greater Kashmir problem is persuading both sides – and now the Kashmiris themselves (whose perception of how time will bring about an acceptable solution is not clear at all) – to examine their own deeper assumptions about how to bring the other to the bargaining table and reach an agreement, and to objectively assess the costs incurred by waiting to address a problem that has crippled both states for over 50 years.

RESOLUTION OR PERMANENT HOSTILITY?

The presence of a paired minority conflict implies that sustaining a dialogue that leads to regional peace will be difficult. It does not imply that war is more likely. Other paired minority conflicts have been moderated; others appear to be on the road to resolution, or at least management. The Indian debate on Kashmir and relations with Pakistan is particularly wide-ranging (far more so than that in Pakistan) and no future can be absolutely ruled out.[41] One arrangement unofficially supported by many Indians is to draw the international boundary along the cease-fire line, although with minor adjustments.[42] This is rejected out of hand by Pakistan, although it keeps cropping up in Indian discussions and has been proposed by third parties.

At one end of the spectrum it is possible to envision a peace process for India and Pakistan that could resolve or ameliorate the core conflicts.

Drawing upon the experience of other regions, as well as South Asia's own history, such a process would require major changes in policy on the part of India, Pakistan, and the most likely outside 'facilitator' of such a process, the United States.[43]

A regional peace process now seems improbable, given the difficulty of getting political acceptance in both countries at the same time on a problem so closely identified with their respective national identities. From India's perspective any such process cannot go very far without running foul of India's hostility towards the two-nation theory – a theory that Indians claim is Pakistan's sole reason for existence. Indians point out that this concept is an incitement to revolt for India's large Muslim population, and encourages other separatist groups, such as the Sikhs, Nagas, and Mizos. If we take the Indian argument at face value, then there can be no real peace process between India and Pakistan as long as either retains its identity. Any peace process is bound to fail if it does not recognize these core differences, yet no peace process that does address them will get very far.

Second, such a peace process would eventually require a change in India's policies towards Kashmir itself. Indians are deeply divided on this question.[44] Some favor absolutely no change in the Delhi-Srinagar relationship, others urge a degree of autonomy for Kashmir, and a few are willing to see the state partitioned, perhaps along the Line of Control. One reason for Indian disarray is the uncertainty over to the actual loyalty of Kashmiri Muslims – if a measure of autonomy were granted to the state, or at least to its more discontented elements – would that not lead to the slippery slope of a renewed movement for a separate state? Given the profound alienation of many Kashmiris, and the growth of extremist Madrassas in the state, some fear that Kashmir is irretrievably lost to a secular India, and a few Hindu extremists have advocated the repopulation of the state by Hindu settlers. The recent defeat of the Taliban and Al-Qaeda in Afghanistan gives new hope, however, that the extremist trend can be halted in Kashmir, but Pakistan's cooperation may be necessary if Islamic extremism is to be marginalized in Kashmir.

The obstacles to the inauguration of a peace process are even greater on the Pakistani side. While the Indian strategic community has debated India-Pakistan relations for 50 years, and has generated dozens of prospective 'solutions' for Kashmir, the Pakistani debate is dominated by the civil and military security establishment, and moderate or doveish views are rarely heard. In recent years an increasingly shrill Islamic element calls for even tougher measures against India, but this is likely to change as a result of the complete misjudgment by Pakistan's Islamist hawks concerning

Afghanistan, and the anger felt by the Pakistan army when Pakistan's Islamist leaders started to attack the army for its support of the American-led operation in Afghanistan. Pakistan could be on the verge of a major re-evaluation of its relationship with Islamic extremism, and will come under increasing American pressure to reduce or eliminate its support for terrorist-inclined groups operating in Kashmir itself.

Complicating the prospect of Pakistan as a partner in a peace process is the intense debate on state identity that Pakistanis have been engaged in for many years. While Pakistan began as a homeland for Indian Muslims, and justified this identity because Hindus and Muslims were 'two nations', the debate over Pakistani identity has moved well beyond this. After the Punjabi-dominated military assumed power, Pakistanis came to see themselves as Fortress Pakistan: a state (that happened to be Muslim) threatened by India. This was a Punjab-centric view of Pakistan. Subsequently, after the loss of East Bengal, Pakistanis turned toward Islam as a way of asserting a national identity. In the midst of a debate over their own national identity, Pakistanis find it essential to agree on at least one point, and that is the unremitting hostility of India.

In the end, a comprehensive peace process may require an outside power or powers. The only state that could now initiate such a process would be America, but since 1964 Washington has been reluctant to become deeply engaged in South Asian conflicts. Recent American studies stopped well short of recommending a regional peace process, and there appears to be little interest in an enhanced American role although since the 1998 tests it has become more active behind the scenes, fearful that events in might slip out of control between the two South Asian nuclear rivals.

More likely than a peace process involving Kashmir are steps that encourage accommodation in other areas – the strategy of the indirect approach. The past 15 years have seen considerable interest in measures that might reduce conflict and increase regional stability. The uprising in Kashmir, the 1998 nuclear tests, and the Kargil war of 1999 all stimulated interest in Track II diplomacy between India and Pakistan, and the role that third-parties might take in promoting the India-Pakistan dialogue.

There has been considerable discussion about enhancing regional economic cooperation, which might create new domestic 'lobbies' in each state. These could eventually provide the political backing for a peace process. Others, especially the European and American foundations, have actively supported Track II and Track III diplomacy (the first being quasi-official, the second involving 'people-to-people' exchanges) in the belief that more contact between Indians and Pakistanis would help dispel misperceptions and point to areas where agreement might be possible. All of these efforts seek to moderate, if not transform, a relationship that seems to be based on fear, hatred, and distrust. They emphasize the gains and benefits that each side may reap from cooperation.

Both India and Pakistan have agreed to a wide variety of CBMs, including pre-notification of troop movements and exercises, the location of nuclear facilities, hotlines between military commanders, regular meetings between prime ministers, and restrictions on propaganda and other steps that might exacerbate India-Pakistan relations.[45] The best that can be said for these CBMs is that neither India nor Pakistan has yet boasted of breaking the arrangements. In time of crisis most have simply ceased to function, and whatever 'lessons' about cooperation have been learned seem to evaporate. Nevertheless, there is a strong feeling in both countries that they can avoid major conflict and that South Asia is not as unstable as outsiders believe.

Besides these long-term efforts to change perceptions, build trust, and clarify areas of agreement and disagreement, the prospect of a major transformation of the India-Pakistan relationship cannot be ruled out. There are several scenarios; some of these seem far-fetched at the moment, but all are worth at least a brief mention.

(1) Pakistan could collapse under the weight of its own contradictions and cease to exist in its present form, perhaps splitting into several states. This seems to be the formula of many Indian strategists who expect the Kashmir problem will be solved in the same way that East and West Berlin were merged, the smaller simply ceasing to exist. Such a Pakistan might continue as a united state (few Indians would welcome the addition of a hundred million Muslims to the Indian union), but it certainly would not be able to stand up militarily and politically to Delhi.

(2) India could cause Pakistan to change its identity or cease to exist in its present form. One precedent is the creation of Bangladesh, an Islamic state which is unwilling to challenge India in any significant way. However, India could alter Pakistan's national identity by other means. Delhi could support dissident ethnic and linguistic groups in Pakistan, especially those who were less 'Islamic' or less anti-Indian than the Punjab.

(3) Some nationalist-Hindu ideologues believe that India's 'civilizational pull' will triumph over the idea of Pakistan, and Pakistanis will simply succumb to India's greater cultural and social power. They do not expect Pakistan to necessarily merge with India, although many Indians who hail from towns and villages that are now in Pakistan

would like to see some parts of Sind and West Punjab reincorporated into India. This school is prepared to wait Pakistan out, and thinks in terms of generations and decades, rather than months or years.

(4) India might underestimate Pakistani nationalism and power, and take some action which would lead Islamabad to actually use its nuclear weapons in a Masada-like last attempt to defend Pakistan, and if that fails, to bring India down with Pakistan by attacking India's cities.

(5) A no less dramatic transformation in the relationship could come about if Pakistan itself changed its priorities, putting development ahead of Kashmir – at least for a while. This would confront India with a peculiar situation: a former enemy seeking peace. The question is whether India would or could, respond in a positive fashion and be willing to negotiate a long-term settlement of the Kashmir dispute. After Kargil, this seems less likely.

(6) India could accept Pakistan's identity as an Islamic state. It could declare that it disagreed with this identity, that it rejects such a theory of religion-based statehood for itself, it could point to the accomplishments of a secular democracy – and the general willingness of Muslim and other religious and ethnic minorities to live in such a state – but it could acknowledge that on this irreconcilable point Pakistanis chose and have the right to continue to choose, to live a different life. It could then move to cooperate on a whole range of shared economic, cultural, strategic, and political interests.

None of these extreme outcomes seems likely, but together they add up to a possibility that the India–Pakistan relationship could take a dramatic and even dangerous turn.

INDIA'S DILEMMA

The most likely outcome to this dispute is one of continuing stalemate. The future is likely be one of hesitant movements towards dialogue, punctuated by attempts on both sides to unilaterally press their advantage in Kashmir and in international fora. This is a conflict that Pakistan cannot win and India cannot lose, a true 'hurting stalemate'. Without some fundamental social or political changes in India and Pakistan, the stalemate is likely to continue indefinitely.

Reinforcing this prospect is the fact that stalemate is more attractive to each side than some solutions that have been put forward. From the perspective of the Pakistan military, which has an absolute veto over any policy initiative regarding Kashmir, the ability to tie Indian forces down in Kashmir is an important consequence of the dispute; cynically, it could be said that Pakistan is willing to fight India to the last Kashmiri. As long as Pakistan sees itself as militarily disadvantaged, it will try to equalize the military balance by any means possible.

This includes the nuclear program, but also a strategy aimed at forcing India to divert important resources to a military front (Kashmir) where the terrain and political situation are in Pakistan's favor. For India, Kashmir has so many links to India's secular political order – especially the place of Muslims – that any settlement which appeared to compromise this order is unacceptable.

Clearly, Kashmir is linked to broader issues of the military balance between India and Pakistan, and the very identity of the two states, and while more could be done to ease the suffering of the Kashmiri people – a cease-fire, and some draw-down of regular and paramilitary forces on the Indian side, and some reduction in support for extremists coming from the Pakistan side – no lasting settlement is possible without dealing with these larger strategic and ideological concerns.

India has much to gain by a normal relationship with Pakistan. Such a relationship could contribute to India's assuming a place among the major Asian and even global powers. It would not be a question, as it is now, of Indian power *minus* Pakistani power, but of an India free to exercise its influence without the distraction – and the cost – of a conflict with a still-powerful Pakistan.

However, events seem to outrun India's capability to adapt to them. In recent years there has been a summit, a war, a coup in Pakistan, another summit, and a major American war in Afghanistan. This war forced Islamabad to abandon its extremist Taliban allies, with potential far-reaching consequences for Pakistan's domestic politics and its support for the radical jihadis in Kashmir. Yet India seems to have responded to the crisis in Afghanistan by reverting to an earlier strategy of encirclement of Pakistan, hoping that its relationship with the United States plus a revived tie with the new Afghan government will again put it in a strategically dominant position. This strategy is only likely to reinforce Pakistani suspicions of India.

The prognosis, then, is yet another decade of deadlock. Both states will continue to acquire – and probably deploy – nuclear weapons. India is likely to remain resistant to outside mediation or facilitation of the Kashmir dispute, and domestic political turmoil in both countries will make it even more difficult for the next generation of Indian and Pakistani leaders to forge a relationship that is not grounded on distrust, hostility, and, now, the threat of nuclear holocaust. There may be limited agreement between New Delhi and its western neighbor, but the most problematic issue is not whether Indians or Pakistanis can be trusted to fulfill obligations incurred in agreements where they had little incentive to comply, but whether, under the influence of a pessimistic vision of the region's destiny, they can be trusted in cases where it *is* in their self-interest to comply.

At best the Pakistani generals may conclude that persistent hostility towards India and an obsession with Kashmir has done great damage to Pakistan, and Indian leaders will conclude that some normalization with Pakistan is necessary for India to play a wider role in the world. This is the basis for a truce between the two countries, but not the basis for a peace. For that to occur, there will have to be more profound changes in their deeper relationship, for they will remain two states allergic to each other without the development of strong economic, cultural and political ties.

NOTES

1. For a fuller explication of the 'India emerging' literature and a more comprehensive assessment see Stephen P. Cohen, *India: Emerging Power* (Washington DC: Brookings Institution Press 2001).
2. This term is my own. The most insightful thinker on how hostile groups or crowds are generated is Elias Canetti, whose book *Crowds and Power* (New York: Seabury Press 1978) is a modern classic. For the perspective of a clinical psychologist who has studied the origins of ethnic conflict and war, see Vamik D. Volkan, *The Need to Have Enemies and Allies: From Clinical Practice to International Relationships* (New York: Jason Aronson 1988).
3. For a sympathetic explication of Jinnah's views after Partition, especially in his speeches of 11 and 14 August 1947, see Akbar S. Ahmed, *Jinnah, Pakistan and Islamic Identity: The Search for Saladin* (Karachi: Oxford University Press 1997).
4. For discussion of this process see Volkan, *The Need to Have Enemies and Allies* (note 2) pp.155 ff.
5. However, several distinguished military experts have discussed the India–China border conflict with insight and imagination. See Maj.-Gen. D.K. Palit, *War in High Himalaya: the Indian Army in Crisis, 1962* (London: C. Hurst 1991).
6. An influential and authoritative Pakistan army interpretation of India can be found in Brig. Javed Hussain, *India: A Study in Profile* (Rawalpindi: Army Press 1990).
7. For a comprehensive statement of this view see the writing of Dr Ayesha Jalal, especially *Democracy and Authoritarianism in South Asia: A Comparative and Historical Perspective* (Cambridge: Cambridge University Press 1995).
8. U.S. Bajpai, *India's Security: The Politico-Strategic Environment* (New Delhi: Lancers Publishers 1983) pp.70–71.
9. For a selection of contemporary Indian writing on Pakistan, much of it by present and former police and intelligence officials, see Rajeev Sharma (ed.), *The Pakistan Trap* (New Delhi: UBSPD 2001).
10. Ibid. pp.70–71.
11. Ibid. p.73.
12. For a fuller discussion of Pakistan's approach to India see Stephen P. Cohen, *The Pakistan*

Army (2nd ed.) (Karachi: Oxford University Press 1998).

13. Ibid. pp.141 ff.
14. For a contemporary Pakistani discussion of Jinnah's secularism see Ahmed, *Jinnah and Islamic Identity* (note 3).
15. This image is vividly conveyed to a second and third generation of Indians (and others) by the portrayal of Jinnah in the Attenborough film, *Gandhi* (1982). A concern with this negative image led the distinguished Pakistani academic-administrator, Akbar Ahmed, to produce several films that offer a more realistic portrayal of Jinnah's personal and professional life.
16. The civilizational gap between Islamic Pakistan and (largely Hindu but formally secular) India was a theme of Girilal Jain, one of India's most brilliant journalists. In the last ten years of his life (he died in 1988) Jain wrote feelingly about Hindu–Muslim affairs and the phenomenon of Pakistan; he was, in many ways, the most successful popularizer of BJP views well before the party came to power. For an overview of his arguments see Jain, *The Hindu Phenomenon* (New Delhi: USBSPD 1994).
17. Lt.-Gen. P.N. Kathpalia, (ret.), 'Indo–Pak Relations: The Concept of National Security', *Indian Defense Review*, Jan.1989, pp.116, 124.
18. See Hussain, *India* (note 6), for a summary of these perceptions.
19. A partial list can be found in Sundeep Waslekar, *Track-Two Diplomacy in South Asia* (ACDIS Occasional Paper, Program in Arms Control, University of Illinois, Oct. 1995) and Navnita Chadha Behera, Paul M. Evans and Gowher Rizvi, *Beyond Boundaries: A Report on the State of Non-Official Dialogues on Peace, Security and Cooperation in South Asia* (Toronto: University of Toronto 1997).
20. Some of these dialogues are more thoroughgoing and reach a younger generation of scholars, strategists, journalists and diplomats, such as the many workshops organized by the Colombo-based Regional Centre for Strategic Studies. See www.rcss.org.
21. In conversations with the author and others, Zia stressed his interest in a long-term agreement with India, although one that would preserve vital Pakistani strategic interests and its heavy moral investment in Kashmir. It was impossible to measure the sincerity of these claims, but he did make a series of extraordinary proposals to India that were rejected – including a desire to purchase Indian-manufactured weapons.
22. The SAARC home page is at www.saarc.com/spotential.html.
23. For an account of the diplomacy of the war see Leo Rose and Richard Sisson, *War and Secession: Pakistan, India, and the Creation of Bangladesh* (Berkeley: University of California Press 1990).
24. For a comprehensive overview, Kanti Bajpai, P.R. Chari, Pervez Cheema, Stephen P. Cohen and Sumit Ganguly, *Brasstacks and Beyond: Crisis Perception and Management in South Asia* (New Delhi: Manohar 1995; Lahore: Vanguard Publishers 1996; Columbia: South Asia Books 1996).
25. For two overviews of the Kashmir problem see Jonah Blank, 'Kashmir: Fundamentalism Takes Root', *Foreign Affairs* November–December 1999 and Sumit Ganguly, *The Crisis in Kashmir: Portents of War and Hopes of Peace* (New York: Woodrow Wilson Center Press and Cambridge University Press 1997).
26. For an excellent survey of these issues see Navnita Chadha-Behera, 'J&K (& L & D & G...): Making and Unmaking Identities', *Himal South Asia*, Nov.–Dec. 1996, pp.26–33.
27. For the Pakistani perspective, see Pervaiz Iqbal Cheema, 'Pakistan, India, and Kashmir: A Historical Review', in Raju G.C. Thomas (ed.), *Perspectives on Kashmir: The Roots of Conflict in South Asia* (Boulder: Westview Press 1992).
28. For an extensive review of the Indian position see, Ashutosh Varshney, 'Three Compromised Nationalisms: Why Kashmir has been a Problem', in Thomas, *Perspectives* (note 27).
29. For a vivid press account see W.P.S. Sidhu, 'Siachin: The Forgotten War', *India Today,* 31 May 1992.
30. For a discussion of the impact of the Cold War on Kashmir and South Asia by one of the chief architects of American policy during the Kissinger era, see Peter W. Rodman, *More Precious than Peace: The Cold War and the Struggle for the Third World* (New York: Scribner's 1994.). For an excellent academic study covering the US-Pakistan relationship see

Robert McMahon, *The Cold War on the Periphery: The United States, India, and Pakistan* (New York: Columbia University Press 1994).

31. This point is made by several Indian and Pakistani authors in Kanti P. Bajpai and Stephen P. Cohen (eds.), *South Asia After the Cold War* (Boulder: Westview 1993). See especially the chapters by Pervaiz I. Cheema and Lt.-Gen. M. L. Chibber.

32. Ganguly, *The Crisis in Kashmir* (note 25) p.27.

33. The distinguished Kashmiri Indian scholar, T.N. Madan, has been a close observer of developments in his home. See T. N. Madan, *Modern Myths, Locked Minds* (New Delhi: Oxford University Press 1997) pp.257 ff. For a remarkable, if sometimes erratic, survey of Kashmir see the voluminous memoir-history by a former Governor of Kashmir, Jagmohan, *My Frozen Turbulence in Kashmir* (New Delhi: Allied 1991).

34. For a brief UN history of the conflicts in Kashmir, plus information about the UN peacekeeping operations in the state see the website of the United Nations Department of Public Information, United Nations Peacekeeping Operations: UNMOGIP (United Nations Military Observer Group in India and Pakistan), www.un.org/Depts/DPKO/Missions/unmogip.htm (31 Oct. 1997).

35. See Stephen P. Cohen, 'US-Soviet Cooperation in South Asia', in Roger Kanet and Edward Kolodziej (eds.), *The Cold War as Cooperation* (London: Macmillan 1990 and Baltimore: Johns Hopkins 1991).

36. For a rare attempt to juxtapose Indian and Pakistani interpretations of Simla see P.R. Chari and Pervaiz Iqbal Cheema, *The Simla Agreement. 1972: Its Wasted Promise* (New Delhi: Regional Center for Strategic Studies and Manohar 2001).

37. One of the most comprehensive accounts of Siachin is to be found in Robert G. Wirsing, *India, Pakistan and the Kashmir Dispute: On Regional Conflict and its Resolution* (New York: St Martin's Press 1994) pp.196–216.

38. See 'Pervaiz Iqbal Cheema 'The Kashmir Dispute and Peace of South Asia', *Regional Studies*, Vol.15/1 (Winter 1996–97) pp.170–88.

39. One of the most important groups to have undertaken a fresh examination of the problem is the Kashmir Study Group, composed of senior retired officials, academics, and other interested parties drawn from America and Europe. See Kashmir Study Group, *A Way Forward* (Livingston, NY 1999).

40. Some elements of the Bharatiya Janata Party have recommended that Kashmir be repopulated with Hindus, once its special constitutional status (Article 370) was eliminated. The Andorra precedent of the thirteenth century – a treaty between Spain and France guaranteeing Andorra's internal autonomy – has been discussed by Jean Alphonse Bernard of Paris; Jagmohan, one of the key principles in the most recent crises in Kashmir, has written that the long-term solution rests in a revival of the Indian spirit. See his own record of Kashmir's crises of Kashmir in *My Frozen Turbulence* (note 33).

41. A survey of centrist thinking, which might well evolve into official policy (if the circumstances were right), can be found in Kanti P. Bajpai and others, *Jammu and Kashmir: An Agenda for the Future* (Delhi: Delhi Policy Group 1999).

42. Nehru suggested this arrangement in conversations in 1953 with John Foster Dulles. See Dennis Kux, *Estranged Democracies: India and the United States, 1941–1991* (New Delhi: Sage 1993) p.116.

43. I have discussed a peace process for South Asia in several places. See Stephen P. Cohen, 'A New Beginning in South Asia', *Brookings Policy Brief No.55* (Jan. 2000), www.Brookings.edu.

44. An excellent source for divergent Indian views on Kashmir is the 'Kashmir' page of the Institute of Peace and Conflict Studies; which offers a succinct presentation of the major Indian positions. See www.ipcs.org.

45. The Regional Centre for Strategic Studies has issued studies on CBMs. See two anthologies edited by its Director, Maj.-Gen. (ret.) Dipankar Banerjee: *Confidence Building Measures in South Asia* (Colombo: RCSS 1999) and *CBMs in South Asia: Potential and Possibilities* (Colombo: RCSS 2000).

4

Toward a 'Force-in-Being': The Logic, Structure, and Utility of India's Emerging Nuclear Posture

ASHLEY J. TELLIS

After a hiatus of almost 24 years, India startled the world by resuming nuclear testing at a time when the international community solemnly expressed a desire through the Comprehensive Test Ban Treaty (CTBT) to refrain from the field-testing of nuclear explosives. On 11 May 1998, the Indian Prime Minister, Atal Bihari Vajpayee, tersely announced that New Delhi had conducted three nuclear tests, one of which involved the detonation of a thermonuclear device. As a stunned global community struggled to respond to this development, India announced two days later that it had conducted two more detonations. In the aftermath of these tests, India declared itself to be a 'nuclear weapon state'[1] and formally announced its intention to develop a 'minimum credible (nuclear) deterrent'.[2]

This decision to create a deterrent, however, did not imply that India would automatically develop an arsenal of the sort maintained by the established nuclear powers. Rather, its traditionally anguished relationship with nuclear weapons[3] almost ensured that its new determination to formally create a strategic deterrent – far from closing the national debate about nuclearization irrevocably – would only focus attention, once again, on the five choices that India had grappled with since its independence in 1947: (1) Renounce the nuclear option; (2) Maintain a South Asian nuclear free zone; (3) Persist with simply maintaining the nuclear option; (4) Acquire a 'recessed deterrent'; and, finally, (5) Develop a robust and ready arsenal immediately.

While the first two alternatives in different forms were vigorously promoted by the international community in the aftermath of the May 1998 tests,[4] the national debate within India focused mainly on the last three alternatives, thus signaling that denuclearization was simply not viable given the new security environment facing the country.

While the proponents of alternative (3) argued that India, despite having tested, ought not to acquire a nuclear force for both moral and strategic reasons,[5] they appear to be marginal in the Indian strategic debate, which has for most part been dominated by proponents of alternatives (4) and (5). The former argue that a 'recessed deterrent', which allows India to constitute a nuclear arsenal within a few months, ought to suffice for Indian security, especially if New Delhi can utilize the threat to overtly deploy nuclear weapons as leverage both to accelerate the pace of global nuclear arms reductions and to secure preferential economic and political gains for India.[6]

The latter, in contrast, argue simply that India has already crossed the Rubicon by resuming nuclear testing and, consequently, should not halt its nuclearization until it acquires a large, diverse, and ready nuclear arsenal that will bequeath New Delhi both security and status.[7] By all indications, and in contrast to the views held by many within and outside India, the Indian government currently has chosen to split the difference between the positions advocated by the proponents of alternatives (4) and (5) (see Figure 1). The Indian nuclear force will be configured neither as a recessed

FIGURE 1

INDIA'S FORCE-IN-BEING IN THE CONTEXT OF ITS STRATEGIC ALTERNATIVES

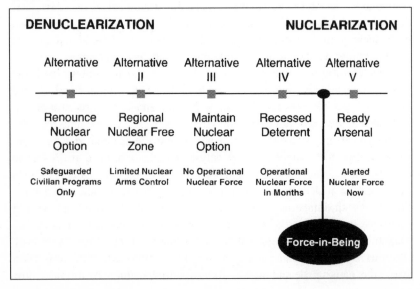

deterrent nor as a ready arsenal but as a *force-in-being*, that is, a deterrent consisting of available, but dispersed, components that are capable of being constituted into usable weapon systems during a supreme emergency.

This article seeks to explicate the logic, structure and utility of this distinctive nuclear force posture. Toward that end, it is divided into three sections. The first section describes why the solution represented by the force-in-being today appears attractive to Indian policymakers in the context of other past efforts to operationalize similar strategic regimes. The second section describes in some detail the anatomy of the force-in-being itself. The third and final section explores the kind of nuclear posture that might replace the force-in-being after it has outlived its current utility as an instrument for safeguarding Indian security.

THE ATTRACTIVENESS OF THE 'FORCE-IN-BEING'

A synoptic comparison of the three alternatives defining nuclearization in the aftermath of the May 1998 tests should indicate why the traditional Indian posture of 'maintaining the option' – Alternative III described earlier – cannot be a destination that New Delhi will return to in its search for a credible deterrent. This alternative, by eschewing the development of an arsenal of *any* sort, simply nullifies the Government of India's decision to create a strategic force and, consequently, has not been pursued. Alternative IV – the 'recessed deterrent' – has been rejected as well, since its emphasis on readying supporting capabilities rather than nuclear weapons and delivery systems prevents the development of those critical components required by a minimum deterrent.

Alternative V, in contrast – a 'robust and ready arsenal' – clearly enables New Delhi to pursue a 'minimum credible (nuclear) deterrent' but, by being too expensive, likely violating its desire for strict civilian control, and possibly being subversive of crisis stability, represents a posture that is much too extravagant for India's deterrence needs.

The decision to acquire a nuclear deterrent configured as a force-in-being, rather than the robust and ready arsenal advocated by many Indian hawks, then represents a *compromise* choice on the part of Indian policymakers that seeks to service many external demands and internal constraints simultaneously. It provides India with *strategic* advantages insofar as the presence of nuclear weapons in some form suffices to prevent blatant blackmail by China and Pakistan. It bequeaths New Delhi with *diplomatic* benefits by exemplifying 'restraint', particularly in comparison with an overt arsenal, and – in so doing – holds the promise of attenuating

US nonproliferation pressures on India.

It offers *psycho-political* reassurance insofar as it bolsters the confidence of India's national leadership, enhances its resolve in crises with local adversaries, and simultaneously provides the country with status as a nuclear weapons power. It buttresses existing *domestic* political structures by enabling India's civilian security managers to institutionally exclude the military from the day-to-day control and custody over the most critical components of India's strategic capability. And, finally, it portends *budgetary* relief insofar as its relatively quiescent force posture avoids all the high costs usually associated with the procurement, deployment, and operation of a ready arsenal.

The key idea encompassed by the notion of a force-in-being is that the entire 'arsenal' functions as a *strategic reserve* – neither fully visible nor operationally alerted – yet nonetheless present and available for employment – after some preparation – when strategic necessity dictates. The weapons and delivery systems *are* developed and produced, with key sub-components maintained under civilian custody, but these assets are sequestered and covertly maintained in distributed form, with different custodians exercising strict stewardship over the components entrusted to them for safekeeping.

The quiescence of the force-in-being at the operational level does not translate, however, into inactivity at the level of strategy. A force-in-being is indeed very active at the grand strategic levels of diplomacy and political choice, but this activity is manifested not so much by its tempo as by its effects. Its very existence as a potentially complete – but dormant – capability serves as a deterrent to possible adventurism by an adversary: it constantly hovers in the adversary's consciousness, commands its attention, keeps it at bay, and prevents it from attempting anything that would result in risk and hazard to itself, while constantly obliging it to think of nothing but being on guard against the terrible attack that would follow in retaliation against any of its provocations.[8]

Not surprisingly, a deterrence posture modeled on the notion of a force-in-being also functioned as the template governing the disposition of other Indian strategic assets. For example, New Delhi pursued a large chemical weapons research, development and production program covertly for almost two decades prior to the conclusion of the Chemical Weapons Convention (CWC), which banned all such weapons universally. The Indian government consistently denied the existence of a chemical weapons program in the early years of the negotiations leading up to the CWC,[9] and even the Indian military was largely in the dark about the character and the extent of these weapons, which were maintained completely under the control of the civilian Ministry of Defence.

Another example relevant to this discussion concerns India's short-range ballistic missiles (SRBM), notably the land-based versions of the Prithvi, which are intended as conventional deep attack systems that will eventually be available in three different range variants with five alternative types of conventional warheads.[10] Fears about the system's nuclear potential raised by both Pakistan and the United States have resulted in India treating the Prithvi force as if it were a strategic asset held in inert reserve. The Indian Army's missile inventory is not maintained by its controlling units in their designated area of operation. Instead, the unit slated to operate the missiles, the 333rd Missile Group, is based in Secunderabad in South India, while the missiles themselves are secured in storage bunkers – unfuelled – close to the Indo-Pakistan border.[11]

Both the chemical weapons program and the Prithvi SRBM force highlight two separate but related characteristics of the future Indian nuclear force-in-being. The former example suggests that the nuclear arsenal will be highly opaque, with great deception, denial, concealment, and mobility, utilized to hide the location of critical assets like weapons, delivery systems, assembly sites, and wartime command posts. Information about all the details pertaining to these assets will be hidden from most, including the Indian military, whose senior officers will be told just what they need to know in order to develop the relevant contingency plans relating to retaliation in the aftermath of India's absorbing a nuclear attack.

The latter example suggests that the nuclear arsenal will be distributed with weapons, and possibly even parts of weapons, kept separately from one another and from the delivery systems. While the delivery vehicles will remain in military custody because they are warfighting instruments *per se*, they are likely to be prepared and secured in secret locations that will neither be easily identifiable nor positioned close to the borders with Pakistan and China. Only when these weapons are required in moments of supreme emergency would the various component parts of the deterrent be brought together, integrated, and released to the end user – the uniformed military – with the objective of executing the acts of vengeance demanded by India's retaliatory response.[12]

THE ANATOMY OF THE 'FORCE-IN-BEING'

Both these examples serve to limn the future shape of India's nuclear deterrent: *a force-in-being that is limited in size, separated in disposition, and centralized in control.* Each of these variables will be analyzed further in some detail but before that investigation is undertaken, one important inference ought to be underscored. The Indian decision to develop a force-in-being implies that New Delhi's post-1998 nuclear posture – despite all the contrary rhetoric and expectations aired in New Delhi, Islamabad, and elsewhere in the world – will not be *radically* different from that which has been in place since about 1992–94.

The biggest difference, of course, is that India today is a declared nuclear weapons power: as such, its national leadership can openly discuss its nuclear capabilities in Parliament and with external interlocutors; the myriad research and development efforts pertaining to India's emerging nuclear capabilities can also be carried out without the pervasive subterfuge of the past; and, planning for strategic nuclear operations too can be pursued far more systematically and without hesitation, embarrassment, or dissembling.

On all other matters, the continuities between its post-1992/94 variant of 'maintaining the option' and its post-1998 posture of a developing a 'force-in-being' will be far greater and much more significant than most public commentators in India, Pakistan, and the United States usually recognize.

Limited in Size

All Indian discussions about their future force posture emphasize one element uniformly: that the desired nuclear deterrent will be limited in size. The Prime Minister, Atal Bihari Vajpayee, using language that is by now fairly common among the country's strategic community, authoritatively staked out this position in Parliament when he asserted that India would not seek more than a 'minimum, but credible, nuclear deterrent'.[13] Leading strategic analysts have amplified this leitmotif, with K. Subrahmanyam, for example, arguing that India is centered 'on minimum deterrence combined with no-first use'.[14]

Very rarely, some commentators have given vent to dissenting views on this question, as for example Brigadier V. P. Naib, who asserted that the need to retaliate against a nuclear strike would require India to have 'in readiness a reliable ability to inflict unacceptable damage at any time during the strategic exchange'.[15]

In a similar vein, one of India's most prominent civilian hawks, Bharat Karnad, said that, for India, the most effective solutions are personified by a 'maximally strategic'[16] deterrence posture built around multiple kinds of high-yield nuclear weapons and numerous, diverse delivery systems which, taken together, would create the 'full and robust deterrent'.[17]

Such arguments, however, do not appear to command a strong following among either the civilian leadership at both the political and the bureaucratic levels, or the higher leadership of the armed services, or the more numerous retired service officers who have written on this subject. Among this last group, a more typical example is represented by Major-General (ret.) Ashok Mehta, who noted that 'minimum deterrence and an NFU (no-first-use) policy allow for the maintenance of a limited nuclear arsenal – warheads and delivery systems – and a small, not-too-elaborate command and control structure. This makes the strategic deterrent affordable and prevents a nuclear arms race'.[18]

While the general consensus in India, both among civilian commentators and the armed services, thus seems to converge on the desirability of a 'minimum deterrent', it is not surprising to find that Indian 'defence experts … seem to be divided over … what constitutes a minimum deterrent'[19] (see Figure 2).

Indeed, the concept of minimum deterrence – being borrowed from Western debates on the subject – has been controversial right from the very beginning of its history. The simplest conceptions of minimum deterrence have defined it as a 'nuclear strategy in which a nation (or nations) maintains the minimum number of nuclear weapons necessary to inflict unacceptable damage on its adversary even after it has suffered a nuclear attack'.[20] Intuitively, this definition suggests that such a nuclear force would be oriented towards countervalue targeting since the small number of weapons presumably entailed by the adjective 'minimal' ultimately requires

FIGURE 2
ALTERNATIVE INDIAN CONCEPTIONS OF 'MINIMUM DETERRENCE'

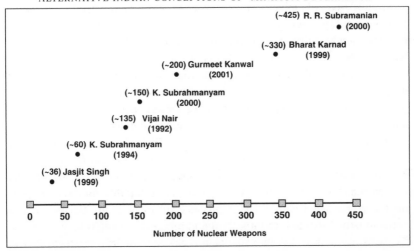

'city-busting' in order to satisfy the need for 'unacceptable damage'.

This predicate of minimal deterrence, however, left many theorists dissatisfied on both moral and prudential grounds and, consequently, a number of alternatives ranging from 'finite counterforce' to 'limited nuclear options' were advanced in order to allow for the possibility of limiting damage and controlling escalation if deterrence were ever to fail.[21]

Each of these alternatives, however, brought new problems in its wake, and ultimately the notion of 'minimal deterrence' – defined as 'a secure second-strike force of sufficient size to make threats of AD [assured destruction] credible'[22] – came to be seen more as an ideal type that was valuable because it provided an eidetic image which contrasted strongly with its polar opposite, 'maximal deterrence'. This was defined as a posture 'capable of fighting, and in some sense winning, nuclear wars across a spectrum of contingencies'.[23]

Since the notion of minimal deterrence did not (and could not) define any unique force size or structure, it was compatible with numerous nuclear architectures ranging from a few dozen warheads to perhaps even a few thousand weapons, all depending on the strength, resilience, and risk-taking propensities of the adversary. Western views on minimal deterrence have traditionally centered on the belief that 'the main challenge [was how] to achieve [stability] at lower nuclear force levels'.[24] The specific problem, then, consisted of appreciating the limits of 'successive build down'[25] or, in other words, the floor beyond which progressively deeper cuts in the number of nuclear weapons could not be safely undertaken.

In contrast to such Western concerns, the Indian approach to minimal deterrence involves exactly the opposite problem. The specific challenge facing New Delhi today is that of a *build-up* – not a draw-down – of its nuclear forces, given that its strategic deterrent hitherto has been largely latent, symbolic, and nominal. This challenge, however, generates a set of questions similar to that engendered by the Western debate, namely, 'how much is enough?' for purposes of both deterrence and stability.

This question exercised Western strategists greatly during the Cold War and a variety of sophisticated analytical techniques were developed in an effort to address this issue satisfactorily.[26] While a consensus solution ultimately proved elusive, at least the framework governing the solution became clear: the number of nuclear weapons deemed to be sufficient were a complex function of the type, yield and reliability of the weapons themselves and the number of targets needed to be held at risk, this last variable being affected, in turn, by the number, types and reliability of the weapons possessed by the adversary and the nuclear strategy it was expected to pursue.[27]

Indian security managers have not thus far defined their requirements with respect to any of these issues publicly, and they will probably never define these requirements openly in the future. But, while the upper and lower bounds of India's strategic requirements are unknown, what is clear is that New Delhi believes successful 'deterrence is not dependent on matching weapon to weapon, but [rather, hinges] on the ability to retaliate with a residual capability'.[28]

This position is obviously borrowed from the writings of K. Subrahmanyam who, in response to the US demand for a quantification of India's deterrent, has argued that 'minimum deterrence is not a numerical definition but a strategic approach. If a country is in a position to have a survivable arsenal, which is seen as capable of exacting an unacceptable penalty in retaliation, it has a minimum deterrence [as] opposed to an open-ended one aimed at matching the adversary's arsenals in numerical terms'.[29] This notion that minimum deterrence is a strategic approach, and hence beyond quantification, has been criticized vehemently by other Indian analysts, however, who note that 'for deterrence to be credible, it has ultimately to be based on numbers'.[30]

Such criticisms overlook the subtlety of the official Indian position. Clearly, both Subrahmanyam and India's security managers amply recognize that deterrence, in the final analysis, *is* about numbers: the numbers of weapons that are possessed by India, the numbers of weapons that can survive a first strike, the numbers of weapons that could be successfully carried to and detonated on target, and the numbers of weapons required to wreak unacceptable damage on an adversary who threatens Indian security.

What they are attempting to suggest, therefore, through their claims that deterrence is not about numbers, is that the number of nuclear weapons judged to be essential to Indian security is not something they are willing to disclose either to their own body politic, or to their adversaries, or to any other interested interlocutors like the United States. In part, this response is conditioned by the fact that they cannot be certain today what their eventual stockpile of fissile materials and the quality of their future nuclear weapons designs would look like.

Even though India's security managers probably have a good idea about where they would prefer to end up, they are quite unlikely to reveal this information – for reasons relating both to the exigencies of public diplomacy and the requirements of deterrence stability – to any one who might have the temerity to ask.

In their public statements, India's security managers have continued to emphasize that the relative number of nuclear weapons possessed by India *vis-à-vis* its adversaries is less important than the fact that even a few surviving weapons would cause more pain than is worth any of the objectives sought by the latter. In some instances, they have explicitly affirmed that India is in fact content to accept nuclear inferiority *vis-à-vis* China, both in terms of numbers and qualitative capability, because such inferiority does not in any way prejudice their ability to preserve India's security and autonomy.[31] Whether a similar position would be maintained *vis-à-vis* Pakistan is unclear, despite Jaswant Singh's insistence that 'the question of an arsenal larger than that of country *X* or *Y* [is] a non-question'.[32]

The only thing worth stating on this matter is that Indian security managers traditionally have always believed that New Delhi's strategic pre-eminence *vis-à-vis* Islamabad was not simply a fact of life but an operating condition that had to be assiduously maintained because of their judgment of Pakistan as a risk-acceptant, if not an irresponsible, state.

On the assumption, therefore, that India continues to enjoy nuclear superiority over Pakistan, even as it remains inferior by many comparable measures to China, New Delhi has repeatedly affirmed that the very notions of 'superiority' and 'inferiority' are politically irrelevant so long as the residual capability to devastate a certain fraction of the adversary's assets always exists inviolate even amidst the carnage of war.[33] Though partially conditioned by the confidence that India already possesses nuclear superiority over Pakistan, this affirmation also draws sustenance from a variety of larger beliefs held in India about: the gradual decay in the efficacy of nuclear threats since the beginning of the nuclear era; the strong presumption already existing against any nuclear use; and the progressively declining thresholds that define unacceptable damage as societies continue to modernize economically.

Irrespective of these expectations turning out to be correct, they still need to be translated into a weapons inventory that is consistent with the overarching concept of 'minimum deterrence'. One of India's most widely read commentators on nuclear matters, Vijai Nair, has attempted to provide just such a numerical estimate of how the country's evolving deterrent ought to be sized. Nair estimates that *vis-à-vis* Pakistan, a nominally weaker nuclear adversary, India should acquire the ability to target:

> six metropolitan centers including port facilities; one corps sized offensive formation in its concentration area; three sets of bottlenecks in the strategic communications network; five nuclear capable military airfields; two hydroelectric water storage dams. A total of 17

nuclear engagements.[34]

Vis-à-vis China, a superior nuclear adversary, Nair argues that India ought to focus on large punishing strikes that would retard postwar Chinese capabilities relative to its other adversaries. This implies that India would need a weapons capability able to pull out 'five to six major industrial centers, plus two ports, to service China's strategic missile submarine (SSBN) fleet. This makes a total of eight nuclear strikes'.[35] Against such a target array, Nair argues that

> the ideal configuration of warhead numbers and yield would be: two strikes of one megaton each for metropolitan centres and port facilities; two strikes of 15 kiloton (kt) each for battlefield targets; one strike with a yield of between 200 and 500 kt each for dams; one strike of 20 to 50 kt each for military airfields; and one strike each of 15 kt for strategic communication centres.[36]

After reliability parameters are factored in, at the rate of two weapons for each autonomous strike, with 20 per cent of the entire force structure maintained as a postwar reserve, the 25 designated targets in China and Pakistan are calculated as requiring an overall Indian arsenal of 132 weapons of varying size and yield.[37]

Other commentators have also offered similar, though sometimes less detailed, assessments. General K. Sundarji, for example, has concluded that against a small country like Pakistan 'up to 1 MTE [megaton equivalent] (say 50 x 20 kt weapons) might do. Even for deterring a large country, one is most unlikely to require more than 4 MTE'.[38] These totals are difficult to translate into specific numbers of weapons because the design yields of India's nuclear weaponry are not publicly known. Sundarji suggests, however, that targeting 15 conurbations in both Pakistan (5) and China (10) should suffice for minimal deterrence: each of these targets could be attacked with 'three fission warheads of 20 kt each, detonated as low airbursts',[39] and from this requirement he deduces that India 'would need 45 warheads (and their delivery means) to survive an adversary first strike'.[40]

These numbers are explicitly based on weapons designs producing nominal yields in the ~20 kt range, and after factoring in reliability parameters and possible losses to an adversary's first strike, Sundarji concludes that 'a low estimate of 90 weapons and an upper estimate of 135 weapons would be reasonable'.[41] K. Subrahmanyam too argues for a comparable class of numbers: in 1994, he declared that India needed only '60 deliverable warheads'[42] which, in practice, probably meant some larger number if the reliability quotient and the possible attrition of these assets are taken into account. General V. N. Sharma, a former Indian Army Chief of Staff, for example, 'believes that around 50 bombs should do, but calls for 'going the whole hog' in delivery systems'.[43]

In sharp contrast to these more moderate estimates, Bharat Karnad has argued that strategic sufficiency for India cannot consist of anything less than the ability to interdict ~60 primary and secondary targets in China and Pakistan and, accordingly, demands a nuclear force of well over 300 weapons by the year 2030 – most of which must be high yield thermonuclear devices.[44]

While the size of the weapons inventory has received some attention, the number of desired delivery systems has not been specified in comparable detail in Indian discussions thus far. In part, this is because deducing the minimal numbers of delivery vehicles necessary requires complex operations research and analysis as well as prior knowledge of many variables like basing modes, relative hardness and mobility, and estimates of success accruing to deception and denial. The kind of delivery system chosen also affects the final force size: while ballistic and cruise missiles, which are single-use vehicles, would correlate with their nuclear payloads in a one-to-one relationship, strike aircraft, being reusable, do not lend themselves to such a simple metric for force sizing.

The lower penetrative capacity of aircraft can increase the gross numbers required, and complex planning tools are therefore necessary if good estimates of operational requirements are to be derived. Given the lack of access to such planning tools, it is not surprising that various Indian commentators have advanced different estimates of the delivery systems required to carry their preferred inventory.

In 1994, K. Subrahmanyam argued that his force of about 60 nuclear weapons be carried on 20 Prithvi SRBMs, 20 Agni intermediate-range ballistic missiles (IRBMs), and the rest on strike aircraft.[45] Two years later, Sundarji, in contrast, argued for a force of ~150 warheads carried on 45 Prithvi SRBMs and 90 Agni IRBMs, with the balance carried by aircraft.[46] Vijai Nair has argued for at least 5 SSBNs, in order to maintain 48 SLBMs ready at all times for use against China and Pakistan, in addition to 36 SRBMs and IRBMs and various other unspecified numbers of manned aircraft.[47]

And, in the most expansive version of all, Bharat Karnad has argued for a force of 4 SSBNs contributing a total of 48 SLBMs, 25 intercontinental ballistic missiles (ICBMs), 40 IRBMs, and 70 manned aircraft, all to be complemented by another 70 air-to-surface missiles and 25 atomic demolition munitions.[48] The exact nature of the calculations leading up to these force architectures is not known.[49]

Despite the lack of consensus among commentators, there are some interesting similarities between these estimates. All posit essentially finite arsenals, that is, weapons inventories and delivery systems that do not inexorably grow in size once the ability to service certain destruction requirements is assured. Further, the level of destruction thought to be sufficient for successful deterrence is relatively small and generally centers around the ability to destroy 8–15 target complexes in China and Pakistan, even though precisely what constitutes destruction may vary from analyst to analyst. Many accept a certain redundancy in capabilities to allow for reliability constraints, attrition as a result of first strikes, and delivery failures, yet none argue for a force posture that is in any way automatically or consistently keyed to the size and character of the adversaries' nuclear capabilities.

In all probability, however, most decisions about the size of India's nuclear arsenal will be made ultimately on considerations *other than merely operational requirements*. It is, in fact, almost likely that the size of the nuclear weapons stockpile will be defined eventually by the quantum of fissile materials available to India – and not necessarily by the size of the target set defined by India's numerous security commentators. Similarly, the yield of the nuclear weapons themselves will be determined fundamentally by the designs that Indian scientists have been able to validate thus far or appear to have the greatest preference for – and not necessarily by the demands imposed as a result of the technical characteristics of the target array.

This by itself should not be surprising because India's political leadership does *not* seek to create a large and complex nuclear arsenal, even if its scientific community yearns to push the envelope with respect to more and more sophisticated weapons designs. Further, the principal criterion for strategic adequacy in Indian eyes is not that the damage inflicted by its weapons ought to be greater than that which can be inflicted by an adversary, but only that the costs resulting from Indian retaliation ought to be greater than any political benefits accruing to the adversary as a result of its nuclear threats or first use.

The requirements for effective deterrence in the Indian context are thus truly low because state managers in New Delhi have already concluded that there are very few political benefits which could be secured by any adversary through aggression – with or without nuclear weapons – against India. Given this generally modest criterion of strategic adequacy, even small numbers of relatively low-yield fission bombs could suffice to provide India with the deterrence it desires.

Although India's nuclear force may therefore be defined eventually more by technical limitations and political constraints rather than by strict operational requirements, Indian policymakers today believe that prudence requires that they keep all their options open. On this issue, both the government of India and security élites within the country at large appear to be of one mind. Both groups are agreed that India's strategic policies with respect to matters affecting the size and quality of its future deterrent ought to have three components.

First, India should not foreclose any possibilities unless the payoffs from foreclosure incontrovertibly exceed the costs. In practical terms, this implies that India will be quite loath to quickly sign and ratify the CTBT and assist the Fissile Materials Cut-off Treaty (FMCT) negotiations to a speedy and successful conclusion, because surrendering the benefits embodied by such actions would occur only if there was some prospect of securing suitable political advantages as compensation.

Second, India should not make any formal commitments to limit the upper bounds of strategic capability. In practical terms, this implies that Indian security managers will not provide any binding assurances to either the United States or the international community that their desired force-in-being will not exceed certain quantitative or qualitative thresholds.

Third, India should not restrain its domestic research, development and production activities relating to nuclear weapons, fissile materials, and delivery systems. In practical terms, this implies that India will continue to press ahead with its existing efforts in all three arenas, although these may be accelerated in some areas – like the production of fissile materials, for example – while remaining more or less constant in others – such as the development of delivery systems.

This threefold strategy is clearly intended to minimize, on the one hand, the extent of the formal obligations restraining India's emerging strategic capabilities while, on the other hand, producing the largest and most effective deterrent force possible within more or less the limits of its current capabilities.[50] The latter objective is not simply to expand the size of the nuclear weapons inventory for its own sake, but rather to increase the extent of the residual fraction that would survive a nuclear strike that might be mounted by its adversaries.

The 'Draft Report of [the] National Security Advisory Board on Indian Nuclear Doctrine' captured this requirement succinctly when it noted that India's operational policy of 'retaliation only' makes 'the survivability of our arsenal ... critical'.[51] The Advisory Board pointed out, quite accurately, that the size of India's nuclear force eventually would be conditioned by many variables, including the capability and the disposition of the nuclear forces maintained by India's adversaries, the demands levied on penetrativity in the face of the incipient transformations in the present offense-dominant global nuclear regime, and the state of political relations: between India and its immediate adversaries; between those adversaries themselves; and between India and other key powers in the global system.

A recognition of these factors led the Board to insinuate that the size of India's emerging nuclear force would have to be sufficiently variable to ensure survivability in the light of the potential changes in these issue-areas.[52] The prospect of such variability, however, cannot imply that the size of India's nuclear force would, by definition, be open-ended. Most Indian security managers recognize that at some point in the future a FMCT, if successfully concluded, would compel them either to terminate the production of weapon-usable materials or at least transparently account for all their future inventories.[53]

This fact, coupled with the constraints imposed by the parlous state of India's nuclear infrastructure, sets a ceiling on the size of India's future nuclear arsenal which cannot be negotiated away unless the country is willing to make a massive investment in new nuclear production facilities right away in the hope that it can dramatically distend its potential arsenal before the decade is out (which is when the constraints emerging from a FMCT could conceivably kick in).[54]

K. Subrahmanyam, in recent writings, has sought to clarify what the outer limits of the Indian minimum deterrent might be by affirming that the country's emerging arsenal will probably be pegged eventually at about a 150 nuclear weapons[55] – a judgment obviously based on the premise that no FMCT restrictions will be operational for at least another decade *and* that India can improve the efficiency of its plutonium production for weapons purposes in the interim.

All this implies that the emerging Indian nuclear deterrent eventually will be quite limited in size: it will be a relatively small force consisting of about 150 weapons (and possibly even fewer) by the year 2010, most of which likely will be capable of producing only comparatively small yields of about 20 kt (if New Delhi persists with its current moratorium on nuclear testing). India will continue to pursue a variety of delivery systems, especially ballistic and cruise missiles, and will acquire as many of these systems as is necessary to deliver its nuclear weapons under a wide variety of operational contingencies.

Because none of the missiles currently existing are ideal vehicles for nuclear payloads, however, it is likely that India will continue to develop these systems to reach ranges that will probably not exceed 3,500 km. This may be so, even as it persists in experimenting with a variety of unorthodox basing modes in order to migrate gradually from the current reliance on air-breathing vehicles that will nonetheless remain the primary carriers of India's nuclear weaponry for at least some years to come.

Separated in Disposition

Although the mature Indian arsenal will remain a relatively small force, the very fact of its existence will become a source of threat to India's adversaries, both China and Pakistan, who in the event of deterrence breakdown may be forced to contemplate a variety of preemptive damage limiting strategies purely for defensive reasons.[56] An important challenge facing India's evolving arsenal, therefore, consists of ensuring its survivability against any first-strike temptations on the part of an adversary, and neutralizing such temptations successfully represents the first key to successful deterrence.

Specifically, this challenge boils down to the question of how a small nuclear force may be preserved inviolate so that, even if first strikes are unleashed *in extremis*, a substantial fraction of the nuclear assets will survive, ready to be reconstituted for the devastating retribution to follow. In general, states that already possess nuclear arsenals have adopted some combination of the following basic solutions designed to ensure survivability: 'physical hardening, geographic dispersion, mobility, redundancy, secrecy, and the active interdiction of attacking weapons',[57] each of which embodies different benefits and costs.

Since India has eschewed the development of a robust and ready arsenal in favor of a force-in-being, it is unlikely to pursue either physical hardening or active interdiction of attacking weapons as the *primary* means of ensuring survivability. It is likely to focus instead on configuring its force-in-being in such a way so as to feature *pervasively distributed capabilities in order that no completed strategic systems actually exist routinely as transparent targets for potential interdiction*. This orientation, exploiting concealment, deception, and mobility, will be defined around distributed capabilities and it is this feature which not only makes the Indian deterrent a force-in-being as opposed to, say, a robust and ready arsenal but also broadly contributes to resolving its problems of survivability – at least in principle.[58]

The concept of distributed capabilities implies that the normal peacetime posture of India's nuclear deterrent will consist of deliberately separated components maintained under conditions of great secrecy. For purposes of analysis, these components may be treated as encompassing: the weapon's core which consists of some kind of fissile material and is usually referred to as the 'pit'; the weapon assembly which consists of all the other non-nuclear elements of the device, including the safing, arming, fuzing and firing (SAFF) subsystems; and the delivery platform, whether that be an aircraft or a missile. If the delivery platform is a missile, there are strictly speaking two components, the missile itself and the launch system: the technical characteristics of the latter will vary depending on whether the missile is designed for road- or rail-mobility, or if it is intended for basing on a sea-based surface or sub-surface platform.

Although the exact extent of separation that will be operationalized in practice is unknown and will never be revealed by India's security managers, it is possible to identify abstractly at least six relatively distinct degrees of separation that could define the routine configuration of India's nuclear deterrent, on the assumption that this force will eventually include only gravity bombs and warheads to be carried either by land-based aircraft or land- and sea-based ballistic missiles. If the inventory were to include cruise missiles of different sorts and various kinds of tactical nuclear weapons, the postures described below would have to be further modified, but since it is likely that India's nuclear systems in the foreseeable future will consist mainly of land and sea-based ballistic missiles – the Agni and, possibly, the Prithvi, in several variants – and land-based aircraft of different kinds, the postures described below should suffice for purposes of analysis (see Figure 3).

Posture I involves a systematic separation of the pit from the weapon assembly both of which, in turn, are stored away from their aircraft delivery system. Posture II involves the same configuration but uses a missile as delivery system; the missile, as well as its launch system, is stored separately. This configuration obviously applies only to the land-based component of the deterrent force, since a sea-based deterrent either does not permit such a degree of separation or permits it only under outlandish technical and operational assumptions so to render it highly infeasible.

The other postures describe various modes of deployment which involve smaller degrees of separation. Posture III involves separating the pit from the weapon assembly and storing these separately from the missile delivery systems which are maintained, however, in integrated form with both missiles and launchers mated routinely. Posture IV involves a further

FIGURE 3

ALTERNATE POSTURES DEFINING THE CONCEPT OF DISTRIBUTED CAPABILITY

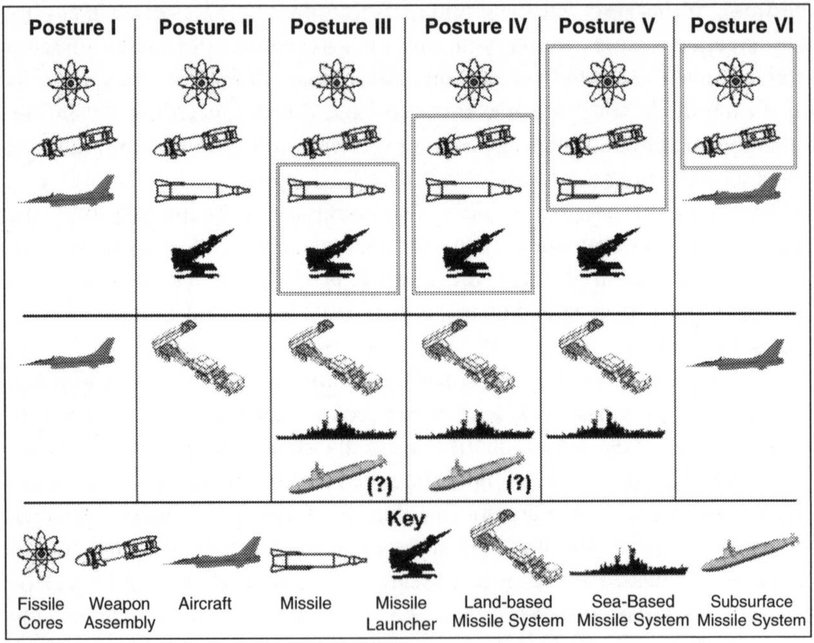

diminution in the degree of separation, with the missile, its launcher, and the weapon assembly, routinely maintained in integrated form minus only the nuclear pit, which is stored separately and away from the rest of the integrated system.

This mode of separation can be adapted for use with respect to both land- and, with greater complexity, sea-based systems. Posture V is broadly comparable to Posture IV in that it would involve the complete mating of the nuclear pit, the weapon assembly, and the missile itself, with these completed units, however, stored separately and away from their associated launch system. This mode of separation is most feasible where land-based missiles are concerned, but is less so in the case of surface ship-based systems, and is practically impossible in the case of submarines.

Posture VI is analogous to Posture V, but applies to aircraft: the pit and the weapon assembly are fully integrated to form complete and ready gravity bombs, but these units are stored separately and apart from their delivery aircraft which, being dual-use platforms, are maintained at relatively high levels of readiness.

It is difficult to assess which model of a distributed capability Indian analysts would either approve or disapprove when they argue about the desirable character of their evolving force posture. Statements made by Indian policymakers suggest an inordinate, though justifiable, concern about the survivability of their nuclear assets.[59] In this context, it is important to recognize that the fact or extent of distribution *per se* does *not* enhance survivability: survivability is best ensured by the lack of transparency about the location of the nuclear assets.

In order to preserve opacity while simultaneously effecting the distribution of components, force planners would need to acquire a far larger number of the potentially more detectable delivery systems than would actually be required by the size of their nuclear weapons stockpile itself. Recognizing this fact, the 'Draft Doctrine of [the] National Security Advisory Board' argues that in addition to 'mobility, dispersion and deception', the 'survivability of [India's nuclear] forces will [have to] be enhanced by ...[the presence of] ... multiple redundant systems...'[60]

While this argument is certainly correct, the key analytical problem identified earlier still remains unresolved. If the only objective is to maximize survivability, it is logical for India to focus on acquiring a larger number of delivery systems than is strictly necessitated by the size of its weapon stockpile, coupled with a force posture that emphasizes higher degrees of separation among components as is exemplified, for instance, by Postures I and II. If the objective of maximizing survivability, however, is pursued concurrently with some other objective, for example, the ability to shift quickly from peacetime deployment to wartime readiness as is recommended by the Draft Doctrine issued by the National Security Advisory Board,[61] then it would be logical for India to consider alternative postures, like Postures V and VI, which incorporate even lower degrees of separation.

A complete solution to the problem of assessing the appropriate degree of distribution, however, will require an analysis of not only the tradeoffs between the survivability-rapid retaliation dilemma but, equally importantly, an analysis of how any solution adopted to deal with this issue also affects India's ability to cope with other challenges, like the threats posed by accidental detonation, unauthorized use, mistaken authorized use, and terrorist seizure.

When these challenges are explicitly incorporated into the analysis, it becomes obvious that Postures V and VI may quickly become subversive of stability insofar as they require nuclear devices to subsist in completed form routinely. The threats emerging from such a posture, however, can be reduced considerably if the nuclear weapon designs incorporate some sort of enhanced nuclear detonation safety system (ENDS) and various kinds of permissive actions links (PALs),[62] but if such technologies are not available (or available only in relatively primitive form), other alternatives will have to be relied upon.

An alternative that resolves the survivability-rapid retaliation dilemma together with the other challenges of nuclear possession, then, can be found only among Postures I, III and IV, with Posture I being optimal for the air-breathing arm and Posture IV being optimal for the land- and sea-based missile arms of the force. Both these postures, however, would require nuclear weapons based on 'insertable pit'[63] designs – hardly the acme of safety technology today.

Regardless of which of the above postures Indian security managers prefer, these will be operationalized not in static but in dynamic form. That is, the many components of the deterrent force which are stored separately may be periodically moved from location to location covertly, and their relatively small size, coupled with the fact that there already exists a ready physical infrastructure designed for storing, maintaining and readying such elements, makes a distributed solution to India's strategic problem eminently feasible. There are, in general, three conditions which are necessary for the success of such an arrangement: first, there must be a large number of storage sites under the effective control of the state; second, the number of individuals with information about the physical location of the actual holdings must be small; third, there must be an organizational system capable of handing both the storage and the episodic, but covert, movements of various components.

All three conditions obtain abundantly in the case of India. While the number of facilities at which India's strategic assets could be distributed is potentially very large, the number of individuals with information about the location and status of these component parts is, in contrast, very small.[64] Those who possess a 'God's eye view' of the entire weapons program are probably less than two dozen in number, though perhaps many more individuals are aware of bits and pieces pertaining to the general effort.[65]

Administrative structures in India, especially those relating to the nuclear weapons effort in particular, cut across organizational realms, and operational directives are invariably communicated informally and without any written record whatsoever.[66] These arrangements work only because the Indian administrative structure spawns very effective, but shadowy, core *networks* which are then superimposed on the existing *institutions*. In such circumstances, strategic decision-making is transacted within the small network, while the larger institutional, bureaucratic apparatus is simply relegated to the business of routine management.[67]

This *modus operandi* certainly does not preclude the development of more formal and institutionalized procedures for managing the Indian nuclear deterrent over time. In the interim, however, it does suggest that the security of the control and oversight arrangements will be very difficult to compromise because low-level actors will *not* possess sufficient information about the status and disposition of *all* the constituent parts of the deterrent, while the high-level actors will be both difficult to identify exhaustively and, even if identified, will not reveal anything more than they choose to about the nuclear posture writ large.[68]

This simple fact makes any counter-control targeting strategy difficult, if not impossible, to execute even by an advanced nuclear power, because even the destruction of every identifiable technical node within the command system may not suffice to prevent control from being reestablished by more primitive means and through the coordinated actions of a relatively small number of individuals who know each other intimately.

What makes the distributed posture potentially effective from the viewpoint of survivability is the fact that routine standard operating procedures already exist both in the civilian and in the military realms. The Indian nuclear program, for example, already has a working set of institutional procedures which regulate the transfers of critical nuclear materials between various facilities and sites as well as a physical infrastructure that enables the appropriate handling of all such materials.[69]

A similar set of procedures and infrastructure exists in the defense research and development organization. Since these communities would have primary responsibility for the custody, storage, and handling of both nuclear pits and weapons assemblies in peacetime, it is not unreasonable to believe that these components would be secured (or moved as the case may be) without any security lapses or compromise. As the components themselves are relatively small in size and can be moved by ordinary forms of transportation, the likelihood that a potential adversary would be able to locate all or many of the storage sites associated with the concealment of these components is extremely remote.

As if to inure against this possibility, the Indian military, too, has a comparable set of procedures and infrastructure governing the storage and movement of critical war materials.[70] If anything, these organizational capabilities are even better developed because the peacetime dispersal of

India's military assets across vast distances of the hinterland has required its armed services to develop both the physical infrastructure and the organizational routines that pertain to the rapid movement of military equipment in an emergency.

All strategic solutions to the problem of survivability involve tradeoffs, and the Indian concept of a distributed force-in-being is no exception. The critical weakness of this posture is not its susceptibility to accidents – because completed nuclear weapons would not exist as such in peacetime – but rather its potential inability to effectively reconstitute in the aftermath of a nuclear attack in order to carry out retaliation. While it is difficult to imagine any successful damage-limiting strikes conducted by either China or Pakistan simply because of the ratio of potential targets-to-weapons involved, not to mention the intelligence requirements needed to support such strikes, it ought to be recognized that such eventualities are possible, at least theoretically, and that they could impose great burdens on the Indian capacity to retaliate.

Should this outcome obtain, it is obvious that India's efforts at ensuring the survivability of its nuclear capabilities were less-than-effective to begin with. This is a risk, however, that Indian decision makers seem willing to take for three reasons: first, because the requirements for successful disarming strikes are deemed to be so gigantic as to render them beyond the pale of possibility in the real world, especially in the context of India's competition with China and Pakistan;[71] second, because neither Pakistan nor China has demonstrated either the technical capabilities or the doctrinal interest in executing damaging-limiting first strikes as a matter of operational policy;[72] third, because the circumstances under which Indian nuclear weapons use becomes realistic is so remote that the risk of being unable to reconstitute effectively becomes a secondary problem, given New Delhi's more pressing interest in assuring the safety of its weaponry, minimizing the costs of its arsenal, and maintaining continual civilian control over all its strategic assets.[73]

What makes a difference in the end is that India does *not* seek to deter formidable nuclear powers like the United States and Russia, merely lesser adversaries like China and Pakistan. Even in these instances, nuclear weapons do not represent New Delhi's first line of defense but remain merely *political instruments of deterrence and reassurance* which acquire effectiveness because the devastation that could be caused by even one of India's modest weapons would be far greater than any of the benefits sought by its adversaries through war. Given these realities, the risk of being unable to reconstitute a overwhelming retaliatory response because of an excessively distributed force-in-being is something that New Delhi can live with.

Centralized in Control

As indicated above, the issue of survivability constitutes only one of the many challenges facing an emerging nuclear power. Among other critical issues is the security of the nuclear force, that is, its resistance to efforts by unauthorized individuals to acquire custody of the weaponry and discharge them without legitimate sanction. Dealing with this problem remains the province of the control system which regulates both the patterns of custody surrounding nuclear weapons and the extent of autonomy enjoyed by their custodians with respect to the issue of legitimate use.

The challenges arising out of these issues have traditionally been termed the dilemma of 'positive' and 'negative' control. As Peter Feaver summarized it, positive control refers to the fact that 'leaders want a high assurance that the weapons will always work when directed',[74] while negative control refers to the equally high degree of reassurance sought by the national leadership that 'the weapons will never be used in the absence of authorized direction'.[75] Since positive and negative control have to be accomplished simultaneously, there has always been a certain degree of tension between these two demands as the requirements of safety could undercut the requirements of survivability and vice versa. These safety-survivability tradeoffs have traditionally resulted in the development of various kinds of innovations intended to simultaneously safeguard nuclear weapons while preserving their effectiveness.[76]

The United States, for example, operating on the premise that achieving successful nuclear deterrence against a revisionist power like the Soviet Union was a difficult and demanding task, attempted to resolve the dilemma by a combination of technical and organizational solutions which always sought to ensure that a sufficient number of nuclear weapons would remain constantly available and ready for instant use even after absorbing a Soviet first strike. To ensure ready availability – or, in other words, continuing positive control – the United States developed an elaborately dispersed force, where ready nuclear weapons were deployed on board a multiplicity of platforms, like land-based missiles, submarines and bombers.

Because this solution essentially implied that the uniformed services had *completed nuclear weapons* (at varying levels of readiness) in their possession at all times, the problems of negative control – that is, the prevention of mistaken or unauthorized use – became a critical issue. The United States addressed this challenge through a combination of technical responses and organizational innovations – all of which were designed to forestall unauthorized use even while the force as a whole remained constantly ready to respond to a nuclear attack.[77] The overall command system then was biased in the direction of positive control, and this tendency was reflected most conspicuously by the highly 'delegative'[78] patterns of authority under which the military enjoyed a high degree of autonomy with respect to the use of nuclear weapons in their possession.

The control system in the case of India would be biased in exactly the opposite direction because New Delhi's strategic requirements are very different from those faced by the United States during the Cold War.[79] Because India is likely to distribute only discrete components of its nuclear 'arsenal' across different locations, the military will likely be tasked primarily with storing, maintaining and manning the delivery systems in the first instance.

This separation by components – which lies at the heart of the Indian version of the distributed solution – will probably be further complemented by a partitioning by organization: the Department of Atomic Energy (DAE) and the Defence Research and Development Organisation (DRDO), both civilian agencies, will retain custody of the fissile core and the weapons assembly (either jointly or separately), while the nuclear-capable delivery system, be it aircraft or missile, will continue to remain in the custody of the military since there is in effect no viable alternate arrangement as far as the dual-capable delivery systems are concerned. Thus, neither the DAE nor the DRDO nor the military would be able to launch a nuclear weapon independently since none of these organizations – acting autonomously – would have all the necessary components to assemble a completed weapon and deliver it to target without explicit authorization from the national leadership.

Without such authorization, it would in fact be impossible for the various custodial teams even to assemble together since there is high degree of organizational separation between the civilian nuclear scientists, the civilian defense technologists, and the uniformed military. Unauthorized assembly of nuclear weapons would require all three groups to collude effectively if deployment postures involving a very high degree of separation among components are chosen by the national leadership.

This is an almost impossible prospect in the case of India because the custodians of these components, being few in number and knowing each other very intimately, share an extraordinarily high commitment to the Indian state and, as such, would be unlikely to undertake any course of action that would imperil the national interest. The lengthy process of socialization that occurs in the civilian bureaucracies, the nuclear weapons research program, the defense scientific establishment, and the uniformed services, in effect, serves as a *de facto* personnel reliability program.[80]

The multiple levels of distribution – first by component and then by organization – which will most likely be institutionalized by the Indian system of managing its nuclear assets, thus, effectively serves as a 'super PAL',[81] an elaborate set of physical and organizational constraints on the unauthorized creation of a nuclear weapon when such is not required by the demands of national policy.

While the character of distribution – by component and by organization – will remain a key difference between the American and Indian solutions to the problems of survivability and unauthorized use, the pattern of ultimate control with respect to the question of who can legitimately order nuclear use will also be similarly divergent. Unlike the United States, the Indian system of control will be highly 'assertive',[82] meaning that the civilian leadership at the very top, in the person of the Prime Minister and his Cabinet, will continue to exercise strict and pervasive control over the structure of distribution of nuclear assets, the authorization pertaining to the marriage of various strategic components in an emergency, and the decision to actually use nuclear weapons as part of a retaliatory response.

By being able to directly oversee the affairs of the DAE, while controlling both the DRDO and the armed services through the civilian Ministry of Defence (MOD), India's Prime Ministers have always been able to exercise – whenever they chose to – close and continuing authority over any developments occurring in these organizations.[83] The acquisition of nuclear weaponry is only likely to make this traditionally tight control even tighter.

Since India's nuclear weapons are intended primarily as political instruments of deterrence and reassurance in the face of possible threats, and secondarily as instruments of retribution in the event of actual use, policymakers in New Delhi believe that their interests are not at all well served by opting for a completely 'delegative' command system where a significant number of completed nuclear weapons are distributed to the military for routine custody and safekeeping, with this end-user being granted the 'pre-delegated'[84] authority for the use of such weapons in an emergency.[85]

Instead, India's declaratory doctrine of 'delayed – but assured – retaliation' can be preeminently satisfied by more or less strong forms of 'assertive' control, which includes the devolutionary, rather than pre-delegated, transfer of resources and authority to the military only under conditions of supreme emergency. Such a command arrangement could be quite satisfactory so long as an adequately distributed nuclear posture, which can assure the survivability of a significant fraction of India's nuclear assets, exists in some form and is complemented by the existence of effective procedures for post-attack reconstitution.[86]

Any assertive command system of the sort associated with centralized control obviously suffers from one specific weakness, namely its vulnerability to 'strategic decapitation'.[87] Strategic decapitation refers to the destruction of the national command authority as a result of enemy action which is intended to paralyze a state's ability to respond rapidly and coherently. Preparing for this contingency certainly concentrates the minds of many Indians: the Draft Report of [the] National Security Advisory Board on Indian Nuclear Doctrine, for example, affirmed that the requisite 'procedures for the continuity of nuclear command and control' ought to be created in order to 'ensure a continuing capability to effectively employ nuclear weapons' even in the face of 'surprise attacks' and 'repetitive attrition attempts' by an adversary.[88]

While such directives are appropriate, there is good reason to believe that the threat of strategic decapitation may not be as overpowering as is sometimes imagined, at least in the case of conflict scenarios in southern Asia. To begin with, there is no reason why Pakistan or China should pursue strategies of nuclear decapitation, even if they are able to do so. Both states, if they were ever in a situation where their nuclear weapons have to be actually used, would most likely employ their weapons for purposes of strategic signaling rather than in pursuit of counter-control objectives. Such employment requires the attacker to deliberately eschew decapitating strikes because the national leadership of the adversary must remain intact if a tacitly or explicitly negotiated termination of conflict is to occur.

This does not imply that India should not treat the possibility of decapitation seriously. It should, and if Indian discussions are any indication, it probably will.[89] The solution to potential decapitation lies in developing a proper system for devolving authority and transferring strategic assets in an emergency. The former would regulate how the legitimate power to authorize the employment of nuclear weapons passes seamlessly from the prewar leadership to various survivors in accordance with some pre-established and publicly recognized procedures. The latter would regulate the myriad procedures defining how nuclear weapons (or the components thereof) would be transferred from their peacetime custodians, assembled for possible use, and finally reassigned to their wartime users for final delivery to target when ordered to do so by the national leadership.

FIGURE 4

INDIA'S LIKELY COMMAND ARRANGEMENTS

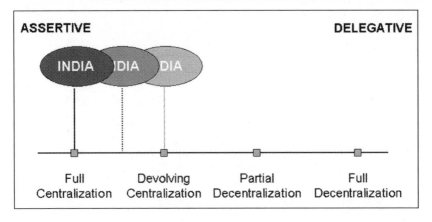

When faced with the set of choices illustrated by Figure 4, India will therefore institutionalize – if it has not done so already – a highly assertive system which involves strict centralized control over both the distributed arsenal and nuclear use decisions in peacetime, with authority and resources steadily devolving to various legitimate successors and operational users respectively in the event of strategic decapitation. This centralization would shift towards more devolutionary alternatives, with respect to decision making in the event of decapitation – just as the custodial arrangement would also mutate as a crisis evolves to the point where India might choose to ready its nuclear weapons for possible use. Figures 5–10 attempt to describe illustratively, and in iterations of increasing complexity, how the assertive Indian command system might operate in a variety of strategic circumstances.

The model of assertive control illustrated in Figure 5 suggests how India might maintain its distributed deterrent both in peace and in war; it attempts to identify the broad pattern of responsibilities both within the civilian and across the civil-military realms. This model is based on the early work of General K. Sundarji, which knowledgeable Indian civilian strategists note has served as the generic blueprint for India's nuclear command and control system.[90] Four specific operational tasks are shown: the command of the force, the custody of the distributed components, the integration of the arsenal, and finally, the delivery of the weapons.

As the graphic suggests, the command of India's nuclear capabilities will remain an exclusively civilian responsibility that resides primarily with the

FIGURE 5

INDIA'S ASSERTIVE COMMAND SYSTEM – THE 'BASELINE' MODEL

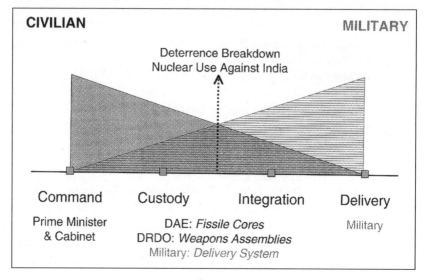

Prime Minister and the Cabinet. Although this responsibility will devolve to other individuals in the event of strategic decapitation, the principle of civilian control will still remain effective.[91] The military will have no *formal* role whatsoever at the level of command, even though they may be consulted by the civilian leadership.[92] The custody of the strategic components would be shared by both civilian and military organizations. In the simplest conception imaginable, the civilians, in the form of the DAE and the DRDO, would retain control, either jointly or separately, over the fissile core and the non-nuclear weapons assembly respectively, while the uniformed military would be responsible for maintaining and stowing the delivery vehicle and potentially maintaining some non-nuclear weapons components.

In this 'baseline' model, the integration and delivery of New Delhi's nuclear weapons does not occur *except after India has suffered a nuclear attack*. Integration, which in this context refers to the many steps involved in mating of the fissile core with the weapons assembly and the delivery vehicle, may involve all the custodial groups converging at the assembly sites directly or, more likely, would require meeting at some intermediate locations.

In either case, the role of the military increases disproportionately at this juncture, since orchestrating the transportation of the various strategic components, together with their custodians, at certain assured levels of security will be a demanding task that is matched only by the military's own exigent obligation to prepare the delivery systems in their custody for prospective nuclear operations – all this occurring amidst the carnage of prior nuclear attacks and, possibly, an ongoing conventional war.[93]

The last task in the sequence consists of the delivery of completed nuclear weapons to their targets. This stage marks the point when civilian contributions essentially come to an end as military operators alone are competent to execute the mission of carrying out the retaliatory strikes. Extensive preplanning will be required to ensure that the delivery vehicles can be moved to bases near the designated assembly areas: under the 'baseline' model, such activities can be initiated even before actual deterrence breakdown occurs.

Figure 6 illustrates schematically how such a command system could be – and perhaps historically has been – operationalized in practice. This illustration is based both on the impressionistic descriptions found throughout in Perkovich's *India's Nuclear Bomb* and Chengappa's *Weapons of Peace*, supplemented by several off-the-record conversations with civilian decision makers and senior military officers in New Delhi.

As Figure 6 illustrates, the orders to integrate India's nuclear assets in preparation for a retaliatory response can be issued only by the Prime Minister, who may choose to consult as necessary the President of the

FIGURE 6

INDIA'S ASSERTIVE COMMAND SYSTEM – A CLOSER LOOK

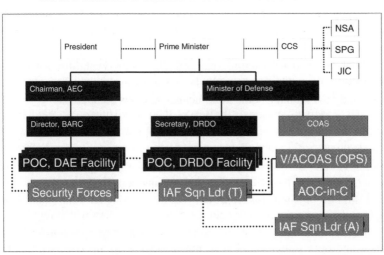

Republic of India and the Cabinet Committee on Security. Once the decision to prepare India's nuclear weapons for retaliation is reached, the Prime Minister can order the Chairman of India's Atomic Energy Commission, the Director of the Bhabha Atomic Research Centre and, through them, the various points of contact at other Department of Atomic Energy facilities where nuclear components may be stored, to prepare their distributed assets for integration.

Through the civilian Minister of Defence – and possibly even directly – a parallel set of orders can be issued, first, to the Secretary, Defense Research and Development Organization and, second, to the Chief of the Air Staff, to support, via prearranged procedures, the fabrication of India's distributed components into complete and usable weapon systems.[94] The Air Chief would be obligated to provide all the major transportation assets necessary to completing the processes of integration as well as to generate the alerts required to prepare the designated attack (and supporting) units for the nuclear delivery mission. The last individual relevant to completing this process is the Chief of Army Staff or the Director-General, Military Operations, who is likely to be responsible for allocating the small security details necessary to escort the various custodians en route to the assembly areas.

While these organizational arrangements exploit what are clearly formal command relationships within the Indian state, the operational dimensions of integrating India's nuclear weapons and preparing them for delivery rely greatly on *informal*, but quite well understood, 'standard operating procedures'[95] which regulate the actions of the various custodians and their supporting cast: the key points of contact within the DAE and DRDO communities, the Air Force transport and attack squadrons, and the Army units committed to the security detail.

What is remarkable about this system in general is how informality, unwritten rules, and 'work-arounds' have been utilized to construct a relatively flexible command system that serves the operational needs of the national leadership even as it preserves the preexisting structural balances within the Indian state.[96] The failure to appreciate the utility of such arrangements within the Indian context often leads to criticisms, both within India and abroad, about the quality of the country's command and control.[97]

Irrespective of how such criticisms are finally evaluated, any analysis of the Indian nuclear command system must recognize that India *does* possess an excellent, entirely formal, national command system which regulates all the activities of the military across research, procurement, training, deployment, and operations. A different, but parallel, system exists – formally –

where controls over the atomic energy establishment are concerned. What the country may currently lack is a formal nuclear command system, that is, an isomorphically structured system which regulates research, procurement, training, deployment, and operations in the nuclear realm through an extremely detailed specification of functional and administrative tasks.[98]

Yet, precisely because India does possess a formal national command system which regulates both the military and the atomic energy domains separately, it is possible for its elected leadership to graft informal, or perhaps even secretly formal, arrangements pertaining to nuclear operations on to what are otherwise two distinct but orderly organizational structures.

India's senior security managers are quite attracted to the idea of institutionalizing a more sophisticated version of the framework illustrated in Figures 5 and 6 as the template for the command and control of Indian nuclear operations in the future. This template, of course, would be modified to accommodate the new delivery systems and the larger number of nuclear weapons that India will acquire over time. It would also incorporate more structured opportunities for the military's participation in affairs relating to the overall deterrent, especially insofar as refining nuclear requirements, conducting targeting analysis, completing contingency plans, and integrating the services' infrastructure, ancillary technologies, and other assorted conventional capabilities in support of nuclear operations, are concerned.

The prospect of such an organizational design forming the basis of India's future command system has not been greeted favorably by the military who, if the reported words of India's Air Chief Marshal (retd.) S. K. Mehra are any indication, appear to be concerned that despite the Prime Minister's repeated declaration 'that adequate C^3I arrangements were in place, ... the Services seemed out of the decision-making loop'.[99] Such statements made by Indian military officers are based on the presumption that New Delhi seeks to deploy a robust and ready arsenal, intended for the conduct of prompt operations, rather than a force-in-being oriented toward ensuring deterrence but also capable of executing retaliatory strikes *in extremis.*

A secret policy paper, *Options for India – Formation of a Strategic Nuclear Command*, reportedly prepared by the Planning Directorate of the Indian military and approved by the three service chiefs after the May 1998 tests, outlined the military's suggested command system (See Figure 7).[100]

If the reporting about this paper is accurate, the higher leadership of the military has called for the creation of a new multi-service body, the National Strategic Nuclear Command (NSNC), which would not only control the entire gamut of nuclear operations in peace and in war but, more

FIGURE 7

INDIAN MILITARY'S SUGGESTED COMMAND SYSTEM

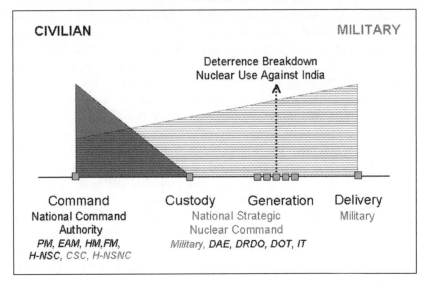

interestingly, would provide an institutional opportunity for the military's claim to representation at the highest levels of *command* itself. This level, which in the 'baseline' model described earlier in Figure 5, was manned exclusively by civilian leaders, is now sought to be expanded, with the service chiefs recommending that the National Command Authority include the 'head of the proposed National Security Council (NSC), the chiefs of staffs committee and the NSNC commander'[101] in addition.

Such a claim is unprecedented, given the traditional pattern of civil-military relations in India and the fact that the service chiefs currently do not have any national command responsibilities. The sketchy reporting about this policy paper further suggests that the reorganization proposed by the military would allow the armed services to acquire physical *custody* of India's nuclear weapons as well, albeit through the creation of a NSNC, which would be manned by military officers in addition to other experts seconded from the Department of Atomic Energy, the Defence Research and Development Organization, and the Departments of Telecommunications and Information Technology.

Precisely because the distension of military power runs counter to the established traditions of the Indian state, it is unlikely to be endorsed by India's political leadership and, in particular, the civilian bureaucracy. The restructuring of India's higher defense organization, which is currently underway in accordance with the recommendations made by the Group of Ministers in the aftermath of the Kargil conflict, in fact confirms that India's nuclear weapons will continue to remain under both civilian command and civilian custody for at least the foreseeable future.

Although the new Indian Chief of Defence Staff (CDS) is vested with 'administrative control' of the country's nuclear forces, this responsibility falls far short of what the armed forces advocated in their 1998 proposal. To be sure, the new reorganization casts the CDS as the 'single point' advisor to the government on all matters pertaining to defense, and it even vests this office with the task of managing India's nuclear forces. This management role however – at least as far as nuclear weapons are concerned – is manifested in three very specific, though highly circumscribed, ways.

First, the CDS will be responsible for overseeing the preparation of all dual-capable delivery systems and physical infrastructure that are currently procured, manned, and operated by different armed services insofar as these are necessary for the conduct of nuclear operations. Second, the CDS will be responsible for overseeing the procurement, organization, training and readiness of all those dedicated nuclear delivery systems that India is likely to acquire in the future. And third, the CDS will be responsible for developing all the plans, both current and prospective – pertaining to conventional joint operations and to the coordination of changing control and custody procedures over nuclear weapon components in an emergency.

While these innovations represent a major step in rationalizing India's capability to conduct nuclear operations, it is important to underscore that they do not give either the CDS or the prospective nuclear command under his authority any control or custody over nuclear weapons (or nuclear weapon components) in peacetime. This means that the country's civilian custodians will continue to maintain at least the fissile cores and possibly even the weapon assemblies routinely.

This fact notwithstanding, the new organizational structures – if they function as intended – could contribute to the effective management of India's evolving nuclear deterrent in multiple ways: first, by providing formal opportunities for military advice with respect to strategic requirements in order to guide the research, development, and acquisition of nuclear weapons, delivery systems, and supporting infrastructure assets; second, by creating a permanent institution tasked with overseeing the development of nuclear targeting and weapon employment plans under civilian guidance; and third, by developing an embryonic joint system intended to systematize all the plans and procedures required to effectively integrate India's conventional and nuclear capabilities under different threat conditions.

If these new institutional arrangements come to fruition in the best imaginable forms, they could pave the way for greater integration of the military in the command function as well over time. Whether this, in fact, occurs eventually will depend on the following circumstances. First, what Pakistan and China do in the interim, since the nuclear force structures, technologies and doctrines gradually becoming visible in these countries may force India to modify its preferred approaches to the management of nuclear weaponry.[102] Second, the kind of delivery systems, that India itself acquires over time, since the shift towards a sea-based deterrent will of necessity transform the force-in-being into something resembling a ready arsenal and, accordingly, will require new methods of management which are closer to the military's preferences than those encoded in the baseline model of control described earlier.

Despite the fact that India's civilian leaders take a different view of the role of nuclear weapons than do many in the military, concerns expressed by military officers about survivability, readiness, and the need to prepare seriously for nuclear operations *in extremis*, however, are not lost on India's senior security managers. Consequently, it is likely that the 'baseline'

FIGURE 8

INDIA'S LIKELY COMMAND SYSTEM IN A LOW-THREAT SCENARIO

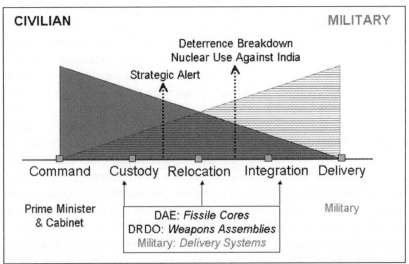

command system illustrated in Figure 5 will actually mutate considerably to accommodate different strategic circumstances. Figure 8 illustrates one possible metamorphosis from the 'baseline' model and suggests how the Indian command system is likely to respond – within the parameters of the basic framework pertaining to the force-in-being – to contingencies that arise within a low-threat scenario.

The first modification likely to be institutionalized relative to the baseline model illustrated in Figure 5 is the development of institutions, like the National Security Council Secretariat, charged with generating a 'strategic alert',[103] which warns security managers about the possibility of an impending crisis. Strategic alerts are different from tactical alerts in that the former signal the possibility of war, whereas the latter signal the imminence of actual military attack.

Since the Indian nuclear force will be routinely maintained as a force-in-being, the possibility of strategic warning becomes critical not so much to its survival – because presumably opacity, mobility, deception and denial in peacetime ought to suffice as far as ensuring survivability is concerned – but to the ability of the Indian leadership to deter threats through possible signaling, if required, and more importantly, to organize for retaliatory actions, should those become necessary.

In truly low-threat scenarios, the baseline model of command is likely to be modified by the search for strategic warning which is then used to organize the relocation of India's dispersed strategic assets, either to increase their survivability, or to signal the readiness to respond, or to prepare for more effective retaliation. Irrespective of the intentions underlying such relocation, Indian security managers would not require the integration of their nuclear devices, even if conventional deterrence breakdown occurred after the receipt of strategic warning, because a low-threat scenario – almost by definition – would leave them confident that they could integrate their weapons without hindrance after riding out a first strike.

In a high-threat scenario, however, it is likely that the 'baseline' command system would be modified in the one consequential way illustrated in Figure 9: India's nuclear weapons would be relocated, if necessary, on receipt of strategic warning. But they would be integrated, ready, and waiting even before nuclear attacks on India occurred – and irrespective of whether conventional deterrence broke down in the interim. If Chengappa's description in *Weapons of Peace* is accurate, the Indian command system did in fact operate in just this fashion during the Kargil crisis in 1998.[104]

As time goes by, however, and as India's own nuclear capabilities mature in different dimensions, it is likely that even the prospectively new

FIGURE 9

INDIA'S LIKELY COMMAND SYSTEM IN A HIGH-THREAT SCENARIO

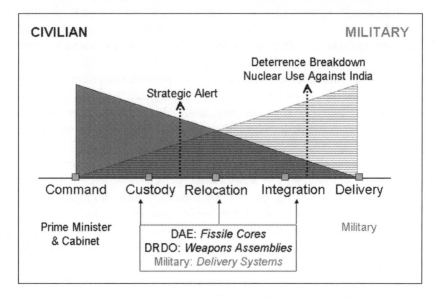

baseline illustrated by Figure 9 will give way to the more complex and sophisticated command system depicted in Figure 10. Under this model, India's most likely command system eventually, New Delhi will still maintain a force-in-being as its standard operating posture in peacetime, with weapons components distributed across a variety of custodial agencies, both civilian and military.

On the receipt of strategic alert, however, it will relocate its assets if required by the specific circumstances facing the force at that point in time. But more importantly, however, it will focus on developing the technical capabilities, the human competency, the infrastructural support, and the organizational arrangements that will enable it to integrate its weapons systems and generate the requisite increases in readiness either before, during, or after conventional deterrence breakdown with the intent of possessing more or less ready nuclear forces even before it absorbs what may be the first of many sequential nuclear attacks on India.

The ability to rapidly alert, relocate, integrate, and ready a larger and more diverse nuclear force even before absorbing a first strike is a capability that Indian security managers will eventually strive for, mostly for prudential reasons deriving from the belief that possessing the option for rapid response is, other things being equal, better for both deterrence of adversaries and reassurance of the national leadership. In this final model of command predicated by the posture of a force-in-being, the actual Indian retaliation after suffering a nuclear attack may still *not* be instantaneous, since the retaliatory response time here will be determined in large part by the extent of damage suffered as result of the adversary's attack. Yet, this command model holds the best promise of allowing Indian security managers to unleash their retaliatory response within a few hours of suffering an attack as opposed to the many-hours-to-a-few-days delay that is inherent in the initial 'baseline' model of Figure 5.

The command system illustrated in Figure 10 thus remains the model that the Indian nuclear deterrent will eventually conform to, although policymakers in New Delhi will not publicly articulate this conception today. Even if they do not aspire to institutionalize this model currently, they are nevertheless likely to reach it once their present development and acquisition plans in the nuclear realm come to fruition.

Although this will take a decade (if not more) to be fully realized, the capabilities that they will have acquired by then will simply allow for the institutionalization of such a command system; it is also not unreasonable to believe that by this point, the current international pressures which make for restraint will have abated somewhat, or at least reduced in intensity, as

FIGURE 10

INDIA'S LIKELY COMMAND SYSTEM EVENTUALLY

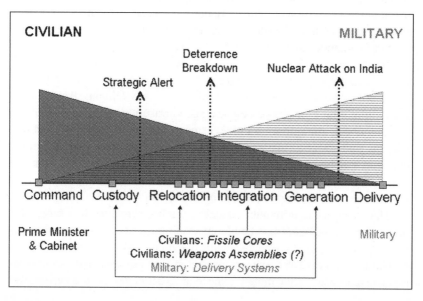

the world grows progressively used to the idea that nuclear weapons in the Indian subcontinent are here to stay. Under such circumstances, the willingness of India's security managers to countenance increasing the rate at which their force-in-being can be reconstituted in the face of imminent threats will also intensify. Even at this point though, it is important to remember that India's nuclear deterrent will still remain a force-in-being rather than a ready arsenal, assuming that no untoward perturbations occur in the interim.

It is obvious that as India moves towards the institutionalization of such a command posture over time it *could* gradually acquire the capability for first strikes in a crisis, something that was *irrevocably* ruled out so long as the baseline command model illustrated in Figure 5 remained operational. This development could become a source of concern to India's adversaries and, if not managed appropriately, could even become subversive of crisis stability.

The saving grace, however, is that even when India acquires the technical, human, infrastructural and organizational competence to ready its forces rapidly in anticipation of an adversary's first strike, it will still lack the political incentives to initiate nuclear first use. More importantly, so long as its nuclear weaponry is more effective for countervalue rather than counterforce missions, it will continue to lack the logical incentives to engage even in preemptive strikes, despite the possible background condition of conventional deterrence breakdown. Consequently, it is reasonable to conclude that as long as India does not possess a true sea-based nuclear deterrent, its currently desired strategic posture – a force-in-being – can endure despite the many variations in reconstitution and readiness timelines that are likely to become visible in the years ahead.

THE FUTURE OF THE 'FORCE-IN-BEING'

The configuration of the force-in-being described above allows India to affirm – consistent with its doctrine – that its nuclear capabilities represent political rather than military instruments, while at the same time remaining tools that can be mutated into weapons of mass destruction if the strategic circumstances so warrant. The force-in-being also lends itself to being *transformed* into a more robust and formidable posture, like a ready arsenal, if India's strategic environment demands such a response over time. This transformation would in fact be likely:

• if China emerged as a true superpower in the future and, as a result of its changed status, dramatically expanded its strategic nuclear capabilities *and* transformed the current conventional balance *vis-à-vis* India to New Delhi's disadvantage;

• if Sino-Indian competition intensified over time as a result of growing national capabilities in both states and if the resulting struggle for power were to generate a high-intensity contest for influence in the middle eastern, southern, and southeastern rimlands of the Asian continent;

• if Sino-American relations were perceived in New Delhi as taking the form of coercive collusion manifested either through joint efforts at 'ganging up' against India on political-strategic issues, or through greater displays of laxity toward Pakistani efforts at increasing its strategic capabilities through proscribed international transactions; or

• if international politics were once again to radically change course and move in the direction of greater nuclearization and even stronger forms of dependence on nuclear weapons for ensuring order and security.

If such circumstances came to pass, the Indian nuclear posture would change and could evolve into something resembling a traditional arsenal. In fact, the genius of the force-in-being is that it allows for such change to take place in a relatively evolutionary fashion. This is because the posture currently favored by India's security managers does not prevent the country from continually improving its delivery capabilities, supporting infrastructure, and procedural systems to levels that could support a variety of nuclear strategies other than delayed retaliation focused on simple punishment.

Nor does it prevent India from continuing to accumulate weapons-grade plutonium and any other special nuclear materials that its evolving arsenal might need in the near term; in fact, depending on the final text of the FMCT, it is even possible, although not likely, that India and all other states might be permitted to continue producing fissile materials, albeit with the stipulation that all post-FMCT stocks of such material be maintained under safeguards.

The currently favored strategic posture also does not prevent the continued improvement of India's nuclear weapon designs through computer simulations and subcritical tests. Ultimately it would not prevent New Delhi from breaking out of any treaty commitments – assuming it signed on to the FMCT and CTBT in the first place – that prohibit either the production of fissile materials or the resumption of field testing for purposes of developing many more potent nuclear weapons.[105]

The solution embodied by the force-in-being thus carries within it the potential for transformation into some other, more lethal, kind of nuclear posture – like a more robust force-in-being or different variants of a ready arsenal – if changes in India's strategic circumstances were to mandate such a transition. In that sense, the force-in-being represents a continuation of the classic Indian preference for 'keeping the option open'.

What is never explicitly stated by Indian security managers but is always on their minds is that the currently favored solution represented by the force-in-being serves the specific purpose of ensuring Indian security in conditions that are best described as being 'between the times' – that is, between the first nuclear era defined by the Cold War and the still-unclear but emerging reorganization of the international system.

If the global order were really to change in a direction manifestly unfavorable to India, exemplified most simply by China's rise as a threatening superpower, Indian policymakers expect that the currently strong wave of American nonproliferation pressures on New Delhi – one of the factors that contributes to maintaining their nuclear capabilities in the form of a force-in-being – would steadily abate and that India would then be free for the first time to return to the business of developing a more robust nuclear posture of the kind the altered strategic environment required.

Under these conditions, they expect that the current US attitude toward nuclear weapons may itself change and that Washington may return to emphasizing the acquisition of even more robust nuclear capabilities than are currently deployed by the United States.

Should such circumstances come to pass, whatever commitments India may have made in the interim to global regimes like the CTBT and the FMCT would slowly become irrelevant and New Delhi could find itself obligated to change course simply to ensure its national security in the new strategic environment. If and until such a point is reached, however, the force-in-being is seen to serve India well, and this solution will in all likelihood subsist as the new 'punctuated equilibrium' for some time to come: a stable way point, but not a permanent terminus in India's slow maturation as a nuclear weapon power.

As Figure 11 graphically illustrates, the history of the Indian nuclear weapon program has in fact been little more than a series of sequentially punctuated equilibria. And if the past is any guide, the defining changes in the character of India's currently preferred nuclear posture – which would materialize only after an extended period of time – will likely be triggered by some sharp, specific external or internal stimulus that cannot yet be discerned with any clarity.

What US policymakers and the intelligence community can do in the interim, however, is continuously monitor the nature of the ongoing Indian

FIGURE 11

HISTORY OF INDIA'S NUCLEAR PROGRAM

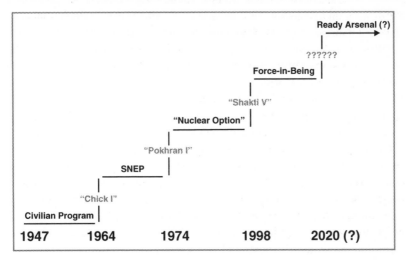

strategic debate, especially with respect to the following questions, because the dominant answers accepted to these queries in the 'official mind' of policymakers and strategic managers in New Delhi will – even more than technical intelligence about India's strategic programs – illuminate the prospect for future changes in India's nuclear posture:

- *What does effective deterrence entail in terms of the numbers of nuclear weapons?*
- *What does effective deterrence entail in terms of the quality of nuclear weapons?*
- *What does effective deterrence entail in terms of the numbers and quality of delivery systems?*
- *What is the 'dominant' solution to the problem of strategic force survivability?*
- *How slow can 'delayed retaliation' be without imperiling deterrence stability?*
- *How formal do C^3I systems have to be for effective deterrence?*
- *How important is military custody of nuclear weapons in peacetime for effective deterrence?*
- *Is stable deterrence best served by certainty or uncertainty of strategic outcomes?*

Depending on how the answers to these questions change over time, the Indian strategic posture could mutate – and although previous discussions posited a ready arsenal as the 'ideal-typical' alternative strategic managers in New Delhi might favor, this choice, like any other, may never be publicly announced or deliberately selected, but may instead appear simply as the end point of a long process of creeping weaponization.

It is thus worth noting – more from a policy standpoint than from a theoretical perspective – that there are some intermediate positions India may pause at along the way.[106]

As Figure 12 suggests, at one end, India could continue to settle for a force-in-being, but one that is *not* limited in size. This posture – a robust force-in-being – would continue to be defined by separated components and centralized control, but it would seek to incorporate the largest and most capable nuclear force India could produce before it is constrained either by bilateral agreements or by multilateral treaties.

At the other end, India could opt for a modest ready arsenal – that is, a force defined by highly integrated weapons ready for prompt operations as well as by a centralized but rapidly devolving command-and-control system, yet one that is nonetheless small at least in terms of the number and

FIGURE 12

FUTURE ALTERNATIVES TO INDIA'S FORCE-IN-BEING

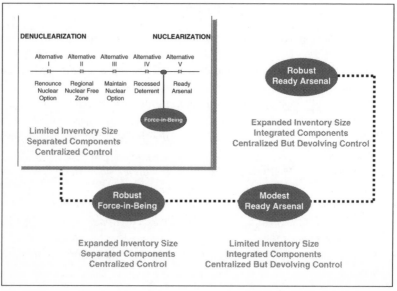

perhaps types of nuclear weapons it involves. Beyond these two sub-alternatives, of course, lies a true and robust ready arsenal, which may be described as a large nuclear force that is fully integrated in disposition, with centralized but rapidly devolving command-and-control arrangements. Since it is impossible to predict whether India will choose to move directly to a ready arsenal of this kind – once it feels compelled to go beyond its current preference for a force-in-being – or even if it will choose to move in decisive as opposed to incremental steps, the only thing that can be said safely at this point is that India's force-in-being still remains a 'work-in-progress' whose final disposition cannot yet be definitively ascertained.

NOTES

1. Prime Minister Atal Behari Vajpayee, 'XII Lok Sabha (Lower House of Parliament) Debates', Session II, 27 May 1998.
2. This phrase has been repeatedly used by Indian leaders as a slogan to define their conception of the country's future nuclear capabilities. See, Mahesh Uniyal, 'No cap on fissile material, says Vajpayee', *India Abroad*, 25 Dec. 1998.
3. The evolution of this complex relationship is best described in George Perkovich, *India's Nuclear Bomb* (Berkeley: University of California Press 1999), and in Itty Abraham, *The Making of the Indian Atomic Bomb: Science, Secrecy and the Post-Colonial State* (New York: Zed 1998).
4. See, by way of example, the P-5 and the G-8 statements issued in the aftermath of the May 1998 nuclear tests and, especially, *Security Council Resolution 1172 (1998) on International Peace and Security*, adopted by the UN Security Council at its 3890th Meeting on 6 June 1998, available at www.un.org/Docs/scres/1998/sres1172.htm.
5. See, for example, Kamal Mitra Chenoy, 'India should beat the nuclear club, not join it', *The Asian Age*, 23 July 1998; Praful Bidwai, 'Sign the Test Ban Treaty', *The Times of India*, 14 July 1998; Praful Bidwai, 'Regaining Nuclear Sanity', *The Times of India*, 5 June 1998; Achin Vanaik, 'Drawing new lines', *The Hindu*, 23 May 1998; Achin Vanaik, 'Hotter than a thousand suns', *The Telegraph*, 26 May 1998; Kanti Bajpai, 'The Fallacy of an Indian Deterrent', in Amitabh Mattoo (ed.), *India's Nuclear Deterrent* (New Delhi: Har-Anand Publications 1999) pp.150–88; and Praful Bidwai, Achin Vanaik, and Arundhati Roy, *New Nukes: India, Pakistan and Global Nuclear Disarmament* (Northampton, MA: Interlink 2000).
6. This position has been affirmed most clearly in Jasjit Singh, 'A Nuclear Strategy for India', in Jasjit Singh (ed.), *Nuclear India* (New Delhi: Knowledge World 1998) pp.306–24. However, echoes of this position can also be found in the writings of other Indian commentators. These are explored in the context of the wider Indian debate on nuclear weapons in Kanti Bajpai, 'India's Nuclear Posture After Pokhran II', *International Studies* 37/4 (Oct.–Dec. 2000) pp.267–301.
7. See, for example, N.C. Menon, 'Subtleties of Sagarika', *The Hindustan Times*, 11 May 1998; S. Chandrashekar, 'In defense of nukes', *The Economic Times*, 17 May 1998; M.D. Nalapat, 'India needs to expand scope of nuclear diplomacy', *The Times of India*, 18 Dec. 1998; Bharat Karnad, 'A Thermonuclear Deterrent', in Mattoo, *India's Nuclear Deterrent* (note 5) pp.108–49; Vijai K. Nair, *Nuclear India* (New Delhi: Lancer International 1992) pp.152–72; Brahma Chellaney, 'Nuclear-Deterrent Posture', in idem (ed.), *Securing India's Future in the New Millennium* (New Delhi: Orient Longman 1999) pp.141–222; and Raja Menon, *A Nuclear Strategy for India* (New Delhi: Sage Publications 2000) pp.177–234.
8. This sentence is based on Rear-Adm. Richard Kempenfelt's famous eighteenth-century

description of a fleet-in-being, cited in Geoffrey Till, *Maritime Strategy and the Nuclear Age*, 2nd ed. (New York: St Martin's Press 1984) p.114.

9.   The Federation of American Scientists notes that 'when the Third UN Disarmament Conference, held in 1988, decided that the next logical step in the disarmament process would be measures to halt production of chemical weapons, Indian diplomats responded by claiming that India had no chemical weapons. Foreign Minister K. Natwar Singh repeated this claim in 1989 in the Paris Conference of the State Parties to the Geneva Protocol of 1925, as did Minister of State Eduardo Faleiro who repeated it at the Jan. 1993 Paris Conference CWC signing ceremony'. See, 'India: Chemical Weapons' at www.fas.org/nuke/guide/india/cw/, which remains the best summary description of India's chemical weapons program.

10. The history of the Prithvi program is very usefully recounted in W.P.S. Sidhu, 'The Development of an Indian Nuclear Doctrine Since 1980' (unpublished doctoral dissertation, Emmanuel College, University of Cambridge, Feb. 1997) pp.246–68.

11. Greg J. Gerardi, 'India's 333rd Prithvi Missile Group', *Jane's Intelligence Review* 7/8 (Aug. 1995) pp.361–4; R. Jeffrey Smith, 'India Moves Missiles Near Pakistani Border', *The Washington Post*, 3 June 1997; 'India's Missile Move', *The Washington Post*, 9 June 1997.

12. For an excellent summary of this particular posture, see K. Sundarji, 'Prithvi in the Haystack', *India Today International*, 30 June 1997, p.49.

13. Tarun Basu, 'Nuclear Doctrine Emerges, but Tension Mounts on Border', *India Abroad*, 14 Aug. 1998, p.26.

14. K. Subrahmanyam, 'Educate India in Nuclear Strategy', *The Times of India*, 22 May 1998.

15. V.P. Naib, 'The Nuclear Threat', *Indian Defence Review* 8/1 (Jan. 1993) pp.61–2.

16. Bharat Karnad, 'A Thermonuclear Deterrent', in Mattoo (note 5) p.135.

17. Ibid. p.133.

18. Maj.-Gen. (retd.) Ashok K. Mehta, 'Case for a Nuclear Doctrine with Minimum Deterrence', *India Abroad*, 28 Aug. 1998.

19. 'India: Defense Experts Differ on Nuclear Deterrence', *FBIS-NES-98-167*, 16 June 1998.

20. H.B. Hollins *et al.*, *The Conquest of War: Alternative Strategies for Global Security* (Boulder: Westview Press 1989) pp.54–55.

21. See, for example, David Lewis, 'Finite Counterforce' in H. Shue (ed.), *Nuclear Deterrence and Moral Restraint* (Cambridge: Cambridge University Press 1989) pp.51–115; Lawrence Martin, 'Minimum Deterrence', *Faraday Discussion Paper No. 8* (London: Council for Arms Control 1987).

22. Barry Buzan, *Strategic Studies: Military Technology and International Relations* (London: Macmillan 1987) p.193.

23. Ibid. p.194.

24. See the remarks of Regina Karp in Serge Sur (ed.), *Nuclear Deterrence: Problems and Perspectives in the 1990s* (New York: UNIDIR 1993) p.122.

25. Ibid. p.123.

26. The history of this search to define nuclear sufficiency, together with a review of all the intellectual innovations it produced, has been usefully reviewed in Fred Kaplan, *The Wizards of Armageddon* (New York: Simon and Schuster 1983).

27. A good analysis of how sufficiency came to be characterized in the United States until the 1970s can be found in Jerome H. Kahan, *Security in the Nuclear Age* (Washington DC: Brookings 1975); from the 1970s until the end of the Cold War, see John M. Collins, *US/Soviet Military Balance Statistical Trends, 1970–1981* (Washington DC: Library of Congress, Congressional Research Service 1982), and John M. Collins, *US/Soviet Military Balance Statistical Trends, 1980–1989* (Washington DC: CRS, Library of Congress 1990). See also, John M. Collins, *US–Soviet Military Balance: Concepts and Capabilities, 1960–1980* (New York: Aviation Week 1980).

28. Jasjit Singh, 'Nukes Have No Prestige Value', *The Indian Express*, 4 June 1998.

29. K. Subrahmanyam, 'Not a Numbers Game: Minimum Cost of N-Deterrence', *The Times of India*, 7 Dec. 1998.

30. Kapil Sibal, 'Toy Gun Security: Flaws in India's Nuclear Deterrence', *The Times of India*, 13 Jan. 1999.

31. Manoj Joshi, 'India Must Have Survivable N-Arsenal', *The Times of India*, 30 April 2000.

32. 'India Not to Engage in a N-Arms Race: Jaswant', *The Hindu*, 29 Nov. 1999.
33. Ibid.
34. Nair, *Nuclear India* (note 7) p.170.
35. Ibid.
36. Ibid. pp.170–71.
37. Ibid. p.181. As Balachandran's analysis points out, however, these small inventory sizes are crucially dependent on India's possessing the high-yield weapons called for in Nair's calculations. Absent such weapons, the number of nuclear weapons required to obliterate these targets immediately goes up from the few tens in Nair's analysis to many hundreds or, more precisely, from 132 weapons of varying yields to upwards of 800 20 kt sized weapons. See, G. Balachandran, 'Nuclear Weaponization in India', *Agni* 5/1 (Jan.–April 2000) pp.42–7.
38. K. Sundarji, 'Nuclear Deterrence: Doctrine for India-I', *Trishul* 5/2 (Dec. 1992) p.48. In later writings, Sundarji reduced these requirements even further arguing that 'all that is needed to deter a small to medium sized country would be about 20 weapons of about 20 kiloton yield each [.4 MTE], and about 50 such weapons [1 MTE] for even a large country'. See K. Sundarji, 'The CTBT Debate: Choice before India', *The Indian Express*, 4 Dec. 1995.
39. K. Sundarji, 'CTBT and National Security: Options for India', *The Indian Express*, 6 April 1996.
40. Sundarji, 'Imperatives of Indian Minimum Nuclear Deterrence', *Agni* 2/1 (May 1996) p.18.
41. Ibid.
42. Subrahmanyam, 'Nuclear Force Design and Minimum Deterrence Strategy for India', in Bharat Karnad (ed.), *Future Imperiled* (Delhi: Viking 1994) p.189.
43. Raj Chengappa and Manoj Joshi, 'Future Fire', *India Today*, 25 May 1998, p.23.
44. Karnad, 'A Thermonuclear Deterrent', in Mattoo, *India's Nuclear Deterrent* (note 5) p.143.
45. Subrahmanyam, 'Nuclear Force Design and Minimum Deterrence Strategy for India', in Karnad, *Future Imperiled* (note 42) p.193.
46. Manoj Joshi, 'Marginal Costing', *India Today*, 1 June 1998, pp.22–3.
47. Nair, *Nuclear India* (note 7) pp.171–2.
48. Karnad, 'A Thermonuclear Deterrent', in Mattoo, *India's Nuclear Deterrent* (note 5) p.146.
49. For still another set of desired numbers pertaining to delivery systems, see Gurmeet Kanwal, 'India's Nuclear Force Structure', *Strategic Analysis* 24/6 (Sept. 2000) pp.1039–75.
50. The entire nuclear infrastructure is detailed in Perkovich, *India's Nuclear Bomb* (note 3) pp.469–72, and the portions relevant to the nuclear weapons production program are briefly described in Manoj Joshi, 'India's Nuclear Estate', *India Today International*, 4 May 1998.
51. 'Draft Report of [the] National Security Advisory Board on Indian Nuclear Doctrine', *India News*, 1 Oct. 1999, p.2.
52. This has also been affirmed by Indian security managers like Jaswant Singh who note that 'this "minimum" … cannot be a fixed physical quantification'. See 'India Not to Engage in a N-Arms Race: Jaswant'. See also Prime Minister Vajpayee's statement in 'Deterrence to Be Evaluated Time to Time: Govt', *Economic Times*, 17 Dec. 1998.
53. As Jaswant Singh phrased it, 'We have, after the tests last year, announced our readiness to engage in multilateral negotiations in the Conference on Disarmament in Geneva for a non-discriminatory and verifiable treaty to ban future production of fissile materials for nuclear weapon purposes. *This decision was taken after due consideration, which included an assessment of timeframes for negotiations and entry into force of an FMCT.* At this stage, India cannot accept a voluntary moratorium on production of fissile materials. Let me add that FMCT negotiations are a complex exercise; it will be important, therefore, as we go along to constantly monitor the pace, direction and content of these negotiations' (italics added). See 'India Not to Engage in a N-Arms Race' (note 32).
54. For more on the terrible state of India's nuclear infrastructure, see Nayan Chanda, 'The Perils of Power', *Far Eastern Economic Review*, 4 Feb. 1999, pp.10–17. The terrible disrepair in both civilian and weapon programs has been further described in T.S. Gopi Rethinaraj, 'In the Comfort of Secrecy', *The Bulletin of the Atomic Scientists* 55/6 (Nov.

1999) pp.52–7.

55. K. Subrahmanyam, 'A Credible Deterrent: Logic of The Nuclear Doctrine', *The Times of India*, 4 Oct. 1999.

56. Gregory S. Jones, *From Testing to Deploying Nuclear Forces: The Hard Choices Facing India and Pakistan*, IP-192 (Santa Monica, CA: RAND 2000).

57. Steinbruner, 'Choices and Trade-offs', in Ashton B. Carter *et al.* (eds.), *Managing Nuclear Operations* (Washington DC: Brookings 1987) p.546.

58. Bajpai, 'India's Diplomacy and Defence after Pokhran II', in *Post Pokhran II: The National Way Ahead*, pp.39–45.

59. See 'Draft Report of [the] National Security Advisory Board on Indian Nuclear Doctrine', p.23; 'India Not to Engage in a N-Arms Race' (note 32).

60. 'Draft Report of [the] National Security Advisory Board on Indian Nuclear Doctrine', p.3.

61. Ibid.

62. For more on these technologies, see United States Congress, House Committee on Armed Services, Panel on Nuclear Weapons Safety, *Nuclear Weapons Safety: Report of the Panel on Nuclear Weapons Safety of the Committee on Armed Services*, House of Representatives, One Hundred First Congress, Second Session (Washington DC: USGPO 1990); Donald Cotter, 'Peacetime Operations: Safety and Security', in Carter, *Managing Nuclear Operations* (note 57) pp.17–74.

63. For more on such designs, see Chuck Hansen (ed.), *The Swords of Armageddon*, Vol.VIII (Sunnyvale, USA: Chukelea Publications 1995) VIII-11-36.

64. See the discussion at various points in Chengappa, *Weapons of Peace* (note 65), and Perkovich, *India's Nuclear Bomb* (note 3).

65. Raj Chengappa, *Weapons of Peace* (New Delhi: HarperCollins 2000) pp.xv–xvi.

66. See Subrahmanyam, 'Indian Nuclear Policy – 1964–98', in Singh, *Nuclear India* (note 6) pp.26–53 and episodically throughout Perkovich, *India's Nuclear Bomb* (note 3) and Chengappa, *Weapons of Peace* (note 65).

67. The failure to distinguish between informal networks and formal institutions as far as decision-making with respect to the Indian nuclear weapons program is concerned often leaves many Western and even Indian analysts puzzled and confused. See, for example, Jonathan Karp, 'India Faces Task of Creating Nuclear-Weapons Doctrine', *The Wall Street Journal*, 27 May 1998. By looking hard for formal institutions and not finding them, they are often led to the erroneous conclusion that an effective Indian nuclear command system does not currently exist. For good theoretical work that highlights the distinction between institutions and networks, see Manuel Castells, *The Informational City: Information Technology, Economic Restructuring, and the Urban-Regional Process* (Cambridge: Blackwell 1989).

68. Chengappa, for example, points out how even India's Defence Ministers, its service chiefs, and important senior bureaucrats, historically often knew what they did about India's nuclear weapons program and activities only because they were specifically told what they needed to know in the context of some incipient nodal event and not because they are entitled to know merely because of the position they held within the Indian state. See Chengappa, *Weapons of Peace* (note 65) p.114.

69. P.R. Chari, *Protection of Fissile Materials: The Indian Experience*, ACDIS Occasional Paper (Urbana: University of Illinois, Sept. 1998) p.57.

70. Menon, *A Nuclear Strategy for India* (note 7) pp.235–61.

71. K. Sundarji, 'Indian Nuclear Doctrine – I: Notions of deterrence'.

72. Subrahmanyam, 'Nuclear Force Design and Minimum Deterrence Strategy for India', in Karnad, *Future Imperiled* (note 42) pp.186–91. On this issue, see also Agha Shahi *et al.*, 'Securing Nuclear Peace', *The News International*, 5 Oct. 1999, and Robert A. Manning *et al.*, *China, Nuclear Weapons, and Arms Control* (New York: Council on Foreign Relations 2000).

73. Subrahmanyam, 'Nuclear Force Design and Minimum Deterrence Strategy for India', in Karnad, *Future Imperiled* (note 42) pp.176–95.

74. Peter D. Feaver, 'Command and Control in Emerging Nuclear Nations', *International Security* 17/3 (Winter 1992/93) p.163.

75. Ibid.

76. Ibid. p.168.

77. For more of these innovations, and their limitations, see Scott D. Sagan, *The Limits of Safety: Organizations, Accidents, and Nuclear Weapons* (Princeton University Press 1993). See also, MSgt. William A. Hodgson, 'Nuclear Weapons Personnel Reliability Program', *Combat Edge* 4/1 (June 1995) pp.22–3.

78. The term comes from Feaver, 'Command and Control in Emerging Nuclear Nations' (note 74) p.170.

79. In fact, it is very likely that, after accounting for all their relevant differences, the Indian command system is more likely to resemble the Soviet command system during the Cold War rather than the American at least insofar as the latter's obsession with system survivability and adequacy of target coverage will be replaced, as in the Soviet model, by equal if not greater emphasis on 'geopolitical considerations, self-preservation, and negative control as [it does on] damage expectancy'. Bruce C. Blair, *The Logic of Accidental Nuclear War* (Washington DC: Brookings 1993) p.59. The Soviet command system and its contrasting biases are reviewed in some detail in this work, pp.59–167.

80. Some Indian scholars have argued for a formalization of this process through the institutionalization of something akin to a 'two-man' rule (see, 'India: Study Recommends Two-Person Rule for Using Nuclear Arms', *FBIS-TAC-98-261*, 18 Sept. 1998), but Indian policymakers, while not ruling out such solutions eventually, do emphasize in private that their current arrangements in fact afford far greater protection than would be offered by a two-man rule, since the necessity for collaboration between at least two organizations to ready India's nuclear weapons itself ensures that more than two individuals would be required to prepare these weapons for delivery. The description at various points in Chengappa, *Weapons of Peace* (note 65) clearly corroborates this claim.

81. This concept, though not this term, is discussed at length in Scott Sagan, 'The Origins of Military Doctrine and Command Systems', in Peter R. Lavoy, Scott D. Sagan, and James J. Wirtz (eds.), *Planning the Unthinkable* (Ithaca: Cornell University Press, Aug. 2000).

82. The term comes from Feaver, 'Command and Control in Emerging Nuclear Nations' (note 74) p.170.

83. This fact is corroborated at various points in Perkovich, *India's Nuclear Bomb* (note 3) and in Chengappa, *Weapons of Peace* (note 65). The capability of the Prime Minister to control the entire defense establishment, both institutionally and operationally, is emphasized in Veena Kukreja, *Civil-Military Relations in South Asia* (New Delhi: Sage Publications 1991) pp.185–228.

84. On the logic and practice of 'pre-delegation' during the Cold War, see Peter D. Feaver, *Guarding the Guardians: Civilian Control of Nuclear Weapons in the United States* (Ithaca: Cornell University Press 1992) pp.44–54. It is important to recognize the distinction between 'devolution' and 'pre-delegation' of command authority: The former refers to the 'orderly transfer of the entire command function, along with a preset chain of command, when the superior in the hierarchy is incapacitated' while the latter refers to the 'a priori delimitation of circumstances under which subordinates in the chain of command can assume that the authorization to use nuclear weapons has been given to them'. Feaver, ibid. p.44.

85. At least one serious Indian analyst has made a systematic argument for what appears to be a partially delegative command system with the uniformed services possessing custody of completed nuclear weapons in peacetime. Whether such a demand for custody is complemented by a demand for pre-delegated use authority is less clear, but it may be implied by the requirement for a launch-on-warning capability discussed in Menon, *A Nuclear Strategy for India* (note 7) pp.177–282.

86. 'India and the Nuclear Question: An Interview with General K. Sundarji, PVSM (Retd)', *Trishul* 7/2 (1994) pp.45–56.

87. This concept is discussed systematically in John D. Steinbruner, 'Nuclear Decapitation', *Foreign Policy* 45 (Winter 1981/82) pp.16–28.

88. 'Draft Report of [the] National Security Advisory Board on Indian Nuclear Doctrine', p.3.

89. Gregory F. Giles and James E. Doyle, 'Indian and Pakistani Views on Nuclear Deterrence', *Comparative Strategy* 15/2 (1996) p.154.

90. The elements of this framework can be found in the many writings of K. Sundarji, with quick summaries available in 'India and the Nuclear Question: An Interview with General

K. Sundarji, PVSM (Retd)' pp.45–56; Sundarji, 'Prithvi in the Haystack'; Sundarji, 'Nuclear Deterrence: Doctrine for India-I and II'. On Sundarji's contributions as constituting the baseline for India's command system and deterrence doctrines, see C. Raja Mohan, 'Sundarji's nuclear doctrine', *The Hindu*, 11 Feb. 1999, and Subrahmanyam, 'Indian Nuclear Policy – 1964–98', in Singh, *Nuclear India* (note 6) pp.38–50.

91. This is alluded to in 'India Not to Engage in a N-Arms Race: Jaswant'.

92. Empirical examples of how this process has been institutionalized historically can be found in various passages throughout Perkovich, *India's Nuclear Bomb* (note 3) and in Chengappa, *Weapons of Peace* (note 65).

93. For a brief, perhaps all too impressionistic, description of how this was attempted during the Kargil crisis, see Chengappa, *Weapons of Peace* (note 65) pp.437–8.

94. Since India's traditional delivery systems were exclusively aircraft, the Chief of Air Staff remained the only service chief with responsibilities to the nuclear command system. As India's delivery systems grow in diversity to include Army and Navy assets, it is likely that the Chiefs of Army and Navy staffs will also be included in parallel arrangements, if the 'baseline' model of assertive command survives more or less unaltered over time.

95. This term, obviously, is used in a very different sense from that appearing in Paul Bracken, *The Command and Control of Nuclear Forces* (New Haven, CT: Yale University Press 1983).

96. A good analysis of how intelligent, informal and non-planned, interventions play a critical role in ensuring the effectiveness of even large, formal, military decision systems can be found in N.F. Kristy, *Man in a Large Information Processing System – His Changing Role in SAGE*, RM-3206-PR (Santa Monica, CA: RAND 1963).

97. See, for example, Clayton P. Bowen and Daniel Wolven, 'Command and Control Challenges in South Asia', *The Nonproliferation Review* 6/3 (Spring–Summer 1999) p.25, and Ashok K. Mehta, 'Need to involve services in decision-making stressed', *India Abroad*, 12 March 1999.

98. The distinctiveness of formal organizations, in contrast to the alternatives, is explored in some detail in Michael I. Reed, *The Sociology of Organizations: Themes, Perspectives, and Prospects* (New York: Harvester Wheatsheaf 1992).

99. P.R. Chari, *Command and Control Arrangements*, Report of the sixth IPCS Seminar on the Implications of Nuclear Testing in South Asia, available at www.ipcs.org/issues/articles/135-ndi-chari.html.

100. Manvendra Singh, 'Who Should Control Nuclear Button? Armed Forces Have a Proposal', *The Indian Express*, 1 Sept. 1998; Rahul Bedi, 'India Assesses Options on Future Nuclear Control', *Jane's Defence Weekly*, 16 Sept. 1998, p.16.

101. Bedi, 'India Assesses Options on Future Nuclear Control' (note 100).

102. Recently, Pakistan announced the creation of its own National Command Authority, an impressive organizational structure which vests control of the country's nuclear weapons in a variety of bodies manned jointly by civilian leaders and the uniformed military. See, 'National Command Authority Formed', *Dawn*, 6 Feb. 2000.

103. For more on this phenomenon in the Cold War context, see Scott Sagan, 'Nuclear Alerts and Crisis Management', *International Security* 9/1 (Spring 1985) pp.99–139; Joseph I. Kruzel, 'Military Alerts and Diplomatic Signals', in Ellen P. Stern (ed.), *The Limits of Military Intervention* (Beverly Hills: Sage Publications 1977) pp.83–99; and, Kurt Gottfried and Bruce Blair (eds.), *Crisis Stability and Nuclear War* (Oxford: Oxford University Press 1988) pp.234–43.

104. Chengappa, *Weapons of Peace* (note 65) p.437.

105. Senior Indian policymakers have already indicated that India could withdraw its unilateral moratorium on explosive nuclear testing should that action comport with its national interests. See 'India Can Still Conduct N-Tests, Says Jaswant', *Indian Express*, 25 Nov. 2000.

106. There are in principle many variants beyond the two alternatives discussed here. These variants can be derived by manipulating the following three variables – the size of the force, the degree of integration between weapon components, and the patterns of command, control, and custody – in different ways.

5

Asymmetrical Indian and Chinese Threat Perceptions

JOHN W. GARVER

ASYMMETRIC THREAT PERCEPTIONS

A curious but important characteristic of India–China relations is the existence of asymmetric perceptions of mutual threat between those two countries. Indians tend to be deeply apprehensive regarding China.[1] Chinese, on the other hand, tend not to perceive a serious threat from India, and find it difficult to understand why Indians might find China and its actions threatening. This paper will analyze these asymmetrical Indian and Chinese threat perceptions.

The following discussion will begin by documenting in three ways the existence of asymmetrical Indian and Chinese threat perceptions: (1) by comparing the official security statements of the two sides, (2) by analyzing the content of élite foreign policy journals, and (3) by looking at the contrasting security views of the two sides apparent at the time of India's May 1998 nuclear tests. After empirically substantiating the existence of symmetrical threat perceptions in these various ways, this article will advance explanations of this phenomena at two different levels of analysis.

The first explanation will be in terms of the nature of the role played by China's public media in China's political system. At this level the argument will be that the mobilization function of the Chinese media leads that media to systematically downplay Indian threats to China's security interests. Since foreign analysts rely on China's public media for explication of Chinese views of India, and since most Chinese must also rely on the same sources for their views of India, the consequence is presentation of a rosy picture of Sino-Indian relations with conflictual elements being systematically downplayed.

The second and more fundamental explanation will be in terms of the history of the relative success of China and India over the past 50 years in shaping the now-existing pattern of international relations in the region. Here the argument will be that China's moves to counter India over the last decades have been essentially successful, while Indian efforts to counter China have essentially failed. This outcome, I will argue, has been the creation of a now-existing status quo fundamentally acceptable to Chinese but gravely troubling to Indians.

The existence of asymmetrical Chinese and Indian threat perceptions has not been fundamentally altered by the international campaign against terrorism unleashed following the September 11, 2001 attacks on the United States. Most importantly, the China-Pakistan strategic partnership emerged intact from those events. As we will see in the following pages, a major basis for Indian fear of China is the close China-Pakistan strategic partnership.

When Pakistan President Pervez Musharraf confronted Washington's demand that he choose between joining with or confronting the United States, Beijing urged him to cooperate with Washington and promised unwavering Chinese support. Over the next several months Beijing urged the United States to increase its assistance to Pakistan and give that country guarantees of long term support.[2] Beijing's interests were greatly served by US re-engagement with Pakistan. No longer would China alone bear the onus of supporting Pakistan – as had increasingly been the case during the 1990s. In short, the survival and continued vitality of the Sino-Pakistan entente during the post-September 11 period is testament both to China's satisfaction and India's deep disquiet with the existing status quo.

CHINA IN INDIAN OFFICIAL DEFENSE REPORTS

Sharply contrasting threat perceptions are apparent in the official defense statements issued periodically by the Indian and Chinese governments. Indian defense reports were issued annually by the Ministry of Defense of the Government of India during the 1990s. The analysis of India's security environment in every one of those reports referred directly to China.

The security environment outlined in India's 1992–93 defense report devoted two full paragraphs to China. China was not interested in negotiations with other countries regarding nuclear disarmament, the report stated. There had been 'No reduction so far in PLA (People's Liberation Army) forces along the Sino-Indian border'. China and Pakistan were assisting Bangladesh in modernizing and expanding its armed forces. To

India's east, 'Myanmar's military relationship with China continues to grow'.[3]

The 1993–94 defense report stated that 'China signed the NPT but broke the year-long global unofficial moratorium on nuclear testing'. China's nuclear test of October 1993 was 'part of China's attempt at further upgrading of its nuclear capability'. China was one of three nuclear powers 'yet to enter the nuclear arms control process'. The reported 'proliferation of missiles in our neighborhood such as to Pakistan, Saudi Arabia, and Iran' was a cause of concern. Pakistan 'has reportedly acquired M-11 missiles from China'.

There had been 'perceptible improvement' in India-China relations, but 'China has embarked on an ambitious programme of modernization of its armed forces. There have been reports to the effect that the Chinese have now significantly upgraded their equipment in many spheres of military equipment'. China was providing weapons to Sri Lanka 'which have enhanced the fire power and mobility of the Sri Lankan armed forces'. 'Sino-Myanmar relations ... in the field of military equipment continued to grow'.[4]

India's 1994–95 defense report stated that while Indian-Chinese relations had been improving and both countries were focused on internal development, 'Some relevant factors also deserve mentioning. Beijing is engaged in building strategic road links from its border towns to rail-heads and sea ports of Myanmar. It is helping to develop these ports. China has also been rapidly modernizing its armed forces and [is] equipping them with sophisticated aircraft, air defense weapons, and enhancing its blue-water capabilities'.[5]

According to the 1995–96 report, China continued its extensive defense collaboration with Pakistan and was known to be associated with Pakistan's nuclear program. 'The acquisition by Pakistan from China of sophisticated weapons systems, including missiles as well as uranium enrichment equipment, has a direct bearing on India's security environment'.[6]

The 1996–97 report stated flatly, 'China has supplied M-11 missiles to Pakistan and is aiding it with technology and manpower as well in the development of its indigenous missile programme'. It added: 'There are also credible reports about China continuing to assist Pakistan in its clandestine nuclear weapons programme'. 'India's concerns regarding China's defense co-operation with Pakistan, its assistance to Pakistan's clandestine nuclear programme, and the sale of missiles and sophisticated weapon systems by it to Pakistan, were conveyed to the Chinese side. The progress that China has made in the recent years in augmenting her nuclear arsenal and missile capabilities will continue to have relevance for India's security concerns'.

'Upgradation of China's logistic capabilities all along the India–China border, for strengthened air operations has to be noted', the report said. 'China's posture in the South-China Sea has implications for the region'. China's 'strengthening defense relations with Myanmar need to be carefully watched, in view of the geo-strategic location of Myanmar'.[7]

The 1997–98 Indian defense report stated that 'India is conscious of the fact that China is a nuclear weapon state and continues to maintain one of the largest standing armies in the world. Its military modernization is rapidly transforming the technological quality and force projection capabilities of its armed forces in all aspects'. China's assistance to Pakistan's nuclear weapons and missile programs 'also directly affect India's security'. India was 'aware of military collaboration between China and Myanmar, including the development of strategic lines of communication'. India would engage China in discussions that 'address all outstanding differences with a view to enhancing mutual understanding and building a relationship of constructive cooperation based on a recognition of India's legitimate security concerns'.[8]

The 1998–99 Indian defense report, issued in the midst of the deterioration of Sino-Indian relations that followed India's May 1998 nuclear tests, toned down the rhetoric about China. Yet a full paragraph was still devoted to China. India 'does not regard China as an adversary but as a great neighbour *with which it would like* to develop mutually beneficial and friendly relations'. [Emphasis added.] The report conveyed India's concern at the still unresolved border issue: 'India has expressed its interest time and again in resolving the boundary dispute with China … as quickly as possible'. China's 'assistance to Pakistan's nuclear weapons programme and the transfer of missiles and missile technology to Pakistan affect the security situation in South Asia', the report stated.[9]

The 1999–2000 defense report doubled over the previous report the amount of space devoted to China. China 'continued the process of modernization of its Armed Forces. The defense cooperation between China and Pakistan also continues. ' 'Sino-Pakistan and Pakistan-North Korean defence co-operation, which encompass transfer of nuclear technology, assistance in the missile development programme and the transfer of conventional military equipment to Pakistan is yet another area of concern and potential instability'.[10]

INDIA IN CHINESE OFFICIAL SECURITY STATEMENTS

There is a stark contrast between the long litany of Indian concerns about China, and the paucity of comparable China's concerns about India expressed in official Chinese defense statements. The People's Republic of China issued its first-ever defense white paper in July 1998. That was just two months after India's nuclear tests and the 'China-threat' justification of those tests, and in the midst of a serious deterioration of Sino-Indian relations that followed those events.

In spite of this, India figured only marginally in China's 1998 defense white paper. The chief threat to China came, the 1998 white paper made clear, from the trend toward interference in domestic politics by 'some big powers', continuing 'cold war mentality' by those big powers, and those same powers' effort to achieve security by alliances and arms buildups. In plain speech, the United States, its actions and alliances, constituted by far the gravest threat to China's security.

There were exactly *three* references to India in the 1998 report. Two referred to Indian *and* Pakistani May 1998 nuclear tests which had 'seriously impeded the international non-nuclear arms proliferation efforts and provoked grave consequences on (sic) peace and stability in the south Asian region and the rest of the world. The task for the international community to strengthen non-proliferation mechanisms has become more pressing now'. The joining of India and Pakistan implied that the threat to China derived from a possible threat of conflict between these two countries, not from any sort of Indian threat to China. The third reference to India came in the section on confidence-building measures (CBM) and described the measures agreed by the two countries in November 1996.[11]

China's second defense white paper was issued in October 2000. This report more clearly and forcefully than the 1998 white paper identified the United States as the greatest threat to China's security. The report also made clear that the US threat to China was increasing. There was exactly *one* mention of India in the 2000 white paper. Toward the end of the report a section on Nuclear Weapons and Missile Defense stressed the importance of securing the 'entry into force' of the 1996 Comprehensive [Nuclear] Test Ban Treaty (CTBT). In this regard, 'Such negative developments in the past two years as the nuclear tests in India and Pakistan and the US Senate's refusal to ratify the CTBT' were noted.

A section on 'frontier defense' made no mention of India even though it specified Mongolia, North Korea, Russia, Vietnam, Laos, Myanmar, Nepal, Pakistan, Afghanistan, Tajikistan, Kyrgyzstan, and Kazakhstan. India and Bhutan were the only two countries bordering China not mentioned. Nor did the section mention the November 1996 CBM agreed to by India and China, even though it *did mention* chronologically prior CBMs agreed to between China and the Central Asian countries in April 1996, and between China and Russia in April 1995.[12] These were strange and conspicuous silences suggesting that there is more here than meets the eye. We shall return to this point in the section on the function of Chinese media.

ASYMMETRICAL COVERAGE IN ELITE FOREIGN POLICY JOURNALS

A second type of data documenting the very different perceptions of mutual threat in China and India comes from analysis of the content of élite foreign policy journals. These journals present thoughtful analytical articles for domestic and foreign readers interested in Indian and Chinese foreign affairs respectively. The authors of many of the articles in these journals reflect, to some degree, analytical interpretation and policy advice given to higher-level decision makers. They also, to some degree, reflect the views of a significant portion of the attentive foreign policy audiences in the two countries. The central point here is that élite Indian journals are very concerned about China while Chinese journals are far less concerned with India.

Four authoritative and roughly comparable Indian and Chinese journals have been selected for comparison over a period of four years, 1997–2000. Two monthly journals selected for content analysis are *Strategic Analysis*, published by the quasi-governmental Institute for Defence Studies and Analysis (IDSA) in New Delhi, and *Xiandai guoji guanxi* (Contemporary International Relations) published by the Chinese Institute of Contemporary International Relations (CICIR) in Beijing. These two journals are comparable not only in terms of their frequency of publication but also in terms of their authoritativeness and their relatively hawkish perspective. IDSA has close links to the Indian defense establishment and shares the threat-oriented view of that establishment, but is independent enough to allow it to speak frankly. CICIR is associated with China's Ministry of State Security, 'China's KGB', an agency deeply apprehensive about foreign threats.

The two quarterlies surveyed are *Indian Defence Review*, published by an independent but very well-connected publishing house in New Delhi, Lancers, and *Guoji wenti yanjiu* (Journal of International Studies) published by the China Institute of International Studies (CIIS) which is under the Ministry of Foreign Affairs in Beijing. *Indian Defence Review* prides itself on being a sober, pragmatic, mainstream journal. *Guoji wenti yanjiu* tends to reflect the relatively moderate perspective of China's foreign ministry. Thus we have a sample of two relatively hawkish and two relatively moderate authoritative journals for each country.

A sample of four elite foreign policy journals is not large, but it is, I believe, representative of a relatively small set of such journals in the two countries. A doubling or a tripling of the number of élite journals surveyed would not, I believe, substantially alter the results.

Figure 1 presents in tabular form the number of other-related articles in *Strategic Analysis, Indian Defence Review, Guoji wenti yanjiu,* and *Xiandai guoji guanxi* over a period of four years based on a review of their tables of contents. All other-related articles, as indicated by listed titles which used the words China, Chinese, India, Indian, Sino, or Indo were counted, whether or not they were security-related. Thus, economic analyses or biographies of national leaders were counted. Articles with general titles which might well have touched on the other country (for example, 'India's Security Environment in the 21st Century', or 'South Asia's Post Cold War Security Situation'), but which did not specifically mention the other country in the title, were not counted.

This particular counting rule eliminated the need to review the actual text of articles and to establish rules for coding the texts of those articles. It also provided strictly comparable data for comparison. It also probably had the effect, however, of *understating* the degree of perceptual asymmetry. Since for reasons having to do with the mobilization role of China's public media (a matter discussed below), Chinese authors of broad surveys were probably less willing to specify India as a threat to China, analysis of ambiguously named articles would very probably have strengthened the tendency toward Indian concern and apparent Chinese non-concern.

Table 1 presents annualized data collected by an analysis of the table of contents of these four elite journals. The data clearly indicates that Indian journals were significantly more concerned with China, than the Chinese journals were with India. For three out of four years, China-concerned articles in the *Indian Defence Review* exceeded Indian-concerned articles in *Guoji wenti yanjiu,* and by a margin of at least 2 to 1. Only in one year, 1997, did *Guoji wenti yanjiu* exceed *Indian Defense Review.* Regarding *Strategic Analysis* and *Xiandai guoji guanxi,* for each of the four years compared, other-concerned articles in the Indian journal out numbered those in the Chinese journals by at least 4.5 to 1, with the difference in two years reaching ratios of 7.5 to 1 and 6.5 to 1.

Comparing the number of other-focused articles by each journal in each publication period yields a more complete comparison, plus a larger number

TABLE 1

NUMBER OF OTHER-FOCUSED ARTICLES ON AN ANNUALIZED BASIS

Quarterly	1997	1998	1999	2000
Indian Defence Review	2	2	2	5*
Guoji wenti yanjiu	3	1	1	2**
Monthly				
Strategic Analysis	9	19	17	15
Xiandai guoji guanxi	2	3	4	2

Note: * Oct.-Dec. issue is missing. This lacuna potentially biases the data toward understating the asymmetry of perceptions.

** In 2000 *Guoji wenti yanjiu* began publishing six rather than four issues per year.

TABLE 2

NUMBER OF OTHER-FOCUSED ARTICLES COMPARED
BY PUBLICATION PERIODS

Quarterly	I	II	III	IV	I	II	III	IV	I	II	III	IV	I	II	III	IV
Indian Defence Review	0	0	0	2	2	0	0	0	1	1	0	0	0	1	4	n.a.
Guoji wenti yanjiu	0	2	0	1	0	0	1	0	0	0	0	1	1*	0	0	1*

Monthly	1	2	3	4	5	6	7	8	9	10	11	12
1997												
Strategic Analysis	1**	1	2	0	2	2	1	0	0	0	0	0
Xiandai guoji guanxi	0	0	0	0	2	0	0	0	0	0	0	0
1998												
Strategic Analysis	4	1	1	2	2	4	1	2	0	1	0	1
Xiandai guoji guanxi	0	0	0	0	1	0	1	0	0	0	1	0
1999												
Strategic Analysis	0	2	4	3	1	0	1	0	1	2	1	2
Xiandai guoji guanxi	0	0	0	0	1	0	1	0	0	1	2	0
2000												
Strategic Analysis	1	0	3	2	2	3	1	0	1	1	1	0
Xiandai guoji guanxi	0	0	0	1	0	1	0	0	0	0	0	0

Note: * In 2000 *Guoji wenti yanjiy* began publishing six rather than four issues per year. The two India-related articles were randomly assigned to the first and third quarters in order to retain comparability.

** This was a combined January-February issue. Again for the sake of comparability, this "1" was randomly assigned to the February period.

of data points thereby permitting statistical tests of the significance of variation. The data is presented in this fashion in Table 2.

The mean number of China-focused articles in the two Indian journals was 1.604. The mean for India-focused articles in the two Chinese journals was 0.396. An n of 47 (with 17 null sets) yields a set large enough to perform simple statistical tests of significance. A T-test on the difference between these two means indicates 99 per cent confidence in significant variation.

As Table 2 indicates, in only seven of a total of 128 publication periods did the number of India-focused articles in the two Chinese journals exceed the number of China-focused articles in the comparable Indian journal. In 36 publication periods, the number of China-focused articles in Indian journals exceeded the number of India-focused articles in comparable Chinese journals. When the number of India-focused articles in Chinese journals was greater, it never exceeded the ratio of 2 to 1. In seven publications periods in which Indian concern with China exceeded Chinese concern with India, on the other hand, in seven cases the ratio was between 3 to 1 and 6 to 1. Throughout the four-year period, there was a total of 77 China-focused articles in the two Indian journals, compared to 19 India-focused articles in Chinese journals. This data makes it clear that Indian concern for China, as manifested in elite policy journals, substantially exceeded Chinese concern for India.

A CASE STUDY OF COGNITIVE ASYMMETRY: INDIA'S 1998 TESTS

A recent and important example of asymmetrical Chinese and Indian threat perceptions came during the imbroglio over India's May 1998 nuclear tests. Indian policy at that juncture reflected deep concerns over threats from China. (This is a proposition that runs counter to much of the accepted wisdom in the United States at the time of India's nuclear tests – a matter we will return to below.) Chinese policy evinced no comparable concern about threats from India.

The reasons for India's nuclearization were laid out in the now-famous 11 May letter by Prime Minister Atal Behari Vajpayee to US President William Clinton and other world leaders. Vajpayee's letter explained India's nuclearization in terms of a deteriorating security environment due largely to activities by China and Pakistan. Neither of those countries was explicitly named, but the allusions were clear enough. China was the chief threat outlined in Vajpayee's letter; 68 words explicated the Chinese threat to India, while 48 words dealt with the Pakistani threat.[13] 'We have an overt nuclear weapon state on our borders, a state that committed armed aggression against India in 1962', Vajpayee's letter said. Although Sino-Indian relations had improved, 'An atmosphere of distrust persists mainly due to the unresolved border problem'. In addition, 'that country has materially helped another neighbor of ours to become a covert nuclear weapons state'.

There was a tendency in the United States at the time of Vajpayee's letter to dismiss it as not genuinely reflective of real Indian apprehensions, but as a disingenuous Indian move calculated to appeal to presumed US fears of China. It is important to note, however, that the threats from China outlined in Vajpayee's letter correspond to the analyses presented in the Ministry of Defense annual reports described earlier. They also correspond to the arguments made by Jaswant Singh to US Deputy Secretary of State Strobe Talbott in their talks during late 1998. A public exposition of Singh's position appeared in *Foreign Affairs*.[14]

Singh's article focused on Chinese assistance to Pakistan's nuclear and missile programs. China's 'proliferation' to Pakistan posed 'a threat to India's security', Singh argued. 'The nuclear era entered India's neighbourhood when China became a nuclear power in October 1964'. Over the following decades, 'Neither the world nor the nuclear powers succeeded in halting the transfer of nuclear weapons technology from declared nuclear powers to their preferred clients. The NPT (Non-proliferation Treaty) notwithstanding, proliferation in India's backyard spread'. During the 1990s, 'India's plight worsened as the decade wore on'. 'The rise of China and continued strains with Pakistan made the 1980s and 1990s a greatly troubling period for India'.

Beijing refused to accept New Delhi's public airing of its concerns about China. Beijing reacted strongly and negatively to New Delhi's 'China threat' justification of the nuclear tests. In the eighteen months after the letter Beijing unfolded a campaign designed to pressure New Delhi to retract its talk about China constituting a threat to India. That effort to influence Indian policy is beyond the purview of this article, but it should be noted that this effort was premised on a fundamental divergence of perspectives on the India-China relation; Beijing's objective was to compel New Delhi to formally, publicly accept China's view that the two countries did not constitute a threat to one another.[15]

China's official words in the months after India's nuclear tests made very clear that, in the view of the Chinese government, India did not constitute a threat to China, nor did China constitute a threat to India. A PRC (People's Republic of China) Foreign Ministry statement issued after

India's tests and after disclosure of Vajpayee's letter to Clinton in no way suggested that Indian nuclear capabilities (or any other capabilities for that matter) might constitute a threat to China. The central objection to Indian actions expressed in the Statement was that India's tests violated the 'international' efforts to prevent nuclear weapons proliferation. Great stress was placed on Indian violation of 'international norms' and 'efforts'; the word 'international' was used five times in the short foreign ministry statement. The statement also objected that India had 'even maliciously accused China of posing a nuclear threat to India'. This was 'utterly groundless' and 'gratuitous' and 'solely for the purpose of finding excuse for the development of ... nuclear weapons'.[16]

A commentary in *Renmin ribao* issued the same day as the foreign ministry statement also made no allusion whatever to any sort of Indian actions constituting a threat to China. The commentary's objections to India's nuclear tests derived from violation of international nonproliferation efforts and norms. 'Even more depraved', however, 'was India's 'suddenly blaming its immoral development of nuclear forces on China', and its 'propagation of the China threat theory'.[17]

In this author's survey of *Renmin ribao* and *Beijing Review* in the months after the Indian nuclear tests, there were no references, even indirect, to India constituting a security threat to China. Again the point was that neither China nor India constituted a threat to the other, and any assertions to the contrary were false and malicious in intent.

Chinese academic commentary on India's 1998 tests also gave little indication of perceived Indian threats to China, much less of possible Chinese threats to India. While opinion among Chinese analysts was not uniform, the dominant point of view among Chinese analysts was that India's 1998 tests had little to do with Indian-Chinese relations at all, but were, in fact, a function of the domestic political needs of the BJP-led Indian government, and/or an Indian drive for hegemony in South Asia. The dominant point of view among Chinese analysts was that an effort to understand Indian-Chinese relations in terms of security was misguided. There were no legitimate, major, security concerns between the two countries, and assertions to the contrary were inaccurate and possibly malevolent.

An article by prominent Chinese South Asian specialist Wang Hongwei typified the mainstream point of view. The BJP government had 'fabricated the 'China threat' as a pretext for their surprise nuclear tests in order, from the perspective of domestic politics, to stimulate Hindu nationalist passions, thus diverting internal contradictions and attention in order to strengthen the weak position of the regime'. From an international perspective, the objective of the Indian tests was to 'strengthen a bit its hegemonist position in South Asia, and especially use the nuclear tests to secure a position equal to that of the ... five nuclear big powers'.[18]

An article by another authoritative Chinese South Asian specialist, Ye Zhengjia argued along similar lines. India's use of 'the China threat' (the term was always put inside quotation marks) was a 'pretext' designed to win Western sympathy and thereby minimize adverse Western reaction to the nuclear tests. India's leaders 'clearly understood', Ye said, that China's nuclear weapons were entirely for self defense and that it was 'inconceivable' that they could ever be used against India. Likewise, 'the assertion that Sino-Pakistan cooperation threatened India is preposterous'.[19]

Other articles by Chinese analysts *did perceive* Indian threats to China. One article maintained that turning Tibet into a 'buffer zone' (*huang chong guo*) between India and China was still the long term objective of Indian military strategy against China. Regarding India's nuclear weapons and missile programs, 'as everyone knows', those weapons were 'mainly directed against China'. India also objected to Sino-Pakistan military cooperation and this could also threaten China's security interests. Because of this, one 'could not exclude the possibility of a worsening' of Sino-Indian relations. In spite of all this, however, the author insisted that India's use of 'the 'China threat' anti-China clamor' in May 1998 was merely a 'pretext'.[20]

Still another article laid out a very realistic view of *Indian perceptions* of security challenges associated with China. Interesting, the piece began and ended with politically correct, unequivocal rejections of 'the China threat' theory.[21] Thus even with the more hard-headed, realistic minority analysts, one got a sense that application of a security perspective to Sino-Indian relations was misplaced. The message was that if only Indian leaders would abandon their unfounded fears of China, Sino-Indian friendship could blossom.

THE MOBILIZATION FUNCTION OF CHINESE OPEN MEDIA

Analysis at the level of bureaucratic process provides a satisfactory if partial explanation of the dearth of Chinese expressions of concern about security challenges from India. The reader will have noticed that all previous discussions of Chinese perceptions of India were based on *publicly available, openly published* Chinese sources. China's two defense white papers issued by the PRC State Council, *Guoji wenti yanjiu, Xiandai guoji guanxi, Beijing Review, Renmin ribao, Nanya yanjiu, Nanya yanjiu jikan,* and *Guoji zhanlue yanjiu*, are all open-source, freely distributed publications. Correct interpretation of the messages conveyed by these sources requires understanding of the function of such media in China.

In China a sharp distinction is drawn between open (*gongkai*) and closed (*neibu*) publications. Closed publications are intended to inform cadre and party members, and are circulated via carefully restricted channels. Closed publications are distributed through special non-public channels, and administrative and legal means are used to ensure they are available only to authorized audiences. Closed publications are intended to inform politically relevant audiences about current affairs. Their content is factual, and often quite frank and even critical of government policies. The purpose of closed, *neibu*, publications is to convey the unvarnished truth to those whose political responsibilities give them a need to know that truth.

Openly disseminated, *gongkai*, sources play a different function. These sources are intended to inform people about Party and government policies once those policies have been decided upon. The key purpose of open publications is to mobilize public support for the implementation of official policies, to explain the wisdom of those policies and encourage people to assist their implementation. With open publications there is almost always a clear line to be followed.[22] A powerful administrative system is in place to ensure that open publications hew to the guidelines laid out by the central Propaganda Small Group and/or the Foreign Affairs Small Group.[23]

The 'line' regarding India followed by all the open source publications reviewed earlier was that 'the China threat' was clearly bogus and a pretext used for ulterior purposes – for purposes other than dealing with real threats from China. Several unstated conclusions followed from this premise. First, it followed that India need not align with the United States to deal with some perceived threat to Indian security. It also followed that there are no legitimate grounds for India to be concerned with, to oppose, or seek to block, the expansion of Chinese ties with the countries of South Asia. Such ties in no way threatened India and were fully in accord with the Five Principles of Peaceful Coexistence, to which India has agreed.

Since the key justification for Indian efforts to restrict Chinese military-security ties with the South Asian countries was a threat to India's security, it followed that open Chinese publications should carry nothing legitimizing Indian security concerns. Discussions of Indian threats to China were apparently not prohibited as long as the article made clear that such 'threats' were merely Indian *perceptions*, that those perceptions were inaccurate, and that there was no substance to 'the China threat'. All articles were apparently expected to explicitly reject 'the China threat theory'. In such a context, it is necessary that Indian threats to China be downplayed – in open source publications. It is quite possible, however, that internal publications convey more realistic, more pessimistic, more conflict-oriented analyses.

The parent organizations of both Chinese journals surveyed earlier, *Guoji wenti yanjiu* and *Xiandai guoji guanxi*, are organs of the Chinese state (the Foreign Ministry and the Ministry of State Security respectively), and are the *only openly distributed* publications of these two agencies. Most of the research products of the CISS and CICIR are distributed via non-public, internal distribution networks to China's decision makers. The two Chinese journals surveyed in the previous section were thus *gongkai* organs of important, authoritative, and closely supervised state organs. As such, they were expected to conform to broad guidelines laid down by central organs of the Chinese Communist Party (CCP) in order to achieve the policy objectives specified by the CCP's Foreign Affairs Small Group.

This is probably one reason why threats to China from India are so little talked about. Beijing's policy objective towards India is to court that country to 'friendship and cooperation' on the basis that neither side constitutes a threat to the other. Talking too much, publicly, about 'threats from India' would not serve this objective.

CHINA'S GREATER SUCCESS IN SHAPING THE EXISTING STATUS QUO: TIBET

The more fundamental factor explaining asymmetrical Indian and Chinese threat perceptions is, I believe, China's relative success in creating the structure of power currently existing between the two countries. This status quo includes the status of Tibet relative to the two countries, India's deep apprehensions deriving from the outcome of the 1962 war, the Sino-Pakistan entente cordiale, and the new Sino-Myanmar strategic partnership. Over the past 50 years China has created a situation in which its own security is fairly secure against challenge by India. The converse of Chinese success, however, has been a status quo deeply challenging to India's security. Contemporary Indian apprehensions of China are, to a substantial degree, a function of the series of setbacks suffered by India at Chinese hands over the past 50 years.

The status of Tibet is a key element of the status quo created by Beijing. Tibet is, and since the early 1950s has been, under effective Chinese military occupation. Large and potent PLA forces are deployed across the length and breadth of Tibet. Those forces are sustained by robust logistic lines linking Tibet to industrial-economic centers in China proper. In short,

Tibet has become a platform for the effective exercise and outward projection of Chinese military power.

Administratively Tibet is under the effective control of China's central authorities. The 'autonomous' nature of Tibet's political institutions is more nominal than substantial, and, in any case, does not permit Tibetan self-rule. Ethnic Tibetans participate in the governance of Tibet only to the extent that they hew to Beijing's line and policies. Any opposition to those policies is suppressed. The indigenous Tibetan population and its distinctive culture are rapidly being over-whelmed by Han settlers, and Tibet's traditional and deeply-Indian-influenced civilization is being swiftly and irrevocably obliterated. Tibet is, in fact, being rapidly transformed into an 'integral part of China' as Beijing has long claimed it was.

India steadily but unsuccessfully resisted Beijing's creation of the status quo in Tibet. The appropriate starting point is that prior to 1951 and going as far back in history as one cares to go, Tibet had not been a permanent platform for Chinese military power or under direct Chinese administration. Tibet had functioned, rather, as a de facto buffer between Chinese and Indian states. Beijing began constructing a new status quo regarding Tibet in 1950–51 when it defeated Tibetan military forces in a series of pitched battles, brought the region under effective military occupation, and began building a network of roads supporting that occupation and tying Tibet ever more closely to China proper.[24]

New Delhi issued a series of diplomatic protests designed to prevent Chinese military occupation of that region. When Beijing rejected these protests out of hand and countered with tough threats, New Delhi backed down. Indian leaders then switched to a policy of appeasement designed, in part, to persuade Beijing that a large PLA presence in Tibet was unnecessary. That policy too did not work. By the mid 1950s PLA forces were pouring into Tibet and in 1959 they displaced the autonomous Tibetan government, assuming direct and permanent administrative authority.

New Delhi then switched to a more hard-line approach of supporting armed Tibetan resistance to Chinese rule.[25] This approach too failed. The PLA waged a protracted and effective counter-insurgency war against the Tibetan rebels that eventually crushed armed Tibetan resistance. New Delhi then tried to persuade Beijing to restore a degree of genuine Tibetan autonomy as part of a process of Sino-Indian rapprochement. Beijing rejected these efforts as interference in China's domestic affairs and manifestation of India's tendency toward regional hegemony. Beijing countered with demands for New Delhi to restrict further the activities of the Dalai Lama and his Government in Exile. New Delhi moved incrementally to accommodate Beijing's demands, convinced, grudgingly, that this was the price India would have to pay for better relations with China.

A counter-factual thought experiment in which we imagine a Chinese failure and Indian success regarding Tibet elucidates the impact of the actual outcome. Suppose that in 1950 India's government had accepted rather than rejected US offers to cooperate on Tibet. Following the onset of the Korean War, US strategists began looking for ways of stepping up pressure on China and in October–November 1950 approached the Indian government about possible cooperation to support Tibet against Chinese encroachment.[26] New Delhi was not interested in the US proposal. US leaders then concluded that without Indian support and cooperation an operation supporting Tibetan resistance to China was not feasible, and dropped the idea – at least for several years. A decade later, circa 1960, when the Indian government finally began taking a benignly permissive attitude toward US covert operations in support of Tibetan forces, the PLA's position in Tibet was far stronger than it had been in 1950.

But let us suppose New Delhi had decided to take a different course in 1950, a course of cooperating with the US and encouraging it to assist Tibetan resistance to Chinese entry into Tibet. The PLA had then not yet entered Tibet. Chinese forces were marshaling in eastern Tibet (then known as Xikang province) to do so, but Tibetan forces (ardently anti-Chinese but primitively armed and organized) still blocked their way. The PLA was also moving toward intervention in the Korean War.

Suppose then that in cooperation with India, hefty US assistance had flowed to the Tibetans. Suppose that US and Indian military advisors had undertaken a crash re-training of Tibetan forces arrayed along the upper Yangtze River. The PLA had not yet built the roads vital to supporting operations inside Tibet. Nor had it yet developed with a decade of Soviet assistance into the potent motorized force that would grind down Tibetan resistance in the 1960s. (PLA construction of roads in Tibet combined with the motorization of PLA forces meant that once a Tibetan guerrilla unit engaged Chinese forces, other PLA units could deploy rapidly to adjacent areas keeping the horse or foot powered insurgents on the run until they became exhausted.) The US and China would soon be engaged in a bitter, intense war in Korea with the US searching for ways of diverting Chinese forces from the Korean theater. Tibetan resistance to Chinese invasion could easily have been roused.

Let us imagine that under these circumstances India's leaders had decided circa 1950 to cooperate with the United States with the consequence that US covert assistance flowed to the Tibetan forces in amounts roughly comparable to those that in fact flowed to Nationalist Chinese remnants in northern Burma. Let us also imagine that, under these circumstances, Tibetan forces had developed adequate strength to thwart or contain the first several PLA thrusts into eastern Tibet. Suppose that Beijing had then hesitated for a period of time, perhaps until the war in Korea was over – just as it did with offensives to retake the off-shore islands once the Korean War began.

Regardless of what happened next, a sequence of events along these imaginary lines would have left China with far greater apprehension regarding India. Even if Indian-US moves had been overwhelmed by superior Chinese force in the mid-1950s, China's subsequent threat perceptions *vis-à-vis* India would have far graver. Indian actions would have been seen as constituting an extremely dangerous threat to China's rule over Tibet.

The consequences of such Chinese perceptions – whether they would have been advantageous or disadvantageous to India – need not concern us here. The point is that more vigorous and effective Indian actions in support of Tibetan autonomy would have led to very different Chinese perceptions of India. As it was, however, India's various efforts to sustain the old status quo in Tibet were ineffectual. Indian actions in the early and mid 1950s were not, in fact, very threatening to China.

COUNTER-FACTUAL PROPOSITION II:
WHAT IF INDIA HAD WON THE 1962 WAR?

The specific outcome of the 1962 war was similarly in accord with China's interests and a manifestation of a successful exercise of Chinese power – and had a profound asymmetrical effect on subsequent threat perceptions. China's leaders decided that India was encroaching on the territory of 'China's Tibet' in collusion with US and Soviet pressure on China, with the intent of fundamentally weakening, or even ending, Chinese rule over Tibet.[27] Warnings to India to desist from its threatening policies were not effective, and China's leaders decided forceful measures were necessary to cause New Delhi to adopt a more sober attitude.

Having decided to move toward use of military force, Chinese leaders paid close attention to such matters as marshaling well-acclimatized forces to strategic areas, pushing roads into forward areas, accumulating adequate material at forward dumps, laying out workable operational plans for swift offensive thrusts combined with appropriate deceptions, engineering situations of local numerical superiority, achieving tactical surprise, the coordination of diplomatic and military means, and last but by no means least, defining achievable war aims together with a war termination strategy in which China held the initiative. PLA forces marshaled local superiority, achieved both strategic and tactical surprise, and struck swiftly.

Indian defenses crumbled and retreat quickly turned into rout. Chinese forces advanced largely unopposed and according to their own timetable to the southern line it claimed as a boundary – on the foothills of the Himalayan range and looking out on the plain of the Brahmaputra River. Chinese forces then stopped unilaterally and withdrew, unpursued by Indian forces, to positions north of what China claimed was the line of actual control prior to the initiation of India's forward policy.

From Beijing's point of view, the 1962 punishment of India was a necessary and salutary, if politically expensive, lesson. The heaviest costs for China were associated with the Indian military buildup that followed India's 1962 defeat, plus deep Indian hostility that would long mitigate against Chinese efforts to normalize relations with India. Yet offsetting these costs was an even greater gain: a far more realistic, sober, and cautious Indian approach toward China. India's moves *vis-à-vis* China were subsequently far more cautious. It was upon this greater Indian sobriety that subsequent Sino-Indian friendship would grow, at least in the Chinese view of things.

Let us again imagine a different outcome in 1962. The outcome that transpired was not inevitable. India had many tactical and strategic advantages which more hard-minded Indian leaders could have seized. China's economy was in a state of collapse. One of the most devastating famines of modern history had just swept across China with perhaps tens of millions starving to death. China was isolated from its erstwhile ally, the USSR; the Sino-Soviet alliance had collapsed. The Tibetan populace cowered fearfully under brutal Chinese repression, and almost certainly would have rallied to a liberation force acting with Indian support and under the Dalai Lama's imprimatur. There was in India a pool of tens of thousands of young Tibetan men who had recently fled Maoist misrule in Tibet and who would have been enthusiastic fighters in a war to liberate Tibet.

China's long logistic lines from Sichuan and Gansu were vulnerable to interdiction. Distances from economic centers in India to the Lhasa-Shigatze heartland of Tibet were far shorter and less rugged than comparable distances from centers in China. The actual outcome of the 1962 clash was not a result of advantages one-sidedly in favor of China. It was, rather, a result of the fact that China had political-military leaders who seized whatever advantages China had, while India had leaders who were positively feckless in their disregard for the realities of military operations.

India's leaders had allowed India's military capabilities to atrophy in the 1950s and then, from this position of weakness, ordered assertive policies designed to expel Chinese military forces from areas claimed by India. This alone was a receipt for disaster. But there was much more; the indictment of India's handling of the 1962 war could hardly be more damning.[28]

Indian leaders ordered Indian forces to defend every inch of Indian territory at the boundary, thereby ensuring that Indian forces would be strong nowhere and could not choose particularly advantageous territory on which to make their decisive stand. Indian leaders deployed to the high Himalayas troops acclimatized to the plains of the subcontinent, gave them inadequate logistic support, allowed their command to drift with an ill and over-age general in charge, and ignored intelligence pointing to a probable Chinese resort to force. India's leaders ordered Indian forces to undertake impractical defensive and offensive operations oblivious to tactical and logistic realities.

Let us imagine that India had had more realistic leaders in 1962. Suppose the broad contours of the planned PLA offensive had been detected by vigilant, Tibetan-aided and perhaps CIA-aided, Indian intelligence services. Suppose that the Indian side had made preparations to allow the planned Chinese offensive to unfold, push through successive but expendable lines of resistance, and than made India's main defensive stand at a supportable southern position, perhaps at Bomdila. Suppose that the planned PLA offensive had transpired and depleted PLA stockpiles.

Then suppose that once China's opening offensive had been contained, and clearly tarred China as the aggressor, Indian forces had opened their counter-offensive. Suppose the objective of that counter-offensive had been a drive directly up the Chumbi Valley by a Tibetan-Indian force to seize Shigatze. Suppose *that* offensive had taken the PLA by surprise and once the Dalai Lama and his Government in Exile was installed in Shigatze the Tibetan liberation army was rapidly expanded with locally recruited ardently anti-Maoist young Tibetans.

Regardless of what happened next, a sequence of events such as imagined here, bold and effective Indian moves to impose Indian interests on China, would have had a deep and abiding impact on Chinese perceptions of threat emanating from India. The fact that this did not happen and than, instead, events went according to Beijing's script meant that China subsequently felt little threat from India. It was India, rather, that perceived threat from China.

COUNTER-FACTUAL PROPOSITION III:
WHAT IF INDIA HAD ABORTED THE SINO-PAKISTAN ENTENTE?

Still another major Indian policy failure – and converse Chinese policy success – has had to do with Pakistan. China was able to establish and maintain an entente cordiale with Pakistan premised on parallel interests *vis-à-vis* India. By keeping Pakistan militarily strong, China kept Pakistan free from Indian domination and confident enough to pose a continual challenge to India. Beginning in 1964 China began supplying military equipment to Pakistan. Following US suspension of arms sales to Pakistan during the 1965 and 1971 wars, China became Pakistan's main supplier of munitions – a situation that continues into the twenty-first century.

During the 1970s Beijing began covert assistance to Pakistan's secret nuclear weapons program. Beijing then began assistance to Pakistan's ballistic missile program, thereby giving Pakistan an assured ability to deliver its new nuclear weapons against Indian targets. By the 1980s and 1990s, China and Pakistan were partners in joint research and development efforts for new model fighter aircraft. Beijing also extended large scale assistance to Pakistani efforts to further develop its military-industrial base. The close strategic partnership between China and Pakistan is one of the defining elements of the international structure of power in Asia at the opening of the twenty-first century.[29]

The depth and durability of the Sino-Pakistan *entente cordiale* compels Indian defense planners to consider the possibility that China or Pakistan will enter any large-scale conflict between India and the other. By doing this Beijing has compelled India to split its military forces. In effect, the Sino-Pakistan *entente cordiale* confronts India with a two-front threat.

India unsuccessfully resisted the creation of the existing status quo of the Sino-Pakistani *entente cordiale*. In the mid-1950s India's leaders hoped to use India's friendship with China to persuade Beijing to keep its distance from Pakistan. By demonstrating Indian friendship for China through fostering China's ties with non-communist developing countries and defending China's interests in the United Nations against United States criticism, while also conceding the essence of Beijing's claim to Tibet in 1954, New Delhi hoped to convince Beijing that China had no need to adopt hostile measures toward India. Indeed, India would create incentives for Beijing to foster continued Indian friendship.

Nehru's strategy of appeasement worked, for a time, on the litmus-test issue of Kashmir; Beijing did not come down on Pakistan's side of that issue until the 1960s. But Nehru's friendship policy toward China did not prevent China's Premier Zhou Enlai and Pakistan's Prime Minister Muhammad Ali Bogra from reaching at the Bandung conference in 1955 a highly effective understanding regarding the parallel interests of their two countries *vis-à-vis* India. Bogra assured Zhou that the enhanced strength Pakistan was gaining from its alliance with the United States would not be used against China. Zhou accepted Bogra's assurances.[30] Several years later this understanding regarding convergent interests would blossom into a solid Sino-Pakistan strategic partnership.

India exerted considerable national effort in 1965 and again in 1971 to punish and diminish Pakistan. In neither case did Indian military victories translate into durable gains. In both cases China helped rebuild Pakistan's shattered military power and confidence (as did the United States). Pakistan's 1971 defeat did indeed threaten to overthrow the structure of power in South Asia (which since 1947 has rested on a balance between India and Pakistan).

But China stepped in with large-scale military assistance. Chinese tanks, warplanes, artillery, small arms, and defense industrial plant. Most crucially, first nuclear weapons technology and then ballistic missile technology flowed from China to Pakistan. By about 1990 Pakistan had acquired the nuclear 'great equalizer' with substantial Chinese help. Indian protests to Beijing, and to Washington, were ineffectual. Pakistan revived from its catastrophic 1971 defeat and within 20 years constituted a greater than ever threat to India.

As the process of Sino-Indian rapprochement gained momentum in the late 1980s and 1990s, New Delhi attempted to persuade China to draw away from strategic partnership with Pakistan for the sake of improved Sino-Indian relations. Beijing threw New Delhi a few concessions; the most important of these was neutrality on the Kashmir issue and other intra-South Asian disputes. During the India–Pakistan nuclear confrontation of 1990 Beijing, under strong Indian pressure, dropped its previous pro-Pakistan position on the Kashmir issue. Beijing also diluted somewhat its verbiage in support of Pakistan against possible Indian attack – as compared to the verbiage it used earlier. But the core of the Sino-Pakistan security relationship remains unaltered.[31] This fact underlies the frequent reiteration in India's annual defense statements about the Pakistan-China relationship. The existence of the close China-Pakistan military partnership confronts India with a serious threat, at least in the views of India's security planners. There is nothing comparable in India's relations with China's neighbors.

This probably need not have been the case. Again a counter-factual thought experiment helps clarify the situation. What would be China's view if India and Japan had formed a warm and deep military relationship in the 1950s or the 1960s? What if New Delhi had decided to match Beijing's partnership with Pakistan by building a comparable partnership with Japan?

Certainly Washington would have been delighted with and encouraged such a development the 1950s and 1960s, and perhaps even later. What if Japan had matched its alliance with the United States with a US-encouraged strategic partnership with India? What if Japan had financed and assisted with transfer of advanced technology major Indian military research and development programs over the decades? What if Japan had come to look on India as a major partner as the Japanese Maritime Self Defense Force (SDF) began developing a more long-legged naval capability in the late 1970s?

Perhaps Tokyo might have dispatched a three-destroyer squadron to pay a friendship visit to Vishakhapatnam in early 1987 during the Sino-Indian border confrontation at Sumdurong Chu and two years after a PLA-Navy squadron paid a visit to Pakistani and Bangladeshi ports. Perhaps Japanese SDF leaders, delegations, ships, and planes paid frequent visits to India, and vice versa, while top leaders of the two countries engaged in frequent consultations about 'issues of mutual concern'. Were such a thick Japan-India security partnership rather than or in addition to the actually existing Sino-Pakistan partnership part of the now-existing status quo, Beijing would feel rather more threatened by India.

Of course China did confront a hostile link-up between India and another of its nemeses, not Japan but the Soviet Union. As Sino-Soviet relations deteriorated in the 1960s, the Soviet Union emerged as India's major backer against China. Existence of this Soviet-Indian link is fundamentally disadvantageous to China. Beijing responded by making it clear to Soviet leaders that cessation of Soviet backing for China's hostile neighbors was the price of normalization of Sino-Soviet relations. Abrogation of the August 1971 Indian-Soviet security treaty was *not* one of Beijing's 'three demands' on Moscow during the 1980s. (Those demands concerned Soviet links with Vietnam, Mongolia, and Afghanistan.)

Yet it does seem clear that Beijing conveyed an essentially similar message to Moscow regarding India. In any case, Soviet President Mikhail

Gorbachev fundamentally redefined (and thereby eviscerated) the 1971 treaty during his 1986 visit to India.[32] This move was an important step in the process of Sino-Soviet normalization that culminated in Gorbachev's May 1989 visit to China. Soviet arms sales to India continued, but it was now clear that Moscow would not endanger Sino-Soviet amity by supporting India against China.

New Delhi chose not to attempt to match the Sino-Pakistan entente with a Indo-Japanese partnership. Regarding the Indo-Soviet link, China was in fact able to uncouple New Delhi and Moscow. New Delhi has failed to achieve any comparable uncoupling of Beijing and Islamabad. Again the point is that China has been far more successful than India in shaping its security environment and this difference is reflected in the asymmetrical security perceptions of the two sides.

CONCLUSION

There seem to be two satisfactory explanations of the phenomena of asymmetrical Chinese and Indian perceptions of threat from one another. The first is the *probable* existence of a calculated but highly classified Chinese foreign policy strategy toward India. This strategy is probably translated into guidelines for public media which prohibit or carefully limit and control public talk about Indian threats to China – much less of Chinese threats to India. Any public talk of one country threatening the other is disallowed. The objective is to delegitimize the framing of Sino-Indian relations in terms of security considerations. It follows from this that India has no grounds to object to Chinese military ties to Pakistan or other South Asian countries, or to cooperate with third powers hostile to China.

We can call this Chinese strategy a 'good neighbor policy', *mulin zhengce* in Chinese. It serves two key objectives. The first is to dissuade India from cooperating with great powers hostile to China – formerly the Soviet Union and now the United States. The operational mechanism for achieving this is cooperation between India and China in constructing a New International Economic and Political Order premised on the interests of the Third World and developing countries. The second objective is to induce India not to object to China's military-security ties with countries of South Asia – Pakistan, Myanmar, Nepal, and Bangladesh. These relations do not in any way constitute a threat to India, Beijing insists, and it is thus unreasonable for New Delhi to object to them.

Both of these policy objectives are served by downplaying talk of security threats within the India-China relations. When translated into guidelines for *gongkai* publications, this policy helps explain why there is so little discussion in Chinese publications about Indian threats to China's security, and why any discussion of Indian-perceived Chinese threats to India is invariably cast in terms of the unreasonableness and inaccuracy of those Indian perceptions.

A second level of explanation of the asymmetry of Indian and Chinese threat perceptions is in terms of the outcome of decades-long application of Indian and Chinese national power to shape the correlation of forces in the Sino-Indian relationship. By and large China seems to have been more effective in shaping the broad contours of that correlation than was India. China mobilized and used its national capabilities in this regard with considerably more vigor and success than India.

The outcome of this is that the existing correlation of forces is far more satisfactory and less threatening to China than it is to India. In 1962 India was taught to fear Chinese military power. The Sino-Pakistan strategic partnership is still strong. Thick security relations have developed between China and Myanmar and China and Bangladesh. The development of China's military links to various South Asian countries has only occasionally met with major setbacks. There is little reason for Beijing to find the status quo threatening. The view is rather different from the Indian perspective.

The adoption of a far more hard-headed and realistic Indian foreign policy after the watershed election of March 1998 may lead to somewhat more symmetrical Chinese and Indian threat perceptions. Under the leadership of Vajpayee and Jaswant Singh, India launched a campaign to collect points of pressure against China. Elements of this new strategy included: overt nuclearization and weaponization; the expansion of military ties with China's eastern and southeastern neighbors via India's 'Look East' policy; a drive to develop and deploy missiles able to reach deep inside China; the forging of a new strategic partnership with the United States; and last but by no means least, stepped-up pressure on Beijing to disengage from missile and nuclear cooperation with Pakistan. The operative assumption underlying this new Indian policy seems to be that if Beijing is more fearful of India, it will become more sensitive to Indian concerns about China's activities in South Asia and the Indian Ocean region.

NOTES

1. The author would like to thank Mr Chunfang Li of the University of Michigan Asia Library, Mr Ron Dial of the Air University Library, and Dr Swaran Singh of Jawaharal Nehru University for their assistance in compiling a complete set of journal table of contents for content analysis.
2. Charles Hutzler, 'China's Quiet, Crucial Role in the War', *Wall Street Journal*, 18 Dec. 2001, p.10.
3. *Annual Report, 1992–93*, Ministry of Defence, Government of India, pp.5, 7.
4. *Annual Report, 1993–94*, Ministry of Defence, Government of India, p.3–5.
5. *Annual Report, 1993–94*, Ministry of Defence, Government of India, p.3–4.
6. *Annual Report, 1993–94*, Ministry of Defence, Government of India, p.4.
7. *Annual Report, 1993–94*, Ministry of Defence, Government of India, p.6.
8. *Annual Report, 1993–94*, Ministry of Defence, Government of India, p.2.
9. *Annual Report, 1998–99*, Ministry of Defence, Government of India, p.2.
10. *Annual Report, 1999–2000*, Ministry of Defence, Government of India, pp.2–3.
11. *White Paper on China's National Defense*, Information Office of the State Council of the PRC, 27 July 1998. *Foreign Broadcast Information Service, Daily Report, China* (hereafter FBIS-CHI) No.98209. http://wnc.fedworld.gov.
12. *China's National Defense in 2000*. Information Office of the State Council. 16 Oct. 2000. FBIS-CHI-2000-1016.
13. The text of the letter is in *New York Times*, 13 May 1998, p.A12.
14. Jaswant Singh, 'Against Nuclear Apartheid', *Foreign Affairs* 72/5 (Sept.–Oct. 1998) pp.41–52.
15. I discuss this in, 'The Restoration of Sino–Indian Comity following India's Nuclear Tests', *The China Quarterly*, No.168 (Dec. 2001) pp.864–88. See also, Ming Zhang, *China's Changing Nuclear Posture, Reactions to the South Asian Nuclear Tests* (Washington DC: Carnegie Endowment for International Peace 1999).
16. China's Statement on India's Nuclear Tests', *Beijing Review*, 17 June 1998, p.7.
17. *Renmin ribao*, Overseas edition, 15 May 1998, p.2. Comments by Foreign Ministry spokesmen in news briefings over the next several months repeated and elaborated these themes. See 'Foreign Ministry News Briefings', in *Beijing Review*, 25–31 May 1998, p.7; 29 July–5 Aug. 1998, p.12; and 27 July–2 Aug. 1998, p.7.
18. Wang Hongwei, 'Ping Yindu de heshiyan' (On India's nuclear tests), *Nanya yanjiu* (South Asian research) 1998, No.1, p.37. Another article along the same lines is, Zhuan Shengfu, 'Zhongguo song wei dui Yindu goucheng weixie (China has never constituted a threat to India), *Guoji zhanlue yanjiu* (Research on international strategy) 1999, No.1, pp.32–5.
19. Ye Zhengjia, 'Wushi nianlai de Zhong Yin guanxi: jingyan he jiaoxun' (Fifty years of Sino–Indian relations: experiences and lessons), *Guoji wenti yanjiu* (Journal of International Studies) 1999, No.4, pp.17–23.
20. Song Dexing, 'Shikan Zhongguo zhoubian anquan huanjing zhong de Yindu yinsu', (Analyzing the Indian factor in China's neighborhood security environment), *Nanya yanjiu jikan* (South Asian Research Quarterly) 1999, No.2, pp.36–42.
21. Yuan Di, 'Yindu he xuanze yu dui hua 'zhanlue siwei" (India's nuclear option and its 'strategic thought' regarding China), *Nanya yanjiu jikan* (South Asian Research Quarterly) 1998, No.3, p.14.
22. Ching-chang Hsiao and Timothy Cheek, 'Open and Closed Media: External and Internal Newspapers in the Propaganda System', and Lyman Miller, 'Politics Inside the Ring Road: On Sources and Comparisons', in *Decision-Making in Deng's China, Perspectives From Insiders*, Carol Lee Hamrin and Suisheng Zhao (eds.) (Armonk, NY: M.E. Sharpe 1995) pp.76–87, 207–32.
23. Kenneth Lieberthal, *Governing China, From Revolution Through Reform* (New York: W.W. Norton 1995) pp.192–99.
24. See John W. Garver, *Protracted Contest, Sino–Indian Rivalry in the Twentieth Century* (Seattle: University of Washington Press 2001) pp.42–53. Also Tsering Shakya, *The Dragon in the Land of Snows, A History of Modern Tibet since 1947* (London: Pimlico 1999) pp.1–91.

25 Regarding Indian support prior to the 1962 war see, John K. Knaus, *Orphans of the Cold War: America and the Tibetan Struggle for Survival* (New York: Public Affairs 1999) pp.248–58. Regarding the post 1962 period see, Satyanarayan Sinha, *Operation Himalaya: To Defend Indian Sovereignty* (New Delhi: S. Chand 1975). John F. Avedon, *In Exile from the Land of Snows* (New York: Knopf 1984) pp.121–30.

26. Shakya, *The Dragon in the Land of Snows* (note 24) pp.22–24. Dawa Norbu, *Red Star Over Tibet* (New York: Envoy Press 1987). Tibet Support Group, *New Majority; Chinese Population Transfers into Tibet* (London: Tibet Support Group 1995).

27. Xu Yan, *Zhong yin bianjie zhi zhan lishi zhenxiang* (The true history of the Sino-Indian border war) (Hong Kong: Tiandi tushu 1993) pp.50, 53. *Zhong yin bianjing zewei fanji zuo zhanshi* (Military history of the Sino-Indian border war of self defense) (Beijing: Junshi kexue chubanshe 1994) pp.39–40.

28. The critique that follows is drawn from Major General D.K. Palit, *War in High Himalaya, The Indian Army in Crisis, 1962* (London: Lancer International 1991).

29. Anwar Hussain Syed, *China and Pakistan, Diplomacy of an Entente Cordiale* (Amherst University of Massachusetts Press 1974). Also J.P. Jain, *China, Pakistan and Bangladesh* (New Delhi: Radiant 1974) p.25. Updated coverage of the Sino-Pakistan link, including Chinese assistance to Pakistan's nuclear and missile programs, is in Garver, *Protracted Contest* (note 24) pp.187–242.

30. Syed, *Diplomacy of an Entente Cordiale* (note 29) pp.57–58, 61–63.

31. John W. Garver, 'Sino-Indian Rapprochement and the Sino-Pakistan Entente', *Political Science Quarterly* 111/2 (Summer 1996) pp.323–47.

32. John W. Garver, 'The Indian Factor in Recent Sino–Soviet Relations', *The China Quarterly*, No.125 (Summer 1991) pp.55–85.

6

Indo-Russian Strategic Relations: New Choices and Constraints

DEEPA OLLAPALLY

Indo-Russian relations have had to be significantly refashioned, if not re-invented, since the end of the Cold War with the collapse of the Soviet Union, and along with it, the foundation of India's decades-old foreign policy framework.

In 1991, India simultaneously faced twin shocks: the undoing of its strategic framework and a financial crisis rooted in the decaying Nehruvian economic model. Russia continues to be plagued by multiple challenges in the security and economic sphere and remains uncertain about the major parameters of its foreign policy. For both states, it is clear that the old era of predictable partners and well-worn issues has dramatically changed. In its place, they have to deal with cross-cutting issues and cleavages, strategic events with enormous flux and no overarching framework, all of which require much more diplomatic finesse and nimbleness in relation to friends and foes who cannot be taken for granted and are no longer fixed.

Both countries continue to be preoccupied with finding their footing on the global scene, but ten years hence, India seems to have weathered the crises better than Russia in refashioning a viable economic and strategic posture. In the process, this period has witnessed a certain amount of experimentation in strategic affairs by Russia and India, with lessons that are not going to be lost on either *vis-à-vis* the limits and possibilities of their future ties.

In considering the contours of Indo-Russian strategic relations in the post-Cold War period and their future prospects, this paper will approach the topic at three levels of analysis: bilateral, regional and global. The main argument of the paper is that while the relationship at the bilateral level has been critical so far, the global level has receded and will continue to do so, while the regional aspects hold the key to future relations. In making this argument, the contribution focuses on various dimensions, including Russia's decline as a global power; the bilateral arms transfers and the commercial character of that relationship; and regional imperatives which were emerging, but are now fully stimulated by the change in American global strategy which has a significant focus on South/Southwest Asia.

THE GLOBAL SYSTEMS LEVEL: LIVING WITH UNIPOLARITY

The end of the Soviet era has meant a radical narrowing of Russia's strategic purview. Whereas Soviet influence and concern extended to far-flung regions such as Angola and Nicaragua, such areas have disappeared from Russia's radar screen. Long accustomed to being defined by its superpower status on the global stage, Russia's search for a new identity has sent it in different directions at various times. The central questions revolve around whether Russia perceives itself first and foremost as a European power or Eurasian one, and what its new position is within a global system that has effectively gone from bipolarity to unipolarity.

While Russia has been 'collecting itself'[1] for the past decade, India has had to craft an entirely new strategic framework with little confidence regarding Russia's reliability or role *vis-à-vis* the subcontinent. In the process, both countries have left behind grandiose and ideologically based foreign policy outlooks and opted for a more pragmatic approach. The Bharatiya Janata Party (BJP)'s pragmatism on foreign policy is well known (exemplified by so-called nuclear realism) and if there was any doubt regarding Russian views, Putin has made clear that 'pragmatism' was only second to 'national interests' as a key principle of Russian foreign policy, followed by 'economic efficiency'.[2]

During the Cold War years, many strategic analysts in India liked to point out a distinction they detected between Soviet and American approaches to India: for the US, relations with India were derivative from the superpower conflict whereas the Soviets appreciated India for its own worth. Post-Cold War, such a sanguine view regarding the Russians seems to have been misplaced or at least overstated. As the historic Russian transformation got underway, India found itself with severe disadvantages, having had intimate ties to the old Soviet Union and few friends among Russia's so-called new democrats who were swept to power with Boris Yeltsin.

Within the Russian establishment, the Foreign Ministry under the pro-western Andrei Kozyrev relegated India to a secondary role. During this initial phase which was to last until 1996, India was forced to take the initiative to try to build new bridges to the Duma and utilize earlier Soviet lobbies. India was able to exploit lobbies against Kozyrev's tilt which had formed in the Russian Federation presidential apparatus, and was aided by such figures as Vladimir Lukin in the Soviet who called for greater attention to be paid to old allies.

There were also economic lobbies who wanted a piece of the Rupee-Ruble account balances which had accumulated in India. India's Ambassador to Russia, Ronen Sen, was an old Russian hand and took the lead in trying to push India to retain its Russia tilt.[3] Yet the Congress government under P.V. Narasimha Rao had no real choice but to diversify India's security links as its most crucial erstwhile strategic ally continued to labor in confusion and anxiety over its economic and political status, with no clear signal regarding its foreign policy preferences.

This trend to enlarge the number of potential strategic partners using a pragmatic rather than ideological approach continued under the successive Indian regimes, reaching its apogee under the BJP which intensified the build-up of India's own military capabilities to gain a measure of strategic autonomy, most notably via nuclear weapons.

Russia's Search for Identity and Impact on India

Even after a decade, the consensus among Russia specialists is that the country has yet to settle on a long term vision or identity.[4] It is generally recognized, however, that the early period under Boris Yeltsin during which Russia was unabashedly pro-western, did not pay off. The country had expected rich dividends in the form of economic largesse and a nod to its great power status in the international system by the remaining superpower.

Instead, Russia's economic health deteriorated sharply, culminating in a severe financial crisis in August 1998. The Russian leadership learned the hard way that little relief would be forthcoming for its huge debt, of which an astounding $100 billion was simply inherited loans from the Soviet Union.[5] Domestic economics under the market system did no better with the resulting hybrid system often popularly described as 'criminal capitalism'. In addition, the first stage of NATO expansion and the large scale military action against Yugoslavia in spring 1999 was a double shock for those Russians who had expected greater sensitivity to Russia's security concerns despite its loss of international stature.[6]

Vladimir Putin, who came to power in March 2000 in a landslide electoral victory, is seen as having a less pronounced fixation on relations with the west, especially the US, though a top priority continues to be economic, political and security cooperation with the broader European Union, particularly Germany. Putin, who is surrounded by former KGB/FSB (domestic intelligence service) colleagues, reflects the fairly widespread view held by Russian elite that they have failed in their drive to join the European community and west in general, and that Russia is no longer an equal partner in the developed world.[7]

The Russians have not been able to develop a clear alternate or replacement perspective, but former Prime Minister Yevgeny Primakov provided some early insight into Russia's options being discussed when he declared that Russia faced a stark choice: be the weakest link in the core powers (that is, the eighth power in the G8 group of countries) or the strongest power within the developing countries.[8]

Under Primakov's influence, Russia made some attempt at resisting unipolarity, the most splashy one being the trial balloon floated on the eve of his December 1998 trip to India regarding the formation of a strategic triangle comprising Russia, India and China.[9] Some Indian analysts heralded this as a welcome antidote to American power, arguing that 'the global advantage of even a loose Moscow–New Delhi–Beijing axis would be to offer prisoners of the unipolar system another option'.[10]

Although the concept went down more or less like a lead balloon, several inferences may be drawn. Russia was clearly willing to use a 'China card' or an 'India card' for its larger objective of pressing for more economic assistance and greater sensitivities in its surrounding security architecture from the US. Just as equally clear were the limits to such Russian global posturing, since neither China nor India was interested in being involved in an exclusionary effort aimed at the US. Despite the rhetoric touting multipolarity, both India and China wanted to stay away from initiatives which could be even remotely seen as directed against the US.

The upshot of the Primakov experiment is the discovery that maintaining good relations with the US takes precedence over the more ideological struggle against unipolarity for India and China. Indeed, even for Russia, the idea appears to have originated more from its unhappiness with the actual rewards for its embrace of the west, rather than strategic rivalry or ideological animosity, although the importance of nationalist sentiment cannot be ruled out. (The August 1998 economic crisis served as a strong reminder that cooperation with the west had not led to expected results.)

Thus for all three countries, whatever their political or ideological impulse may be regarding US global preeminence, their preference appears to be adjustment to the realities of unipolarity by avoiding conflict with the

US. Under these circumstances, there is little room for maneuvering, plotting or strategizing for these states at the global level. Instead, the strategic game becomes reduced to the bilateral level between the individual states and the leading superpower and between themselves.

It is not surprising then that following the September 11, 2001 disaster and America's apparent rethinking of its strategic priorities placing combating terrorism at the top, there has been little to no resistance. While the so-called war on terrorism certainly holds immediate and specific attractions for Russia, China and India, support is likely to have been forthcoming even in the absence of such interests. The choices Pakistan faced, and the decision it took to back the US, is emblematic of this new global order.[11]

Reconciling Global Differences

The evolving positions of Russia and India on the American missile defense system are also instructive in understanding the changed global environment and its effect on Indo-Russian relations. Russia has strongly opposed the change in the traditional deterrence posture of the US implied by missile defenses, which in turn holds serious uncertainties for Russia.[12] India had generally been supportive of Russia on this score, agreeing that missile defenses would be too destabilizing and likely to foment further arms build up by others such as China.

Yet, in the spring of 2001, as the incoming Bush administration announced its intentions to move forward with developing missile defenses, India conspicuously went out of its way to state its support.[13] That the Indian leadership chose to take a public stand on this in spite of the fact that a senior Russian minister was on a trip to India, and that it went against India's own stand which was historically faithful to the Russian position on missile defense, was telling. While it may be seen as India playing the 'American card' *vis-à-vis* the Russians, the reality is that India's main aim is to consolidate its growing ties with the US without particular reference to Indo-Russian relations. From the global perspective, what is most interesting is that there is in fact increasing evidence that the Russians themselves might be willing to live with the US missile decision and that they are largely playing for time and *quid pro quo*.[14]

While it is difficult to sketch out a specific role for India in Russia's plans given the Russians' persisting uncertainty about their ultimate identity and global posture, the fairly indifferent attitude toward India taken at the beginning of the transition has perceptibly changed. With the ascendancy of the India-oriented Primakov in place of Kozyrov, first as Foreign Minister in 1996, and then as Prime Minister, followed by President Boris Yeltsin's visit to New Delhi, developments suggested that though well into its transition and late in the tenure of the Yeltsin team, Russia was re-discovering India as part of its overall policy reassessment.

The extensive trip to India by President Vladimir Putin in October 2000 served to reinforce this trend in important ways. For example, this slow but discernible shift has been mirrored in Russia's more open acceptance of India's declared nuclear status. In response to India's nuclear tests in 1998, Russia had joined the chorus of condemnation by the west, though in more muted tones.

Putin's trip to India included a high profile stop at India's premier nuclear research institution and the country's nuclear nerve center, the Bhabha Atomic Research Centre (BARC). Putin visited BARC with R. Chidambaram, then Chairman of the Atomic Energy Commission and Anil Kakodkar, Director of BARC, both closely connected with the 1998 Pokhran tests. The Russian premier spoke before the scientific community with surprisingly little rancor about India's tests or its lack of progress on signing the Comprehensive Test Ban Treaty (CTBT).

Putin noted that 'I would like to see India participate in the CTBT', but added, 'However, we realize that the signing of the CTBT should be based on strategic vision and interest of India and the local populace.'[15] This visit under-scored how far the Russians had traveled in accepting India's new status, evidently without having received any political concessions from India.

However, some ambivalence remains in Russia's position reflecting to a large degree international pressures which the Russian leadership is struggling to reconcile. The Russian reaction to some Indian commentators' suggestion that Russia might circumvent restrictions on cooperating in the nuclear sector with a non-nuclear state that does not adhere to full scope safeguards by 'temporarily' declaring India a nuclear state, is telling. Putin made the following observation: 'We do not believe that new nuclear weapon states have emerged on the global arena and we do not think that our recognition of this fact will lead to positive consequences for those states that claim for such recognition'.[16]

Yevgeny Adamov, the former Atomic Energy chief had offered the opinion during a visit to India in December 2000 that he viewed sanctions by the west on India 'unconstructive' in forcing India to forfeit its nuclear option, and pointed out that 'We are against a policy of sanctions and did not impose them even when India conducted its nuclear tests'.[17] On the contrary, within three months of Pokhran II, an agreement was signed to sell India $15 billion worth of Russian arms over 10 years.[18]

As for Russia's role in India's global strategy, the post-Cold War Indian leaderships seem to have made a virtue out of the difficulties forced on them by the loss of their principal ally. P.V. Narasimha Rao's government as early as 1992 began chalking out a 'look east' policy which attempted to redress the longstanding neglect of the Asia-Pacific region, by cultivating ties in particular with Singapore, Korea and to a lesser extent, Japan. The most dramatic shift was the breakthrough achieved in Indo-US relations culminating in Bill Clinton's hugely successful visit in March 2000 – despite the nuclear tests two years before, and the beginning of what has been termed 'an India first' policy by some Americans.[19]

If anything, the Bush administration has been pressing forward even more vigorously, with a decision to lift nuclear tests related sanctions placed on India well before the September 11, 2001 terrorist attacks and the attendant decision to lift them against both India and Pakistan, in light of the American need for Pakistan's cooperation against the Taliban in neighboring Afghanistan.

While the post-September 11 turn by the US toward Pakistan is surely going to complicate India's foreign policy, there is little doubt that India wants to maintain its move toward casting the US as a critical, if not the primary, partner. The momentum in Indo-US relations may slow since the attacks in New York and Washington with India taking a 'wait and see' attitude.

Some Indian commentators have been urging the Vajpayee government to be more vocal in pointing out Pakistan's historic complicity with the Taliban, but officials have demurred, with Foreign Minister Jaswant Singh pointing out that 'now was not the time to shout from the rooftops about Pakistan'.[20] There is no reason to expect that the upswing in Indo-US relations, in part based on a shared concern about a rising China, but also rooted in economic logic, cannot be sustained independent of the US need for Pakistan. Conversely, there is no reason to expect India to shift gears toward the Russians simply because of an understandably rough patch in Indo-US relations, since the calculus of gains to be had from closer ties to the US over Russia in its current discombobulated state seems to have been understood by New Delhi.

At the global level, it may be said that Indo-Russian relations have suffered in the post-Cold War period due to the absence of significant variables that would inexorably pull the two countries together, but by the same token, there are no overriding strategic divergences either. This lack of any serious disagreements together with some very real material benefits that they could derive from a techno-commercial relationship is becoming evident at the bilateral level. Unlike their past special relationship though, the new bilateral ties are largely devoid of genuine strategic content and the question is the extent to which sufficient momentum can be generated to take the new relationship to an enhanced level.

The end of the Soviet era posed special difficulties for India, particularly in the military realm given its huge dependency on Soviet arms transfers for spare parts and equipment. During this crunch, the Indian Defense Ministry was even forced to turn to Ukraine and East European states as a stop gap measure.[21] As Indo-Soviet ties unraveled at a dizzying speed, India faced multiple crises in the security and economic spheres, with not only its strategic framework in shambles, but also in the financial sector, where the country was left with just enough foreign exchange to cover a fortnight's worth of imports.

Russia could offer no help for the latter emergency even if it wished to do so, revealing its stark limitations and lopsided development. Indeed, the rupee-ruble arrangement that had earlier been viewed as innovative and uniquely helpful, became a burden to both countries and only complicated India's financial situation. Besides, in India's view, Russia was unceremoniously dumping its erstwhile 'special' partner with unseemly haste in the new Russia's rush into the western fold.

The early years (1991–96) in which Russia's policy toward India amounted at best to 'benign neglect', have left a deep mark on Indian policymakers, in particular providing a rude awakening for those who imagined that Indo-Russian relations were strong enough to weather any circumstances that might emerge. The partial recovery of their ties since then is explained in large part by the techno-commercial arms trade which has proved to be the only real enduring aspect of their earlier 'special' bilateral relationship.

The manner in which the rupee-ruble balance came to haunt India and Russia is emblematic of how the very logic of earlier ties, has crumbled. By the end of the Cold War, India had accumulated a debt of near $15 billion owed to the Soviet Union for weapons purchases. The Russians, who had previously gone along with accepting rupees, became reluctant to do so resulting in a dispute over the type of currency and exchange rate. Without much of a demand in Russia for Indian goods, approximately one half of the rupee debt remained in Indian banks.[22]

The inability to find a mutually satisfactory way out of this quandary led to a virtual collapse in trade in 1992. Even after prolonged negotiations, the agreement reached led to charges of corruption and manipulation of the rupee fund by Russia's banking oligarchy. At issue was the Russian decision to auction off large sums of rupees at a 15 per cent discounted rate to stimulate Russian investor interest in importing Indian goods. By 1994, Indo-Russian trade had dropped to just one-fifth of the level of 1990. During his visit to India in 2000, Putin made it a point to address a large gathering of big industrialists in Mumbai (Bombay), and invite them to assist Russia in certain areas of Indian expertise such as information technology, management and financial services.[23]

Arms Link

It has turned out that the engine driving post-Cold War Indo-Russian relations is a familiar one – that is, the arms trade – but without the overt trappings of geopolitics or ideology as before. The commercial aspects are dominant, with the accompanying constraints of a narrower focus in the bilateral relationship. For India, however, arms trading with the Russians, along with new possibilities for greater cooperation in the nuclear realm, could represent an important element in its larger strategic vision. As such, there is some potential built-in imbalance between the interests of the two countries.

The arms link between the two states has been not only resurrected, but taken to a new level in recent times. The stimulus for this regeneration after the initial uncertainty, was largely determined by Russia's pressing need to earn hard currency and to safeguard its embattled defense industry. On India's part, the need to upgrade its Soviet-made conventional weapons arsenal and to step up the modernization and expansion of its defense capabilities (made more acute since the 1999 conflict with Pakistan in Kargil), has logically led it back to the Russians.

Although bereft of political compulsions *vis-à-vis* Russia, and despite India's long standing objective of diversifying its defense suppliers (70 per cent of India's military arsenal is Russian), the Indian leadership perceives defense deals with Russia as holding the advantages of price competitiveness, cutting-edge technology and the potential for technology transfers, as well as the Indian forces' familiarity with Russian equipment.

Russia's commercial imperatives in the defense sector are understandable, having inherited a huge military-industrial complex comprising 1,600 defense enterprises with nearly two million personnel. Political leaders had initially thought reforms in the economy and military-industrial complex could be done quickly and well, and to that end, elaborate programs were adopted for restructuring the armed forces, conversions of defense institutions, and revitalization of military R&D. But the transition has been far from easy, with the emergence of a confused system exhibiting some of the worst features of both planned and market economies including a weak state, insecure property rights, barter and rampant crime and corruption.[24]

The reality of this situation is recognized in the highest political circles, with Ilya Klebanov, Russia's Deputy Prime Minister, declaring that arms sales 'are the life buoy for our defense industries now that the defense budget is so small and military state orders are so few'. Klebanov has promised that 'big contracts, joint work and joint production of arms are waiting for us [India and Russia] in the future'.[25] Large Russian firms such as MiG MAPO have been given the right to engage in arms transactions directly. From India's point of view, this type of openness is extremely attractive given its persisting commitment to improve indigenous capability toward achieving greater strategic autonomy.

The importance of India for the Russians may be gauged by the fact that the Indians buy more hardware from the Russian defense industry than do Russia's own military forces. During Putin's visit, the bilateral defense relationship was taken much further than before. The most ambitious defense deal relates to India's purchase of more than 300 T-90S main battle tanks (MBT) with anti-tank guided missiles. The Indian Army has expressed reservations about the indigenously built Arjun MBT; besides the delay in its delivery has led to frustrations in the Army. Included is the option to transfer technology and set up a manufacturing unit in India. Another contract allows India to assemble Sukhoi Su-30 fighter aircraft under license from Russia. The Indian Air Force chief, Air Marshal A.Y. Tipnis, has described the Su-30 as the 'best aircraft available in its class'.[26] Russia has also agreed to lease four Tu-22 Backfire bombers (maritime reconnaissance and strike aircraft).

The Indian Navy stands to gain significantly as well. Russia indicated its willingness to sell the aircraft carrier *Admiral Gorshkov*, including refitting her according to India's specifications so that Indian naval planes such as the Sea Harrier can land on her deck. India has a pressing need for an aircraft carrier since the INS *Vikrant* is aging and under repair. The Navy's potential blue water capability would be seriously challenged without another carrier. The Navy's close links to Russia are illustrated by New Delhi's plan to purchase a fighter regiment of Mikoyan-Gurevich MiG-29K aircraft for *Admiral Gorshkov*. As a senior Russian diplomat put it, 'The teeth of the Indian Navy will continue to be Russian.'[27]

Nuclear Cooperation

Putin's visit to BARC exemplifies Russia's evolving position on military-technical cooperation with India. He was the first Russian leader to tour BARC, joining only two other foreign leaders before, Chinese Prime Minister Zhou-en-Lai and British Prime Minister Margaret Thatcher. Putin's high-powered 70-member delegation, which included Deputy Prime Minister, Ilya Klebanov, Foreign Minister Igor Ivanov and Defense Minister Igor Sergeyev, attests to the importance the Russians give India in this new phase of their defense industrial strategy.

India's former Atomic Energy Chairman Chidambaram has sought to portray Indo-Russian cooperation in the nuclear realm as far-reaching and part of an Indian plan to give significant impetus to the nuclear program. India's target, as outlined, is to generate 20,000 MW of nuclear-generated electricity by 2020. Chidambaram stated that although India had a self-reliant nuclear power program based on indigenized pressurized heavy water reactors (PHWR), the objective was to develop fast breeder reactors (FBRs) and thorium utilization in a closed nuclear fuel cycle, as well as modern light water reactors (LWR).[28]

The current production is limited, and the Indian nuclear program has come under criticism in terms of cost, efficiency and safety. So far however, the nuclear power establishment has warded off such criticism, in part pointing out the need for reducing the country's energy dependency, a view shared by successive Indian leaderships. The exigencies of working under external sanctions, imposed on India in light of its nuclear activity, has also allowed the nuclear energy program to enjoy a more exalted position than it might otherwise have had.

It is precisely in the context of sanctions and other international regimes that Russia's role in the nuclear field becomes critical for India. India has been looking toward other suppliers such as France, but without immediate results. As a leading Indian strategic analyst commented, 'The reality is that Russia today is the only great power which is ready to cooperate with India in the atomic energy sector'.[29]

Nuclear cooperation is not without costs for Russia, and Russian policy has not been entirely predictable *vis-à-vis* India. So far, Russia has been able to circumvent some of the most restrictive clauses of key relevant regimes of which Russia is a member because of loopholes and creative interpretation. At the moment, India does not appear to have much choice but to bank on Russia's stated and implied intentions. A critical testimony to the desire of the Russians to deepen future relations is the Memorandum of Understanding on peaceful nuclear energy uses signed along with the

Declaration on Strategic Partnership during Putin's visit to India. While the latter has been made public, the former remains unpublished.

Russia has been careful about not appearing to deviate from the most important nuclear export control mechanism, the Nuclear Suppliers Group and its guidelines. Russia itself has enacted national export control legislation, most notably the Federal Law 'On Export Controls' adopted in June 1999 by the Russian Parliament and signed by the President. There is also an Export Control Commission which has an impressive high level roster of representatives: the Federal Security Service, Ministry of Foreign Affairs, Ministry of Economy, Ministry of Defense, Ministry of Industry and Trade, the States Customs Committee, State Committee on Nuclear and Radiation Safety of the Russian President and the Russian Academy of Sciences. The Commission determines whether contracts and agreements and some licenses comply with Russia's international commitments.[30]

According to some leading Russian critics, 'whole ministries are closely associated with certain companies in pursuing their short-term economic interests and ignoring long term Russian national interests'.[31] A campaign against corruption was launched in Spring 1999 by then Prime Minister Primakov which coincided with his other campaign to force Russian oligarchs to follow the law. This may have led to his downfall when he was removed in May 1999.

The most export-oriented ministries are the Ministry of Atomic Energy, the Russian Aviation and Space Agency and the Ministry of Economics which stands in some contrast to the Russian Foreign Ministry. The greatest Russian lobbyist for nuclear collaboration with India in recent times was the former Minister of Atomic Energy, Yevgeny Adamov, who ignited a storm of controversy when he indicated in an interview with the newspaper *The Hindu* in December 2000 that Russia might consider withdrawing from existing export control regimes.[32]

Adamov was making an oblique reference to the Nuclear Suppliers Group (NSG) which was formed in 1975. Adamov cited China as an example since it is not a member of the NSG, but is part of the Zangger Committee which does not require full-scope safeguards. The NSG's Guidelines for Nuclear Transfers did not demand full-scope safeguards for non-nuclear states until 1992 following the discovery of Iraq's clandestine nuclear weapon program. President Boris Yeltsin signed Decree No. 312, which paralleled the NSG guidelines – though it exempted Russia's 1988 agreement with India to build two nuclear reactors at Kudankulam that provided for facility safeguards, thus meeting the requirements governing deals prior to 1992.

In 1996, Yeltsin reaffirmed Russia's commitment to the NSG Guidelines. However, Putin took a step soon after he took office distancing the country's policy from NSG by amending Russia's export control legislation; in May 2000, Decree No. 312 was modified to allow nuclear supplies to non-nuclear weapon states whose activities were not under full-scope safeguards 'in exceptional circumstances'.[33]

The position of Russia's Minatom (Ministry of Atomic Energy) was that the new Decree significantly expanded Russia's nuclear export capability and that it was linked to Russia's intent to assist the Indian program. Indeed, Putin said as much when he noted in New Delhi that two more reactors in addition to Koodankulam were distinct possibilities.[34] This was consistent with Adamov's promise in *The Hindu* interview that 'We will do our best to participate in India's ambitious program to generate 20,000 MW of nuclear power by 2020'.[35]

In another positive signal, Russia came to India's rescue when China stopped badly needed supplies of enriched uranium fuel to Tarapur after India's 1998 nuclear tests. India turned to Russia which began delivering supplies in February 2001, despite criticism from the west. For example, *The Economist* took the Russian leadership to task, calling 'Russia's nuclear dalliance with India', a result of 'the fissile nature of Russian politics'.[36] The Russians were accused of falling back on old Soviet connections with India, allegedly often with the connivance of officials who are supposed to police any irregularities.

Adamov, who was close to Putin, seems to have exerted strong influence on Indo-Russian nuclear policy. The Atomic Energy head apparently not only had Putin's ear but was also close to certain influential business communities. According to some analysts, Putin's decision to sign the Decree in May 2000 allowing nuclear supplies to non-nuclear countries which did not have full-scope safeguards may have been a political move to support Adamov as the nuclear energy chief tried to increase nuclear sales abroad.[37]

Critics argued that the head of Minatom had a foreign policy all his own, and that concerns expressed by foreign ministry officials were more often than not overridden by the drive for sales. Indeed, Adamov was perceived to have been replaced in March 2001 partly for his outspokenness (for example, his interview to *The Hindu*), and enthusiasm for deals with Iran. His ouster gave rise to speculation that the Ministry of Atomic Energy may abandon its attempts to 'substitute its corporate policy for state policy in nuclear non-proliferation' thus providing an opportunity for the Ministry of Foreign Affairs.[38]

On the contrary, Adamov's successor, Alexander Rumyantsev, has come out firmly in favor of Russian nuclear assistance to India (and Iran for that matter). Rumyantsev, a former head of one of Russia's top nuclear labs, left no room for confusion, and in a news conference, stated that cooperation with Iran on the Bushehr nuclear power plant was strictly civilian and in keeping with international commitments. Indeed, he indicated that the Russians were considering a second reactor at Bushehr and vowed to catch up if work was lagging behind schedule. Regarding India, Rumyantsev took the long view and noted that 'India is our strategic partner. We want to ensure that there are no reproaches (from the international community) in this regard'.[39] He stated that Russia intends to build a nuclear power station in India despite international concern.

Rumsyantsev's statements so far should put to rest any sentiment that the replacement of Adamov would have negative repercussions for Indo-Russian relations in the nuclear sector as initial analysis might have suggested. Indo-Russian nuclear cooperation would seem to have support at the highest levels of Russian leadership, at least for now. But it is no secret that India would prefer to get nuclear assistance from France or even the US, and to that extent, India might be betting that the bait of its deals with Russia might eventually draw in the others. Moreover, India is not likely to forget Russia's backtracking on the cryogenic engine technology contract in 1993 suggesting that it is not the most reliable partner.[40] Thus while the stage is being set for a higher level of nuclear cooperation, there is no guarantee that other interests and preferences will not take precedence in the future for either India or Russia.

REGIONAL LEVEL: THE EURASIAN AND ASIAN BALANCE OF POWER

While the global pulls and pushes for Indo-Russian relations remain mixed and in flux (for Russia in particular), and the bilateral arena provides a somewhat limited economics-driven basis, the national and strategic imperatives which are emerging at the regional level are likely to prove the most influential in determining the nature and direction of Indo-Russian ties.

America's renewed attention to Southwest Asia since September 11, 2001 has essentially only hastened the day of reckoning with Islamic militancy-based terrorism that several countries in the region have been confronting to varying degrees. At the same time, it is important to keep in mind that the shared terrorism/militancy threat is overlaid by over-the-horizon geopolitical competition which may be submerged for the immediate term, but is highly unlikely to disappear.

Unlike the global or bilateral levels, regional strategic interests hold much greater clarity for both India and Russia. Territorial integrity itself is at stake for these two states exemplified by the Kashmir and Chechnya conflicts, with an important part of the problem perceived to be rooted in their worrisome neighborhood. Indeed, shortly after the Taliban's takeover in Afghanistan in 1996 when it became evident that Kabul was harboring terrorists whose targets extended around the region, India and Russia sought ways to monitor and control terrorist organizations with ties to Islamic radicalism. As the Taliban's chief regional supporter, Pakistan was viewed as heavily contributing to regional instability and part of the larger problem.[41]

Vis-à-vis the Taliban in Afghanistan, Russia and India shared the objective of containing the Taliban's strand of political Islam with the Iranian government, which was wary from geopolitical and religious perspectives. However, India seems to have become unconvinced about the ability of the Russians to mount any serious effort against terrorism in the area, and instead had begun looking to the US as a more potent partner.[42]

The Russian-Indian (and to a degree Iranian) coincidence of interests also extends to the Central Asian area where Pakistan and Turkey are viewed as competitors in Russia's traditional sphere of interest. The geo-economics of Central Asia (gas and oil reserves) has predictably brought in the US as well which does not want to cede the fate of the region's wealth to the neighboring powers, Iran and Russia.

While not very active, the American policy objective has been to separate and insulate Central Asia's economic interests from Russia. This has had the exact opposite effect on the Russians who find it all the more reason to remain engaged in the region.[43] Meanwhile, the Chinese have been increasingly insinuating themselves into Central Asia, lured by the energy supplies which they desperately require in the future, and mindful of the need to have a buffer of friendly states on its sensitive western borders across Xinjinag, where it is confronting Islamic radicalism and separatism.

In 1996, Russia, China and the three bordering Central Asian states of Kazakhstan, Kyrgyzstan and Tajikistan formed The Shanghai Five, a formal structure aimed at confidence building measures on the borders and other forms of cooperation. The group has had its share of tensions, especially as the Central Asian states' relations with China became more bilateral in nature, to the dismay of Russia.

The China Factor

Although Russia, India and China have a common fear of Islamic militancy within their borders and separatist threats, regional competition also weighs heavily and militates against making a common cause that would be trusted by all three. In terms of the regional dynamics, Russia and India share similar concerns about the potential threat that China could pose, though clearly not to the same degree.

As far as India is concerned, the Chinese threat looms larger than ever, and while it may have been impolitic and undiplomatic of India's Defense Minister George Fernandes to openly cite China as a major justification of India's nuclear tests, he verbalized publicly what many Indians privately express (much like many Americans). Indeed, Indian analysts are increasingly asking the question as to why the US finds it difficult to take India's security concerns regarding China seriously when Americans themselves are worried about China, although the Bush administration appears to be redressing this anomaly.

India is also faced with the unsettling knowledge that since the end of the Cold War, Russia's relations with China have been warming considerably. Currently, India and China are Russia's two largest arms recipients, trading places over the 1990s for first or second place.[44] Russian leaders have termed both China and India as 'strategic partners' during respective visits to Beijing and New Delhi, a noticeable departure from the past when there was no question that Russia saw China as a strategic competitor, with the special relationship reserved for India.

Russia has indicated some sensitivity to India's concern about the massive build up of Chinese military capabilities via Russian weapons sales, but in practice, the Russians are doing little to address the repercussions for India. In 1996, India ordered 40 Su-30 multipurpose aircraft, with Russia prepared to upgrade them to Su-30 MK according to Indian specifications, utilizing Indian, French and Israeli avionics, which apparently the Chinese were also interested in. During a visit by Indian Defense Secretary Ajit Singh to Moscow in November 1998, the Russians assured him that they would not sell the Su-30 MK multipurpose fighter to China or any other neighboring country in deference to India. Subsequently however, the Russians changed their mind and decided to go ahead with sales to China, fitting the aircraft with avionics according to Chinese specifications.[45]

So far, India has not appeared to be unduly concerned about the Russo-Chinese arms ties, but such cooperation might well reach a level that India may find hard to ignore. India may be counting on Russia's own self-interest to provide a check against unrestrained help to China since there is a strong opinion in Russia that it is a mistake to elevate Chinese capabilities which could be turned against the Russians. After all, China has been

Russia's traditional foe and is seen as the only other regional power that can seriously challenge or potentially deny a dominant Russian role in the Eurasian balance of power.

There is also widespread opinion in Russia that implicitly undercuts the notion of allying with an autocratic China directed against a democratic west.[46] The Russians may be calculating that China, which has serious gaps in its military arsenal and lags behind Russian capabilities by 15 or more years, can continue to absorb substantial quantities of Russian weaponry for the near future without shifting the balance. Conversely, India which does not have such luxury *vis-à-vis* China, may have no choice but to augment its own arsenal, thereby allowing Russia to continue reaping a double windfall and alleviate some of its financial pressures in the process.

The Pakistan Factor

India's concern is at two levels with respect to China: a direct potential threat from China and indirect one via China's assistance to Pakistan in the nuclear and missile arena, as well as possible re-export of arms from Russia.[47] There is also the possibility that Chinese-Pakistani joint military production could rely on Russian weapons design transferred to China. Ostensibly, Russia's policy is to avoid selling arms to two parties who are involved in a dispute, and the leadership has openly declared that it would refrain from selling arms to Pakistan. However, arms to India and China are justified on the grounds that the two countries have engaged in confidence building measures related to the disputed border.[48]

Russia's commitment not to sell arms to Pakistan (at least not directly or openly) appears firm enough though it is not out of the question that the Russians may reconsider its hands-off approach to Pakistan for other reasons. In this connection, Putin's decision to send his special envoy, Sergei Yastrzhembsky, to Pakistan on the eve of the Russian leader's trip to India in October 2000, and the revelation that Putin himself had accepted a Pakistani invitation, no doubt gave India a jolt. Pakistan took the initiative in reaching out to Russia, but the Russians appear very receptive. A major reason is that Russia believes Pakistan can play an important role in containing Islamic fundamentalism in the region.

On the Pakistani side, the military leadership had been seeking ways to overcome the international isolation it faced prior to September 11, especially as the US discovered much stronger convergence of economic and political interests with India. Playing into Russia's vulnerability, General Pervez Musharraf dispatched the Inter-Services Intelligence (ISI) chief, Lt. General Mahmood Ahmed, to Russia in August 2001, signaling that Pakistan may be ready to address Russia's concerns on terrorism and drug trafficking emanating from Afghanistan.

At the same time, Putin's message to the Indian Parliament left little doubt that Russia and India were besieged by the same phenomenon and that they needed to join forces in the fight against terrorism. He revealed serious misgivings about Pakistan's role in encouraging terrorism which are unlikely to disappear, and stated that 'The same people are organizing terrorist attacks from the Philippines to Kosovo, including Kashmir, Afghanistan and Russia's north Caucusus...'[49]

Russia's newly apparent willingness to deal with Pakistan, after keeping it at arms length for decades, may also be motivated by what it sees as India's warming up to the US. Prime Minister Vajpayee's description of India and the US as 'natural allies', along with specific steps such as India's readiness to jettison its opposition to the National Missile Defense (NMD) in a break with Russian preferences, must have stimulated some concern in Moscow about the wisdom of a purely India-centered approach to the subcontinent. In the context of America's re-entry into Pakistan after the September 11 incidents, the question that arises for India is whether Pakistan's utility for the US (and Russia) is going to reorder their priorities to the extent that it will come at the expense of India.

POST-SEPTEMBER 11, 2001 STRATEGIC SHIFTS

US policy shifts in the wake of the September 11 terrorist attacks on American soil evoke images of past Indo-US ties which tended to swing between optimism and pessimism, mostly shaped by the extent to which the US contributed to Pakistani 'borrowing power' to undercut India's natural advantages on the subcontinent. In the fight against terrorism, if the US ultimately limits its focus to terrorist groups with a global reach (that is, America), both Russia and India may find a point of convergence against such US approach given the particular regional threats they face.

It is becoming evident that despite the critical turnaround in American policy toward Pakistan, there is little inclination on the part of the US to slow, let alone reverse, the momentum in Indo-US relations. Prior to September 11, the US objective in Pakistan was limited to preventing Pakistan from spiraling out of control given its ongoing political, economic and strategic turmoil. In contrast, American policy toward India was ambitious and geared to significantly improving bilateral ties in the long run.

There has been no shift in the latter, and for the first time, both India and Pakistan can count themselves as important partners of the US. There is no intrinsic reason why the US cannot have good relations with India and Pakistan simultaneously, especially if General Musharaff's declared commitment to shut down terrorist groups in Pakistan including those aimed at India, and move the country in the direction of moderate Islam, is genuine and effectively implemented. India having a larger Muslim population than Pakistan, the promotion of moderate Islam in the region can only be a welcome development for India.

In the short run at least, the Bush administration seems serious about eliminating terrorism wherever it emanates from, seeing the logic of interconnected networks which may have multiple targets, including the US. The US pressure on Pakistan to fully abandon groups linked to terrorism is in part a result of the desire to meet India's demands, but is also driven by its own objective of closing down possible future terrorist breeding grounds.

At the regional level, as an informal coalition in combating terrorism, Russia, India and China may emerge as clear *status quo*-oriented powers that specifically do not want to see borders changed by force. It is notable that one of the key results of Chinese Premier Zhu Rongji's visit to New Delhi in January 2002 was the establishment of a joint forum against terrorism.[50]

Meanwhile, despite China's long-standing relationship with Pakistan, the growing ties between the US and Pakistan may lead to a reconsideration of a purely Pakistan-centered policy toward South Asia by China. Sino-US convergence on the terrorism front is unlikely to be sufficient to negate other clashing interests. The Bush administration's decision to withdraw from the Anti-Ballistic Missile (ABM) Treaty and pursue missile defences has the greatest impact on China which fears that it could degrade the relatively small Chinese nuclear arsenal (unlike Russia's). In mirror fashion, the palpable improvement in Indo-US relations may stimulate the Russians to cultivate better ties with Pakistan in a reversal of past policy.

In addition, a long-term American military presence in Central Asia, including bases, runs counter to traditional Chinese and Russian preferences. Equally important is the growing US influence in Central Asia[51] and the disposition of oil and gas in the region which has the potential to marginalize Chinese and Russian prospects (and Iran for that matter), and lead to new resentment. A new game of pipeline politics seems inevitable, and India and Russia could find themselves at odds or in the same camp, depending on the route that the pipeline ultimately takes.

CONCLUSION

India and Russia appear to have navigated the worst dips of their post Cold War relations, restoring their ties to a respectable level, though not approaching anything like their previous unique strategic partnership. There are no overarching convergences of interests at the global level that are genuinely strategic, and motivations at the bilateral level are essentially economic, thus more likely to be dictated by market logic where a greater degree of substitutability exists. Given that the economic dimension is based firmly on arms transfers however, this constitutes a partial strategic link, especially from India's perspective. The absence of any geopolitical antagonisms between the two countries can only reinforce this techno-commercial link.

This paper has suggested that regional level calculations will prove to be most decisive for India and Russia in their mutual relations. This thesis is even more salient after the September 11, 2001 policy shifts. While Indo-Russian interests are likely to converge most significantly at the regional level both in terms of combating terrorism and being wary of a rising China, neither India nor Russia is going to give primacy to the other in the development of foreign policy. This is in large part dictated by the need to go beyond the black and white politics of the past.

In its place, a more nuanced cross-cutting issue-based politics is evolving, which means that no fixed balance of power is going to emerge on the Eurasian or Asian landscape. The idea of pragmatic, issue-based foreign policymaking seeking appropriate international coalition partners rather than fixed allies seems to be increasingly taking hold in the Indian establishment.

Given that outside the subcontinent India is a weaker power than many of its Eurasian and Asian neighbors, India may opt to not join any tacit or explicit grouping such as that proposed by Primakov, but rather learn the fine art of balancing in the more fluid strategic environment it faces. This would work best if, under dire circumstances, India could count on an ultimate powerful ally, but there is no evidence to indicate that Russia would or could play this role.[52]

US policymaking after September 11 calls into question its potential role in this connection as well. In any event, one important strand of thinking among India's strategic elite seems to be that in order for India to prove its worth as a potential ally or partner for any state, it needs to develop its military capability even further, and keep up its economic growth. Russia is likely to prove critical in doing the former and appears ready to do so; likewise with the US for the latter.

NOTES

1. This is a historical reference to Russian Prince Aleksandr Gorchakov's comment after the humiliating defeat in the Crimean war that 'It is said that Russia sulks. Russia does not sulk. Russia is collecting itself.' Quoted in Celeste Bohlen, 'Putin the Power Broker', *New York Times*, 26 Aug. 2001.
2. Ibid.
3. Hari Vasudevan, 'Russia as a Neighbor: Indo-Russian Relations 1992–2001', Lecture at the Conference on 'Russia – Ten Years After', Carnegie Endowment for International Peace, Washington DC, 9 June 2001.
4. See for example, Michael McFaul, 'West or East for Russia', *Washington Post*, 9 June 2001; Dimitri Trenin, 'Russia's Foreign Policy Under Putin', Paper prepared for the Conference on 'Russia – Ten Years After', Carnegie Endowment for International Peace, Washington DC, 7–9 June 2001; and Robert Legvold, 'Russia's Unformed Foreign Policy', *Foreign Affairs* 80/5 (Sept./Oct. 2001).
5. *SIPRI Yearbook 2000: Armaments, Disarmament and International Security* (Oxford: Oxford University Press 2000) p.253.
6. See for example, Alexi Arbatov (a member of the Duma Defense Committee), 'Russia and NATO – Ten Years After', Paper prepared for the Conference on 'Russia – Ten Years After', Carnegie Endowment for International Peace, Washington DC, 7–9 June 2001.
7. Alexi Malashenko, 'The Nationalism of the Russian Elite: Mentality and Political Practice', Paper for Conference on 'Russia – Ten Years After, Carnegie Endowment for International Peace, Washington DC, 7–9 June 2001.
8. McFaul (note 4).
9. Legvold (note 4) pp.64–5.
10. Sunanda K. Datta-Ray, 'Suppose Russia, India and China Could Really Get Together', *International Herald Tribune*, 5 Jan. 1999.
11. An alternative outcome might have been for Pakistan to fall back on its relations with China and stimulate a China-Pakistan-Afghanistan alliance based on Chinese competition with the US and India.
12. The American withdrawal from the Anti-Ballistic Missile Treaty in late fall of 2001 has only accentuated Russian concerns.
13. The Indian leadership couched it by giving support to the arms reduction part of the Bush administration statement, but the support was obvious.
14. See for example, David R. Sands, 'Russia Sees Missile Shield as Inevitable', *The Washington Times*, 6 Sept. 2001; Bohlen (note 1); and McFaul (note 4). Russia's ideal *quid pro quo* list includes: debt relief, no NATO expansion in Baltic states, and silence on Chechnya.
15. T.S. Subramanian, 'Koodankulam Calling', *Frontline* 17/21 (14–17 Oct. 2000) p.1. See also Celia Dugger, 'Putin Joins India in Vow on How to Use Atomic Plants', *New York Times*, 6 Oct. 2000.
16. Vitaly Fedchenko, 'The Russian-Indian Nuclear Cooperation: More Questions Than Answers', *Yaderny Kontrol* 6/3 (Summer 2001) p.23.
17. Vladimir Radyuhin, 'India, Russia Nuclear Cooperation Will Continue', *The Hindu*, 17 Dec. 2000.
18. Ashley Tellis, p.87. See also 'India to Buy Russian Arms Worth $15 Billion in 10 Years', *The Indian Express*, 12 Nov. 1998.
19. There is a large literature explaining the improved relations between India and the US Examples include: Stephen Cohen, *India: Emerging Power* (Washington DC: Brookings 2001) and Gary Bertsch, Seema Gahlaut and Anupam Srivastava, *Engaging India: US Strategic Relations with the World's Largest Democracy* (NY: Routledge 1999).
20. *Times of India*, 25 Sept. 2001.
21. Vasudeven (note 3).
22. Jerome Conley, *Indo-Russian Military and Nuclear Cooperation: Implications for US Security Interests*, INSS Occasional Paper 31, Proliferation Series, USAF Institute for National Security Studies, USAF Academy, Colorado (Feb. 2000) p.27.
23. Gulshan Sachdeva, 'Reviving Economic Interests', *Frontline* 17/21 (14–27 Oct. 2000) p.2.
24. For a good discussion, see Christopher Davis, 'The Defense Sector in the Economy of a Declining Superpower: Soviet Union and Russia, 1965–2001', book manuscript, 22 Aug. 2001, pp.43–6.
25. Baidya Bikash Basu, 'Trends in Russian Arms Exports', *Strategic Analysis* 23/11 (Feb. 2000) p.1923.
26. Quoted in John Cherian, 'The Defense Deals', *Frontline* 17/21 (14–27 Oct. 2000) p.1.

27. Ibid.
28. Subramanian (note 15) p.3.
29. C. Raja Mohan, 'India, Russia to Discuss Nuclear Issues', *The Hindu*, 3 Oct. 2000.
30. Vladimir Orlov, 'Export Controls in Russia: Policies and Practices', *The Nonproliferation Review* 6/4 (Fall 1999) pp.145–6.
31. Ibid. p.147.
32. Vladimir Radyuhin, 'India, Russia Nuclear Cooperation Will Continue', *The Hindu*, 17 Dec. 2000.
33. Vitaly Fedchenko, 'The Russian-Indian Nuclear Cooperation: More Questions Than Answers', *Yaderny Kontrol* 6/3 (Summer 2001) p.21. The International Atomic Energy Agency does allow for export of nuclear supplies to non-nuclear states without full scope safeguards if there are exceptional safety reasons to do so.
34. Ibid. p.20
35. Vladimir Radyuhin, 'India, Russia Nuclear Cooperation Will Continue', *The Hindu*, 17 Dec. 2000.
36. 'Russia Breaks Its Word', *The Economist*, 27 Jan. 2001.
37. David Hoffman, 'Russia to Allow Nuclear Exports', *The Washington Post*, 12 May 2000.
38. Vladimir Orlov, 'Undoing Adamov', *The Moscow Times*, 2 April 2001.
39. Hanuska Emerick, 'Russia Commits to Iran Reactors', Reuters, 17 April 2001. See also 'Russia Vows Speed on Iranian Reactor', *International Herald Tribune*, 17 April 2001.
40. For a discussion on the repercussions of technology controls on Indo-Russian relations, see for example Brahma Chellaney, 'The Implications of the Wassenaar Group', in Deepa Ollapally and S. Rajagopal (eds.), *Nuclear Cooperation: Challenges and Prospects* (Bangalore: Tyrox Press 1997) pp.84–5.
41. For a superb discussion of the links, see Ahmed Rashid, *Taliban: Militant Islam, Oil and Fundamentalism in Central Asia* (New Haven, CT: Yale University Press 2000) *passim*.
42. Jaswant Singh seems to have been a prime mover for a more US-oriented approach in this regard. See Vasudevan (note 3). This may be seen as having paid off with the establishment of the Indo-US Joint Working Group on Terrorism.
43. See for example, National Bureau of Asian Research, 'Energy, Weapons Proliferation and Conflict in Central Asia and the Caucasus', Conference Proceedings, US Institute of Peace, Washington DC, 20–21 April 1999, and Martha Brill Olcott, 'Unfulfilled Promises in Central Asia', Paper at the Conference on 'Russia – Ten Years After', Carnegie Endowment for International Peace, Washington DC, 7–9 June 2001.
44. India has had a slight edge if calculated in terms actual deliveries of major conventional weapons between 1995 and 1999. See *SIPRI Yearbook 2000: Armaments, Disarmament and International Security* (Oxford: Oxford University Press 2000) p.341.
45. Jyotsana Bakshi, 'Russia-China Military-Technical Cooperation: Implications for India', *Strategic Analysis* 24/4 (July 2000) p.637.
46. McFaul (note 4). The brittleness of Sino-Russian amity is discussed by Robert Scalapino, 'The People's Republic of China at Fifty', *NBR Analysis* 10/4 (Oct. 1999) pp.17–18. One area of increasing tension between China and Russia which has yet to be explored in depth is the Chinese migration into Russia's Far East and its demographic, economic and political implications.
47. For a discussion of re-export of Russian weapons through other countries to Pakistan and the potential for Russian temptations to turn a blind eye, see Vadim Kozyulin, 'Re-Export of Russian Conventional Arms May Intensify', *Yaderny Kontrol Digest* 12 (Fall 1999). The saga of Ukraine's sale of 320 Russian-developed T-80 UD tanks to Pakistan in 1996 and the ultimate benefit to Russia despite its protestations is detailed. Apparently, Russia received a large slice of the sale via inter-firm cooperation agreements and also an urgent large-scale order from India for T-90 tanks to maintain its balance with Pakistan. Pakistan has a current gap in new fourth-generation aircraft which MiG-29 or Su-27 could conceivably meet.
48. Bakshi (note 45) p.634.
49. B. Muralidhar Reddy, 'The Pakistan Card', *Frontline* 17/21 (14–27 Oct.) pp.1–2. The ISI's patronage of the Taliban is well recognized.
50. *The Hindu*, 15 Jan. 2002.
51. For a good discussion of American build up of its presence in Central Asia, see *New York Times*, 9 Jan. 2002.
52. Russian analysts have suggested that Russia learn this fine art of balancing given the combination of its weakness, and its unwillingness to play a junior partner role. See Dimitri Trenin, 'Russia's Foreign Policy Under Putin', Paper at the Conference on 'Russia – Ten Years After', Carnegie Endowment for International Peace, Washington DC, 7–9 June 2001.

7

The Indo-French Strategic Dialogue: Bilateralism and World Perceptions

JEAN-LUC RACINE

In his concluding address to a seminar on 'India and France in a Multipolar World' organized in February 2000 in New Delhi, French Minister of Foreign Affairs Hubert Védrine, after recalling the main initiatives taken by both countries during the past two years for developing their bilateral relations, took care to locate them in a larger, global framework: 'It was high time that our two countries, both which are committed to making their own assessments of world relations and autonomous decision-making with regard to the major issues affecting the planet, take the time for an in-depth dialogue. A start has been made. The benefits are obvious. We must continue.'

This study will try to evaluate the rationale and the content of this dialogue, and to assess the benefits it generates for both countries in light of the expectations both sides may entertain. The historical background of the bilateral relationship will be quickly recalled in section I, before giving emphasis in section II to the developments which marked the 1990s, particularly the French presidential visit to India in 1998.

Section III will focus on the strategic dialogue which developed after France had shown a greater understanding of India's open nuclearization than most Western countries.

Two regional policies, regarding Kashmir and the Indian Ocean, will draw our attention in section IV.

Section V will address the unmet Indian expectations, the first of them, besides the limited enhancement of economic relations, being the issue of dual technology constraining a possible cooperation in nuclear energy. The last section will comment on the shared quest for multipolarity.

French immediate geopolitical interests in South Asia are not the most important for Paris, which has nevertheless developed in recent years a special relationship with India. Besides the search for new markets, is the main rationale at play a principled quest for a more balanced world order, moving a relatively small but powerful country to acknowledge the need to accommodate the billion-plus India in global geopolitics? What is New Delhi, on its own, looking for in Paris? Was it, after the nuclear tests, a way to avoid diplomatic isolation? Another entry point to Europe? A provider of technology and defence equipment enabling India to diversify, politically and strategically, her access to decisive instruments of power? Or, on the longer run, a partnership founded on a partly common reading of international relations?

The opening of a strategic dialogue with France in 1998 must be seen as a testimony of a paradigmatic change in Indian foreign policy. Going beyond the old privileged Russian connection, New Delhi, after asserting India's ambition through nuclearization, had to develop a much more active multidirectional diplomacy, a step to the high table India wishes to have access to, far different from the Non-Aligned Movement or the G77 tradition.

The opening of Indian economy also had to be matched by the opening of her geopolitical horizon. While the US entered a dialogue with India, focused on what was seen in Washington as the negative impact of the tests, France offered a very distinct, overarching perspective, much more open to India's expectations. The opportunity was seized, and later on New Delhi entered in comprehensive strategic dialogues with other relevant countries as well, after the consternation about the test had receded.

Beyond the strict bilateral frame, the enhanced Indo-French relationship offers therefore an opportunity to address much broader issues, which define the present debate on what the global order should be, and which illustrate as well the Indian quest for a higher status in the community of nations. Realpolitik is at play, which is said to cultivate national interests. But it remains to be seen how national interests call for adjustments to the evolving international chessboard.

THE BACKGROUND

It is something of a common joke in the fringes of Indo-French seminars to remember, with a touch of false nostalgia, that if Dupleix had beaten Clive during the Carnatic Wars of the eighteenth century, the French East India Company would have taken the lead over its British competitor, Clive would not have established himself as the new rising force in Bengal after the Battle of Plassey (1757), and, to cut a long imagined story short, India would have today French, and not English, as her lingua franca. Two centuries after Dupleix, France handed over to India its colonial settlements (Pondicherry and additional small remnants of empire), not too readily but gracefully enough on the whole for keeping a foot there, with the approval of Pandit Nehru, who expected, so he said, to see the former French port town to become 'India's window to Europe'.[1]

Nothing of that sort happened. In the post-World War II context, France and India choose different options. France's NATO membership was not in line with India's non-alignment paradigm. Worse, its painful decolonization wars, in Vietnam first, then in Algeria, put Paris on the wrong side of history. While the leading figure of Nehru faded away after the Indo-Chinese war of 1962, before disappearing two years later, de Gaulle was re-emerging as a name to remember. The general brought the Algerian war to a close by conceding Independence, launched in French Africa a quick and peaceful decolonization process, and defined a nuclear doctrine based upon national autonomy. But Nehru passed away in 1964, and when Indira Gandhi really confirmed her hold over India's political scene, de Gaulle had already resigned.

On the whole, the bilateral relationship, all along the 1960s to the 1980s, was not bad but somewhat indifferent, André Malraux's exalted visits and the hard work conducted by French indologists notwithstanding. The relationship could have been much more substantial, and not only on the economic front. Since the inception of the Indian Atomic Energy Commission, France had offered support to India's nuclear energy program, when the dual technology issue was not the constraint it became later on.

The first French nuclear test in 1960, followed by the development of a national 'force de frappe' relying upon a land/sea/air triad, the elaboration of the French nuclear deterrence doctrine, and the 22 years-long reluctance of Paris to join the Non-Proliferation Treaty (NPT) were followed with interest by Indian security experts. India took note of de Gaulle's decision to step partly outside NATO, by deciding in 1966 to withdraw from the integrated military command of the Alliance, in order to preserve the free use of French forces.

As a medium-sized country willing to assert herself and having her say despite the major Cold War divide, France was sending a message which was not lost on New Delhi. The delivery of spare parts during the Indo-Pakistan war of 1965; France's overall support to the cause of Bangladesh and India in 1971, in contrast to the entering of US aircraft carrier *Enterprise* in the Bay of Bengal, seen in India as an act of intimidation;

Paris taking over from the US the supply of heavy water to Tarapur nuclear plant in the early 1980s – all had positive consequences.

The Scope for Improvement

Potential affinities and limited shared interests were not enough, however. French foreign policy directed to what has been called the Third World was by tradition focused on Africa, the Middle East, and Latin America. India was not much in the radar screen of the French decision makers, who were certainly selling her armaments, but were known for having in this field strong if not stronger links with Pakistan.

French-speaking Indira Gandhi had met French presidents from de Gaulle to Mitterrand, but her visits never upgraded significantly the bilateral relationship, nor did Giscard d'Éstaing's visit in 1979 – the first testimony of a growing interest nonetheless – or Mitterrand's two official visits to India in 1982 and 1989. India's Year in France, in 1985, was an image building exercise not much different from what it has been in other major countries: India chose to privilege her past and present culture. Four years later, France's Year in India was somewhat different, for Paris was eager to promote, besides culture, French technology.

On the economic front, the bilateral relations were not what they should or could have been. French banks and French companies have been present in India for decades. The new economic policy launched by the Congress government in 1991 attracted attention. Almost every French major set foot in India, if it was not already present. Besides well-known high-technology companies such as Dassault, Aerospatiale, Alcatel, dozens of other names could be cited in many fields.

But on the whole, France was lagging behind not just in term of foreign direct investment, but also as far as trade was concerned. On the eve of President Chirac's visit to India in January 1998, the Franco-Indian Chamber of Commerce and Industry could only stress the weakness of a stagnant relationship: in 1996, India was ranked 35th among exporters to France, with 0.41 per cent of French imports, and was France's 43rd client, buying a mere 0.37 per cent of French exports.[2] While high-profile deals such as the sale of Mirages and avionics, or the launch of Indian INSAT satellites on Ariane space rockets from French Guyana were under way, the overall economic relationship was disappointing.

The French President's visit to India was to change the substance of the relationship not so much on the economic front, although Chirac came along with the biggest corporate delegation ever. The visit was a watershed, mostly at the political level. Significant signals sent during the visit were confirmed after the Bharatiya Janata Party (BJP) came to power and decided to conduct nuclear tests. The strategic dialogue this paper tries to assess was then firmly put on rails.

1998: THE WATERSHED

The year 1998 qualitatively changed the nature of the Indo-French relations on two accounts. First, the French President's state visit, in January, set the tone, and announced a number of new developments expressing the enhanced consideration given to India by the French decision makers. Second, these announcements materialized after the moderate French reactions to Indian nuclear tests, which set Paris apart from other major capital cities. This gave a new strength to the Indo-French relationship which owes much to the international framework in which the two countries are located. India and France are not simply expanding bilateral ties, but pursuing a dialogue on global issues.

A New Awareness

The visit of President Mitterrand to India in 1989 brought no dramatic breakthrough, but it helped to reaffirm a shared goodwill, which offered the basis for a more sustained dialogue. In 1992 Prime Minister P. V. Narasimha Rao visited France, and discussed the economic reforms he was implementing, as well as India's concerns regarding the new world order heralded after the 1991 Gulf War. He called for investment, cooperation in nuclear energy, space and oil research, and drew attention to the issue of terrorism.[3]

In 1994 Alain Juppé, French Minister for External Affairs came to India, and defined the French agenda: to restart the political dialogue and to develop the economic relationship. Both countries could build up on what had already been achieved. Politically, New Delhi and Paris were always keen to remember that France and India were democracies sharing affinities, if only their past common unhappiness with the sharp divide of the Cold War years and their concern for North-South relations.

Economically, though more could be done, at least France had secured a noticeable market both in civil aviation and defence (in 1994, 40 Airbus and 49 Mirage aircraft were flying in India). Even though Indo-French interests or policies diverged in several areas, for instance the French position favoring the extension of the NPT; the decision to stop the delivery of enriched uranium to Tarapur nuclear plant;[4] or commercial litigations opposing Indian and French trade partners on energy projects;[5] such differences would not hamper, said the Minister, the willingness to give 'a new push' to political and economic bilateral relations.[6]

Four years later, the situation had somehow improved. In 1997 India could boast over her highest-ever growth rate (7 per cent). The Third Front Government in power after the 1996 elections showed that the process of reform, if not greatly accelerated, was at least not subjected to political changes at the top. By then, a regular dialogue had been established between the Confederation of Indian Industries and its French counterpart, the Confédération Nationale du Patronat Français (now renamed as Mouvement des Entreprises de France or MEDEF). At the diplomatic and strategic level, Paris was also duly taking note of India's new assertiveness, particularly voiced during the debates which ended with her rejection of the NPT in 1995 and her rejection of the Comprehensive Test Ban Treaty (CTBT) in 1996.

People in power probably played a positive role as well. Alain Juppé, as Minister of Foreign Affairs, happened to have for key aides two career diplomats who had been posted in New Delhi: Dominique de Villepin, as Cabinet Chief, and Maurice Gourdon-Montagne as Deputy Chief. When Juppé became Prime Minister in 1995, Gourdon-Montagne took over as Cabinet Chief, while Dominique de Villepin moved up, to become the General Secretary of the Presidency, said to be one of the closest advisers to Jacques Chirac.[7]

Interestingly, the man who held this top job at the end of Mitterrand's Presidency (1991–95), after having been the President's diplomatic adviser during his first mandate (1981–88) was Hubert Védrine, who became Minister for External Affairs when Lionel Jospin set up his Leftist government in 1997. As a fiery proponent of a multipolar world, Védrine was to favor a higher status for India in world affairs. In the specific context of the French 'cohabitation' system which applies when a French president works with a government from the other side of the political spectrum, the political differences between the two sides were therefore irrelevant as far as the Indian policy was concerned.[8] Juppé's New Delhi speech of 1994 referred to 'a new multipolar world' one could hope for, a theme dear to Védrine, and a concept Chirac underlined as well during his presidential visit.

President Chirac's Visit

President Chirac's state visit in January 1998 was rich in symbolism. The French President had been invited as the Chief Guest for Indian Republic Day, the year India was celebrating her 50th anniversary as an independent state. To have the Head of State of one of the Permanent members of the UN

Security Council was significant. The fall of the Third Front Government led by I. K. Gujral by the end of 1997 might have affected, if not the visit, which after due consideration was confirmed, but at least its message. Paris decided not to downgrade it to a purely formal exercise.

While Boris Yeltsin had chosen to postpone a visit planned to New Delhi, Paris opted to address India as a partner, regardless of regime shifts in New Delhi. There was in France no pro-India lobby comparable to the Indo-US Business Council, nor any Indian caucus active in the political circles, for the Indian diaspora in France, if rich in 'People of Indian Origin' – most of them from Pondicherry – is rather unlike the powerful and wealthy 'Non-Resident Indians' in the US. Their limited presence has not prevented French analysts from taking note of what was at stake as far as India was concerned.

In November 1996, Thierry de Montbrial, Director of the French Institute of International Relations, the best known French think tank, had called for looking at India with 'a different eye', and asserted that France 'has everything to gain' in answering India's quest for a new relationship with Europe. On the eve of Chirac's visit opinions were published in major printed media, which concurred at various levels, be they focussed on economy, on strategic perspectives or on larger bilateral issues.[9]

Arriving in Mumbai (Bombay) along with a galaxy of CEOs of French major companies,[10] the French President began by addressing the business communities of the two countries. He defined his visit as 'a confidence vote' in favor of 'a new India, modern, inventive, creative, liberating its initiatives and eager to occupy its due place in the world economic scene'.[11] In New Delhi he proposed to India to build up with France 'a global partnership developed on [our] complementarities and [our] shared interests'. France, 'the fourth world economic power', was eager to 'reinforce considerably its industrial, trade and financial links with India'. As a world leader in nuclear energy, France, said Chirac, could also address this field 'if certain conditions were met'. The point, particularly sensitive because of international regulations, was to be commented upon at length by the Indian press.

Besides a vast panorama of scientific and technical cooperation, and the creation of an Indo-French Initiative Forum expected to elaborate 'a common Franco-Indian vision',[12] Paris was officially proposing, in a significant move, to set up a strategic group, in order to facilitate 'a better understanding of our defence doctrines and an increased military cooperation'.

At the global level, Paris favored a regular consultation between India and the G8 on issues related to IMF and WTO. It pleaded, as did New Delhi, for a regulated globalization respectful of the existing cultural and linguistic diversity, and recognized that India was a global power. 'The treaties and the practices which regulate the international political order should consequently' be altered: a restrained but clear support for India's quest for a permanent member seat in an enlarged UN Security Council.[13]

These propositions were well received in India. A leading commentator concluded that 'Chirac visit restores warmth in bilateral relations', and added: 'his call for a strategic and political dialogue with India was backed by appropriate statements'.[14] Beyond statements, the real issue was implementation. I. K. Gujral's transition government then in power could not do much, as it was running current affairs and preparing the next general elections. Once the BJP came to power two months after Chirac's visit, and decided a few weeks later to conduct nuclear tests adverse to the global dominant security order, Paris could have decided to revise its policy. It did not, and choose on the other hand to confirm, as it has done during the presidential visit, that France was eager to engage India as such, and not a particular regime in power.

After the Nuclear Tests

Among all Western powers, France was by far the most understanding after the new BJP-led government conducted two rounds of nuclear tests at Pokhran on 11 and 13 May 1998. Paris did join other members of G8, European Union, and UN Security Council in their condemnation of the tests. But the tone of statements emanating from Paris as such was different, although India was said to be 'on the wrong path'.

The French Foreign Affairs Ministry expressed on 13 May its 'preoccupation' and called for restraint by all states in the region, but found 'encouraging' the Indian declaration in favor of non-proliferation. The French Defence Minister added that India seemed to have conducted her tests by relying upon her own capacity, and that she was not willing to export her technical knowledge. In addition, the Minister for Parliamentary Affairs declared that the French government would 'not encourage' the Americans in slapping sanctions against India, 'because this is not the right way for seeing India joining nations willing to sign non-proliferation treaties'. This was to no avail of course, for President Clinton, bound by the Glenn Amendment, imposed the same day sanctions upon India. But this was more than India could expect. 'A French kiss makes up for global bitterness', commented *The Economic Times* the next day.[15]

Effectively, the new BJP-led government was facing at that time strong condemnation for having opened the nuclear Pandora's box in South Asia. Russia was as understanding as Paris, but the Yeltsin years were not the best for Indo-Russian relations. China was stiff, for Indian Prime Minister A. B. Vajpayee had mentioned in his letter to President Clinton 'a northern neighbor' challenging India's security, a few weeks after his defence minister's controversial definition of China as 'India's threat number one'. In this context, France's comments were offering some breathing space to a government whose image was still in doubt, and which had strained, by conducting nuclear tests, the established relationships with a number of important partners, such as those with the US, Japan, Germany, Canada and Australia.

By contrast, the French leadership recognized in India's willingness to strive for an independent nuclear force a rationale akin to the Gaullist policy of strategic autonomy implemented by Paris almost 40 years before, and now accepted by the Left in power. However, this understanding could not be equated with a blank check. Paris invited India to sign the NPT. It appeared quite a rhetorical proposal, for the French administration never believed that India – nor Pakistan after she conducted her own tests on 28 and 30 May – would roll back their nascent nuclear forces, nor accept the NPT as it stands, because article IX recognizes only as nuclear weapon states those states who were such in 1967. More important for Paris was the CTBT, the coming negotiations on the Fissile Material Cut-off Treaty (FMCT) and the need for restraint, responsibility, nonproliferation, and strong command, control and communication facilities.

The political and strategic dialogue envisaged during President Chirac's visit to New Delhi could now be started with an India who, not recognized as a nuclear weapon state as per the NPT, was then defining herself, to quote Air Commodore Jasjit Singh, as 'a state with nuclear weapons'.[16]

THE NEW RELATIONSHIP TAKES SHAPE

The French reaction to the nuclear tests once known, the new bilateral relationship between Paris and New Delhi could develop on the lines defined in January 1998, before the arrival of the Bharatiya Janata Party in power. A strategic dialogue was engaged and developed. It was broad enough to allow bilateral and international issues to be discussed with, the concept of 'security' covering much more than the strict defence field.

In June 1998, barely three weeks after the nuclear tests, Brajesh Mishra, Special Envoy and Principal Secretary to Prime Minister A. B. Vajpayee, conducted in Paris the first visit to a P5 (five permanent member nations of the UN Security Council) member by a very high-profile member of the Indian administration. The Indo-US dialogue, conducted between Jaswant

Singh (not yet External Affairs Minister) and Strobe Talbot, the US Deputy Secretary of State, started the same month. If the Indo-US dialogue was obviously the most potent, engaging the French was relevant for New Delhi.

First, Paris was offering precious elbow room to Indian diplomacy at a difficult time (the French were said to have mellowed the P5 and G8 statements condemning India's tests, and were clearly not toeing the US line).

Second, France was a possible provider of high technology. On both accounts, geopolitical and technical, France was seen as a way to balance whatsoever, even if on unequal terms, the necessary dialogue with Washington.

The Strategic Dialogue

On his way back from the UN General Assembly held in New York, Prime Minister A. B. Vajpayee conducted in Paris, in September 1998, his first official visit to a major foreign state after assuming power. Economic prospects were not forgotten, but strategic issues were on the top of the agenda: CTBT and terrorism, amongst other points, were discussed. The idea of a strategic dialogue was formalized. The first session was held in New Delhi one month later.

Since October 1998, two meetings a year are regularly organized between Brajesh Mishra, later on nominated National Security Adviser, and Gérard Errera, the French Special Emissary. The dialogue is not seen as a negotiation round. It is a process aiming less at immediate results than at developing trust and mutual understanding on all types of geopolitical issues. Paris shares India's willingness to discuss freely all matters of global interest (and not just bilateral or regional problems), and values good relations with a country seen as a stabilizing force in Asia, and a future great power. New Delhi appreciates the French openness, its dedication to a multipolar world order.

Both countries object to what Hubert Védrine defines as 'the counterproductive aspects' of the US 'hyperpower'.[17] Both countries are also exchanging messages and clarifications, including between the biannual official sessions. Paris has for instance clarified why France has not supported Madeleine Albright's attempt to round up, in Warsaw in June 2000, democratic countries around the United States (for multipolarity is not supposed to rely upon democracies only).[18] India, on her own, has briefed French authorities after US Deputy Secretary of State Richard Armitage's presentation of the ballistic missile defence (BMD) policy to New Delhi in May 2001, as well as before and after the Agra summit with Pakistan in July 2001.

Essential as it is, the strategic dialogue conducted since 1998 is only a part of the comprehensive mechanism which now exists between France and India. Besides the regular meetings between foreign secretaries, working groups address technical and economic issues (such as information technology, energy, and scientific cooperation) while the Indo-French Initiative Forum, launched even before Vajpayee's first visit to Paris, goes organizing high-flying seminars focused on the way both countries look at global issues. Among the field of cooperation upgraded after 1998, science and technology appear prominent. Among the new mechanisms set up in 1998, the Indo-French High Committee for Defense deserves special attention.

The Science and Technology Links

The Indo-French cooperation in science and technology started soon after independence, including sensitive nuclear research. The arena covered expanded after the two governments established in 1987 the Indo-French Centre for the Promotion of Advanced Research, supporting hundred of joints projects in fundamental and applied sciences.[19] Cooperation in biotechnology and information technology is fast developing.

In a different field of special relevance, the relationship between the Indian Space Research Organization (ISRO) and the Centre National d'Études Spatiales (CNES) is well established. The two conduct joint research on a new satellite for climate and weather applications, to be launched in 2005 on India's Polar Satellite Launch Vehicle (ISRO and Arianespace signed an agreement on PSLV in 1998). Further cooperation is also expected in the fields of aerospace, aeronautics and space science, under the twin umbrella of the Society of Indian Aerospace Technologies (SIATI) and the 'Groupe des industries françaises aéronautiques et spatiales' (French Aerospace Industries Group: GIFAS), representing hundred of high-tech companies, while the new INSAT-3B ISRO satellites are still launched from French Guyana.

However, in dual technology sectors, the 'substitution' policy of the past does not apply any more, and India can no longer knock at the French door for getting easily what Washington does not want to provide.[20] In fields open to joint research, the prospects of cooperation are large. When transfer is sensitive, France sticks to the international rules, particularly those related to nonproliferation. This severe restriction does not prevent however the development of a growing Indo-French defense relationship.

The Defense Relationship

Meeting once a year, the High Committee for Defense goes beyond exchanges of views on defense perceptions. One of its three subcommittees conducts a dialogue on strategic issues, the other two pay attention respectively to military bilateral relations and to defense equipment. This is on the whole an area where the bilateral relationship, which has definitely a long history, has known steady progress, as a cursory look at the calendar of high level visits would confirm.

In January 1999, George Fernandes, on his first trip abroad as Indian Defence Minister, came to Paris. In May the High Committee for Defense met for the first time. In September came Air Chief Marshal A. Y. Tipnis, and in December Chief of Army Staff General V. P. Malik. In February–March 2000, vessels from the Indian Ocean French Fleet sailed to Mumbai, then to Visakhapatnam, on the Bay of Bengal, for joint exercises with the Indian Navy, an operation defined in the Indian press as 'India's first post-Pokhran naval exercise with a UN Security Council member'.[21]

In April, General Kelche, French Chief of Defense Staff, was in India, followed in May by Alain Richard, French Defense Minister, and in July by a parliamentary mission discussing nuclear and ballistic missile proliferation. In February 2001, the French Navy was back in India, for the first International Fleet Review organized off Mumbai's coast. Significantly, the antisubmarine frigate *Dupleix* and the nuclear submarine *Perle* were present.

Beyond the upgraded visibility of ministers' and military top brass' visits, what is the substance of the Indo-French defense cooperation? While the broad geopolitical parameters discussed between the two countries are basically the preserve of the top-level strategic dialogue, the armed forces and the ministries involved do carry on their own consultations on military doctrines, in order to define more precisely the pattern of service to service cooperation.

Posting officers in the partner country is going on, although on a limited way. More numerous are the experts' missions or the short-term joint exercises. On the whole, the High Committee for Defense has been able to expand considerably the number of cooperative actions between the two countries, which have more than tripled in three years.

One of the most decisive fields of discussion and negotiations is in the area of defense equipment. If the Indian forces have mostly bought Russian armament for decades and continue to do so, France has always been an alternative source of supply, particularly for the Indian Air Force. Today, the scope is not just sales and delivery, but local construction under license, transfer of technology, joint research, and industrial cooperation. This policy is followed as well by Russia, which signed during President Putin's visit to India in October 2000 not only a Strategic Partnership Declaration but also a 10-year Indo-Russian agreement on military technical cooperation.[22]

Indian requirements are large and growing in number and sophistication. The demand for high technology is vital, for the successes of the Defense and Research Development Organization (DRDO), one of the key participants to the Indo-French High Committee for Defense, if remarkable, are not always as quick as expected. DRDO insiders recognize that in many fields India 'tries to catch up with others', rather than producing outstanding new defense equipment.[23]

Taking into account the opportunities, and the rise of the successive Indian defense budgets, (in fact lower than it seems when assessed in real terms), Indo-French defense deals have developed recently. Most prominent in this regard was the order, concluded in 2000, for 10 new Mirage 2000 jets (to be delivered in 2003), in addition to assistance in constructing an indigenously designed submarine, avionics for MiG-21 and GPS navigation packages for Sukhoi-30 aircraft. Consultations are on for Alpha Advanced Jet Trainers (challenged by British and Russian competitors) and for the French-made *Scorpen*-class submarine, the next generation after the *Agosta* series delivered to, or under construction in, Pakistan. Battlefield surveillance radars and new systems for T-72 tanks are of interest for the Army. A detailed list would be long, for 54 armaments systems are said to have been identified for joint production.[24]

The sensitive issue of French arms sales to Pakistan is no more a matter of acrimony. The agreement signed in 1994 for three *Agosta* 90B submarines, to be equipped with Exocet missiles, has been hardly appreciated in New Delhi. But India had to accept that Paris felt fair to honor past contracts, hoping that in the present context of Indo-French 'active strategic partnership' no new major deals affecting the regional balance would be signed between Paris and Islamabad. Looking at the total orders of French defense equipment passed by New Delhi and Islamabad all along the 1990s, it appears that, although the value of Pakistan's orders was more than twice India's share, the trend turned in favor of India after 1996.

Before General Musharraf joined the US-led war against the Taliban and Al-Qaeda in September 2001, Pakistan saw herself as neglected by all Western countries courting India's emerging market. The international community is certainly looking differently to Pakistan today. Even before this shift, an Indian realist taking a long-term view acknowledged that 'France is capable of sustaining multiple relationships with China, India,

TABLE 1

ORDERS FOR FRENCH DEFENSE EQUIPMENT PASSED BY INDIA AND PAKISTAN
DURING THE NINETIES (BILLIONS OF F.F.)

	1991	1992	1993	1994	1995	1996	1997	1998	1999	Total
India	0.490	0.520	0.956	0.546	0.368	4.708	0.679	0.864	0.965	5.866
Pakistan	0.643	1.813	0.835	6.216	1.042	1.773	0.313	0.344	0.338	13.377

Source: Délégation Générale pour l'Armement. *Rapport au Parlement*, Paris, 2001, annexe 6,
pp.81–2.

Pakistan. (…) Expecting France to renounce its relationship with Pakistan
for us is being unrealistic'.[25] New Delhi would however expect from France
as well as from any other friendly country, that in a context of regional
persistent tension, no defense sale would alter the balance of power between
the two South Asian rivals.

REGIONAL ISSUES

The strategic dialogue conducted between France and India covers all
geopolitical issues, including those of immediate regional interest for New
Delhi and Paris. Out of them, Kashmir and the question of militant
Islamism, and the Indian Ocean should be briefly addressed here.

Kashmir and Terrorism

On the sensitive Kashmir issue, New Delhi can, on the whole, praise Paris,
which seems to have adopted the traditional Indian diplomatic mantra: the
less we talk about Kashmir, the better it is. Contrary to the US, France has
never presented herself as a potential mediator, and does not encourage
Track II or Track III diplomacy on the issue, or on India-Pakistan relations
at large. Basically, the French position, as expressed by Foreign Minister
Alain Juppé in 1994, has not changed: 'the internationalization of the
(Kashmir) question must be avoided. A solution must be found in a bilateral
frame, between India and Pakistan'.[26]

Paris similarly does not criticize publicly the human rights record of
Indian forces in Kashmir, does not refer to 'the wishes of the Kashmiris' nor
does it present the Line of Control as 'a nuclear flashpoint', although
concerns have been voiced in various ways, particularly after the military
tension which has followed the attack on Indian Parliament in December

2001. Just after the Kargil crisis, the French position was reiterated in parliament: no mediation.[27]

South Block could have written the brief, although up to a point. First, Paris has always called for the resumption of the Indo-Pakistani dialogue when it was frozen. More generally, and whatever could be their own reservations on Pakistan's policies, successive French governments have always considered it wise to keep Islamabad engaged. This was done after the tests, and done as well after General Musharraf's coup in 1999, in order to avoid the pitfalls of a dangerous isolation.

Second, and for the same reasons, while Paris had and is still 'condemning all sorts of violence, terrorism and external interferences',[28] it stops short of referring to 'cross-border terrorism'. Along with other major countries, France has never defined Pakistan as a terrorist state, as India was expecting at a time.

India's agenda on terrorism is mostly focused on Pakistan and by implication on Taliban' Afghanistan, both having been presented by New Delhi does as 'the single largest gene-pool of global terrorism'.[29] The Indian concern about terrorism has been reiterated consistently, at the highest level, by Indian President R. K. Narayanan, both during his state visit to Paris in April 2000[30] and when he received the credentials of the new French Ambassador Bernard de Montferrand four months later.[31]

Not much was officially said after Home Minister L. K. Advani visited Paris, and the Interpol headquarters at Lyons, in June 2000. Advani was seeking support for the India-sponsored convention on international terrorism at the UN, a step forward from the French proposal for an International Convention for the Suppression of the Financing of Terrorism, adopted by the UN on December 1999.

For years, New Delhi had expected to get from Paris a stronger indictment of the Pakistan-Taliban-*jihadis* nexus. In the post-September 11 scenario, France has naturally strongly voiced her condemnation of terrorism targeting India after the attacks on Srinagar and New Delhi by suicide commandos. The word 'terrorism' itself has found a new recognition in the context of Kashmir. But New Delhi is certainly not too happy with the way Paris, and the world community at large, see in Musharraf a Pakistani leader doing his best to contain extremism in his country. India would like her doubts and distrust regarding the Pakistani leadership better understood. The Indo-French Joint Working Group on Terrorism, which met in Paris on 7 September 2001 for the first time, is offering an additional framework for a sustained dialogue on the point.

The Maritime Dimension

If France has no direct interest in Kashmir, she does have overseas territories in the Indian Ocean, and in the Pacific Ocean as well. The French fleet cruises in both of them, and French troops are stationed in Djibouti, on the Gulf of Aden. India has denounced in the past these legacies of colonial empire, the nuclear test site of Mururoa (now dismantled) in the Pacific, and the presence in the Indian Ocean of war vessels from outside powers. Times have changed, and New Delhi is not unhappy, to say the least, to have joint naval exercises with the French, and to discuss with them the way to expand her Navy, including its submarine component, expected to play an enhanced role in India's new nuclear-related strategy.

The concept of 'expanded neighborhood' underlines the range of Indian geopolitical and geo-economic interests. It includes, in its maritime dimension, the entire Indian Ocean, and more particularly its northern waters, the oil sea routes extended from the Gulf to the Malacca Straits, the gateway to South China Sea and the Pacific. The setting up of a new Andaman and Nicobar Command at Port Blair asserts Indian strategic interests in the region: a signal to ASEAN, and to China.

This maritime dimension is part of the Indo-French strategic dialogue. Besides the service-to-service cooperation between the two Navies and the question of defense equipment, two issues deserve comment. In 1997, the Indian Ocean Rim Association for Regional Cooperation (IOR-ARC) was launched with India, Australia and South Africa as key-members. It suffered a setback after India's nuclear tests, but may strengthen itself in the future. Since the inception of the Association, Paris has conveyed to New Delhi France's willingness to be co-opted as a member of the regional grouping, which include today 19 rim countries. France has been accepted in 2001 only as a dialogue partner.

More immediately relevant, whatever its shortcomings, is the ASEAN Regional Forum (ARF), the only strategic grouping accommodating India. The European Union is a member of ARF, but France would like 'to participate on a national basis in the activities of the ARF'.[32] Here again, the decision is not in the hands of India alone. Here again, India's commitment is not quite explicit.

ASKING FOR MORE: UNMET EXPECTATIONS

Although the Indo-French strategic dialogue might go on very well, and the atmospherics of the military relationship might be warm, India is not obtaining complete satisfaction from Paris. This is true up to a point at the political level: New Delhi would appreciate stronger statements from Paris regarding Pakistan's policy in Kashmir. This is true also as far as the overall economic cooperation is concerned. This is equally true for the most sensitive dimensions of trade, covering defense equipment and civil nuclear energy.

Looking for More Investments

It has been said repeatedly, all through the 1990s, that bilateral trade and French investments in India are not what they should be. The Indian quest for international status cannot ignore economic parameters, and the extended notion of security encompasses not just energy supplies but also access to technology and capital for developing infrastructures. Another matter of debate, not just confined to bilateral relations, are the issues debated upon in the World Trade Organization, which partly affects the way India deals with what is sometimes labeled as 'Fortress Europe', a definition contested by French authorities.

For the past ten years, between France and India, innumerable ministers' visits, business associations meetings, industrial seminars and trade fairs have been conducted, and the economic departments in respective embassies have been remarkably active. The results, if encouraging, are however not yet meeting expectations. Bilateral trade turnover did rise from 9.16 to 15.18 billion FF from 1990 to 2000, the balance of trade favoring India since 1994. Indian exports to France, along the 1990–2000 decade, rose much more (from 3.68 to 9.44 billion FF) than French exports to India (from 5.48 to 6.15 billion).[33]

French investments in India have certainly expanded, from a mere US $2.5 million in 1991 to US $70.2 million in 2000.[34] That year, FDI approvals set France at the ninth position in overall country ranking. Power, petroleum, telecom, pharmaceuticals, and water management projects attracted French interests, but the bilateral relationship is still mostly dependent on large projects, the network of dynamic middle-sized companies being rather weak. Despite progress, the difficulties underlined by Ambassador Ranganathan in 1994 remain partly valid. On one hand, India still suffers from the competition of China and other markets. On the other hand, French businessmen remain less India-oriented than a number of their European counterparts. Many consider that the process of investing in India is still too intricate, and too uncertain.[35]

It is difficult to evaluate how the overall substance of the Indo-French dialogue is affected by this relatively slender economic relationship. In a way, the political dialogue stands by itself, as it addresses world geopolitical visions. Nonetheless, one cannot underestimate the ambit of economic cooperation and trade interest in strengthening a political and strategic relationship, as the US-China duet testifies.

Between these two perceptions, there is room for adjustment, for at least two reasons. First, France is an important player in the field of infrastructure: her expertise in roads, electricity, ports, railways is recognized in India, but the point is to attract (and to keep on) the companies. Second, and more importantly, India's interest for French civil or military technology remains high, despite existing constraints.

Defense Equipment Constraints

As far as defense equipment is concerned, three restrictive elements have to be taken into account. First, regarding arms exports, the French Defence Ministry favors now a much greater coordination between the General Delegation for Armament (DGA), which offers its technical support, the Inter-Ministry Commission for the Study of Export of War Materials (CIEEMG) and – here is the new dimension – the Delegation for Strategic Affairs (DAS), more concerned with the political dimension of the exports.[36] This does not affect India specifically, but adds to the list of clearances.

Second, is the issue of cost. French military products are said to be of high quality, but costly. More costly than the Russian goods; more costly than the US equipment, which is generally produced in larger series. The general evolution of arms production in France must be considered as well. A sizeable share of the production is now in the hands of the private sector. While these private companies depend heavily from the State, which places the most important orders, the government cannot define their entire production line. Faced with the prospect of declining defence budgets, a part of this production has turned to civilian customers, a process which may drive up the cost of defense equipment. On the other hand, the fact that a part of French avionics fits as well on Russian planes, as on French ones is useful to the Indian market.

Third, the European dimension is bound to interfere more and more. For defence equipment which is not one hundred per cent French, the co-producing countries have to be consulted before sales are decided. Among its priorities, the European Common Foreign and Security Policy addresses the question of 'Armaments Europe', and France would like to see a European Armament Agency promptly established. The growing cooperation between European countries in defense production, including through new European corporations, implies that the clearance for export defence contracts will more and more involve several European countries.

The Dual Technology Issue and the Nuclear Energy Conundrum

Besides defense production per se, the international context affects the Indo-French relationship, particularly as far as dual technologies are concerned. Of prime interest here is India's quest for nuclear energy. As noted above, the French Commission for Atomic Energy had been in close touch with its Indian counterpart, since the heroic days of the first Indian leader in the field, Dr Homi Bhaba. France later on supplied heavy water to Indian nuclear plants, substituting herself to American or Canadian providers. French expertise in nuclear energy, which produces today 75 per cent of France's requirements, adds to India's interests in technology transfer.

The French President revived India's expectations in 1998 when he stated that the bilateral cooperation could also, 'in due time, address the production of nuclear based electricity'.[37] In clear words Paris would consider selling India either nuclear plants and/or the know-how and/or important components. Expecting 'returns from the French connection' after the first strategic dialogue meeting had been held, an Indian commentator noted: 'While America has walked away with the cream of the Chinese nuclear market, France now has a chance to make a big breakthrough in India.'[38] But no firm commitments were made, for India does not fully adhere to the safeguards and verification procedures set up by the International Atomic Energy Agency and by the Nuclear Suppliers Group (NSG), which Paris finds binding.

Would the bilateral committee set up for discussing energy issues be able to find, as Chirac diplomatically put it, 'solutions which reconcile our common willingness to cooperate with the necessary respect of the rules fixed by the international community?'[39] India expects some flexibility, arguing that France's rigidity on that matter is not realistic. After all, Washington has for years turned a blind eye to Chinese proliferation, because trade prospects appear sometimes more important than the rules of sanctions.

Russia, on her own, has certainly bent over US pressure regarding the proposed technology transfer related to cryogenic engines, said to violate the Missile Technology Control Regime (MTCR). Finally, Moscow did sell such engines to India which needed them for its Geosynchronous Space Launch Vehicle, which took off in May 2001. The basic argument goes that if France sticks to the theology of regulations regarding nuclear energy or dual technology, she might lose her share of the Indian nuclear energy market, estimated at $30 billion for the next 20 years, to the benefit of less rigid competitors. However, Moscow, said to be understanding, is careful as well. Russians made a deal with Washington on the cryogenic engines, and the India-Russian cooperation agreement on Koodankulam nuclear power plant, signed in 1988, has not yet materialized.

France is therefore not alone in paying attention to international regulations in this field. She is said to try to have them somehow relaxed in favor of New Delhi, pleading India's case at the NSG. This would be in line with a second argument advanced by New Delhi, which suggests that the rational view is to consider India as a responsible partner. Officially, Paris believes that the responsibility invoked would be better established if New Delhi were sending what Minister Védrine called 'signals'.[40] Unofficially, Indian insiders suggest that some French key players admit that the dual technology constraints regarding civil nuclear energy have no valid rationale when applied to India, a country which already and openly possesses nuclear weapons.

The matter expresses well the present transition stage India is passing through. She asserts herself as a future big power, but asks perhaps more than other nations are ready to agree to for the time being. This is precisely this transitional stage which gives their value to the dialogues currently engaged by New Delhi with many countries. To put back the Indo-French bilateral dialogue in its larger context will finally help to assess its contents, and its significance.

GLOBAL VIEWS AND SECURITY DOCTRINES

The Nuclear and Ballistic Missile Issues

France has pleased New Delhi by understanding, if not approving, India's rationale for going openly nuclear, but divergences remain on nuclear issues. Both countries plead for disarmament; both, in the present circumstances, believe in nuclear deterrence. But their views on the international nuclear regime are still apart. Immediately after India's and Pakistan's nuclear tests, the French Minister of Foreign Affairs stated in Parliament that 'these tests change absolutely nothing in the French nuclear doctrine', and that the first priority would be 'to restore the credibility of the NPT'.[41]

Three years later, the official statement on France's defence policy, set out by President Chirac, remains unambiguous. 'Nuclear deterrence is the crux of the resources enabling France to affirm the principle of strategic autonomy from which derives our defense policy', and is above all 'an important factor of global security'. As far as global rules are concerned, Paris considers that the NPT, 'a vital instrument for stability' which must not be weakened, 'constitutes the basis for implementing nuclear disarmament'. France calls as well for 'the entry into force of the CTBT and the opening of negotiations on FMCT'.[42]

By contrast, India holds that the inequitable NPT regime is a failure. Commenting upon the NPT Review Conference in May 2000, Jaswant Singh reiterated: 'the nuclear weapon states (NWS, France being one of them) parties to NPT and their allies have not diminished the role of nuclear weapons'.[43] 'The NWS have either been active collaborators in or silent spectators to continuing proliferation', and instead of beginning 'any kind of collective, meaningful negotiations aimed at global disarmament', they have arrogated themselves 'a permanent special right to possess nuclear weapons and only for their exclusive security'.

Yet, 'though not a party to the NPT, India's policies have been consistent with the key provisions of the NPT that apply to the NWS'.[44] When India's Minister of External Affairs argues that 'India cannot join the NPT as a non-nuclear weapon state', must we understand that she would be ready to do so, if the NPT was altered in order to accommodate new members? It is difficult to imagine the NWS accepting officially the new nuclearized countries in their fold, a process which would be seen as encouraging other countries to nuclearize themselves.

The alternative lies in the search for a new global security order. This is precisely what Brajesh Mishra called for when stating that 'the old arms control precepts, which also underline the NPT, have to give way to new equations if multilaterally negotiated arms control has to succeed'.[45] Is President Bush's BMD project an acceptable 'new equation' for India? The hasty support extended by the Indian Ministry of External Affairs, two days after Bush's historic speech at the National Defence University in May 2001, surprised many in India and abroad. It was seen by most observers as a complete shift from the established Indian position on the matter, which supported the Anti-Ballistic Missile (ABM) treaty and opposed the BMD project, which was seen as conducive to a new arms race and the militarization of outer space.

While most European countries, including France, have voiced strong reservations about BMD, India endorsed a 'highly significant statement by the Bush administration (...) transforming the strategic parameters on which the Cold War security architecture was built', for 'there is a strategic and technological inevitability in stepping away from a world that is held hostage by the doctrine of mutual assured destruction'.[46] But two days later, when Russian Foreign Minister Igor Ivanov was in Delhi, his Indian counterpart made clear that the 'ABM treaty of 1972 cannot and should not be abrogated unilaterally'.[47] Fortunately for New Delhi, the opening of bilateral discussions between Moscow and Washington on this point eased India's position, often described in the country as a shaky equilibrium between Russia, her old friend, and America, her new one.

The rationale behind India's reaction is easy to explain. As a fine observer noted, Bush's proposal is akin to 'a tectonic movement in geopolitics'. 'As an 'outcast' in the old nuclear order, India has every reason to herald its demise and welcome the construction of a more credible global nuclear arrangement'. It remains to be seen, however, if the 'rewriting the rules of the nuclear game' will effectively offers India 'a chance to be a part of the nuclear solution and not (of) the proliferation problem'.[48]

This is not the place to debate upon the US missile defence policy implications *per se*, nor to evaluate its impact on South Asia. However, the episode and its follow-up help to locate the Indo-French new dialogue in its overarching context, defined not only by the global parameters, but also by the new relationship New Delhi is establishing with key powers, particularly the US.

France and the India-US Rapprochement

The successful visit of President Clinton in India, in March 2000, heralded a new chapter in the bilateral relations between the US and India. Both countries pleaded, in a joint statement expounding a common 'Vision for the 21st Century', for 'working together for strategic stability in Asia and beyond', as 'partners in peace'.[49] The new relationship was expanded by the Bush administration, particularly at the strategic level.

In May 2001, the US Deputy Secretary of State Richard Armitage came to Delhi, after Tokyo and Seoul, for briefing the Indian Government on US's BMD policy. In July, the first visit ever of a Chairman of the Joint Chiefs of Staff, General Henry H. Shelton, ended with the decision to restart military cooperation with India and to revive the Indo-US Defence Policy Group, stalled since 1997. The same month, the new Assistant Secretary of State for South Asia, Christina Rocca, confirmed that the review of sanctions imposed upon India after the 1998 tests was 'underway'. No new US administration has put India 'on its radar screen' so quickly and never had the US discussed global strategic issues with India in such a way.[50]

Is Paris concerned with such a development, which may deprive France from the benefits of having been the first Western power to recognize the legitimacy of India's new assertiveness? The views of the French administration are in fact congruent with its search for multipolarity. First, insiders in key ministries remark that the new US perception of India proves Paris' Indian policy was right. Second, France cannot expect to be the only

Western country to develop good relations with India. Third, it is believed that the Indo-French relationship, no more alone in its category, but still the first in time, will preserve its specificity.

Beyond the 'community of democracies' New Delhi and Washington are now fond to invoke, Paris would still concur with Jaswant Singh's statement that both France and India 'pride themselves on a tradition of independent thought and action in foreign policy'.[51] Fourth, and perhaps more importantly, both sides know that India would not put all her eggs in the same basket. This choice would be not just contrary to the established Indian practice, but also difficult, for the pro-US stance has also reluctant supporters if not opponents in the Indian administration.

It would also be unwise, considering the fluctuations of US policy, bound by Congressional votes or Presidential decisions. In the US vocabulary, 'friends' is sometimes a transient concept, as the Pakistanis know well. The US is seen as too demanding, too hectoring, too conditional, too prone to reverse gear, to accustomed to double standards, for India choosing to be one-sided. To get access to US technology, to US surveillance data or even to the US BMD shield – eventually extended not just to allies but to friends – is appearing promising, but other parameters are not forgotten.

India would gain to strengthen her links with Washington, but not at the cost of her Russian connections (hence the adjusted position on BMD). She could make use of her new relations with Washington for enjoying a certain leeway *vis-à-vis* Beijing, but would not accept being used as a pawn against China. However important the relationship with America turns out to be, India needs other partners as well. The expected relation might not be much different from Védrine's description of the US-France partnership conveyed to an Indian audience: to be friends of the US does not imply to be 'aligned with them'.[52]

The European Dimension

France is not seen in India as a global military power, but her diplomatic standing is acknowledged. Besides carrying her P5 status and her defence and nuclear technologies, France is seen also as having a certain imaginative vision, a tradition of 'intellectual inquiry',[53] manifest in her statements on nuclear issues or on multipolarity. At both levels, this French vision has identified India as part of a global equilibrium, more clearly than other European powers have done. After President Chirac's visit to India, senior journalist K. K. Katyal commented: 'So far, Germany was the only entry point for India's dealing with the European Community. Now France becomes another such point.'[54]

Two years later, the same observer compared India's engagement with each of the two European countries. He considered that on most points – tests, sanctions, Security Council membership – 'it flowed smoothly and effortlessly from the French stand on the tests, but as regards Germany, it was the result of persistent efforts', Bonn, then Berlin, having generally taken a primarily hardened stand.[55]

While Germany is seen as the economic powerhouse of Europe, sharing with France the political leadership of the European Union, France appears more involved in global issues. Among the three most important European countries, Great Britain is seen in India as being simply aligned with Washington, and certainly not a model. To quote from the wry but insightful presentation on Indo-American relations made by Jairam Ramesh in New York in 1999: 'We do not want to be a Tony Blair who we see as your poodle, but we do want to have a special relationship with you, on our terms.'[56]

By these standards, Germany is seen somewhere in between: not a NWS, not a Security Council permanent member, not as close to Washington as Great Britain is, but perhaps too close nevertheless – the old NATO legacy. And when Germany asserts herself and move away from the US, it is partly through the political empowerment of the Green Party, not exactly happy with India's nuclearization. By contrast, France offers an image of particular interest: close to the US, but touchy on her autonomy, looking for recognition as a noted player, but accepting differences and pleading for multipolarity.[57]

That said, France is certainly not competing with her neighbors at the cost of the European idea, far from it. The French administration misses no opportunity to stress the decisive relevance of the European Union for constructing a new multipolar order. This intimate conviction is repeatedly conveyed to the Government of India and to Indian think-tanks. When he received President Narayanan in Paris in April 2000 – the first ever state visit by an Indian President to France – Jacques Chirac did not dissociate the prospect of India emerging as 'one of the foremost centres of powers in the world of tomorrow' from the growing assertiveness of the European Union eager to establish 'the political means to make (her) voice heard in the concert of nations'. Hence, 'the international balance of powers needs a strong relationship between India and the European Union'.[58]

One month later, Defense Minister Alain Richard visited India. In his key speech, he choose to comment not on the running reform of French forces, but rather on the 'emergence of a new political player', the European Union, and her Common Foreign and Security Policy. CFSP, he clarified, aims at crisis prevention, crisis management, peacekeeping in Europe and in its margins, for 'regional issues are regionally dealt with' (draw the conclusion for Kashmir). Richard clarified the rationale of the Kosovo war so strongly criticized in India:'we put out fire in (our) own backyard'. He underlined the evolving relationship between the European forces, still made up of national armies, and NATO, which is no more entitled to 'exclusiveness for defense issues in Europe'. This development, added the defense minister, 'is an essential contribution to the stability of a really multipolar world, more balanced than the present one, with the emergence in Asia and Europe of new key players'.[59]

MULTIPOLARITY AND THE INDO-FRENCH DIALOGUE: BETWEEN PRINCIPLED VISIONS AND REALPOLITIK

The Indo-French dialogue on multipolarity deserves attention for three reasons.

First, it offers a wide common ground between the two countries. It pleased India to be acknowledged as one of the 'emerging new great powers in Asia'[60] and as one of the future poles structuring a more balanced world order. However, India was expecting more than statements on her 'vocation' to join the permanent members of the Security Council. Finally, the French President said it publicly in Paris to his Indian counterpart in April 2000: 'India is naturally destined to become a permanent member of the United Nations Security Council. France supports and will support your candidature.' New Delhi, however, wanted more and got it when, on 1 November 2001, France backed openly India candidature during the UN General Assembly debate on the expansion of the Council.[61]

Second, the Indo-French dialogue on multipolarity addresses, by definition, the question of emerging powers and global balance. We have noted the French comments on the parallel assertiveness of Europe and India. In this regard, the EU-India Business summit held in Lisbon in June 2000 appears as an acknowledgement by India of the 'need to review India-EU relations', not just a call for investment.[62] What is at stake here are the Indian perceptions of what is sometimes defined as Eurasia. New Delhi criticized NATO expansion to Eastern Europe. The relationship with China is too uncertain for providing much credit to the proposed Moscow–Beijing–New Delhi triangle once proposed by Yevgeny Primakov, but the Indian administration is certainly concerned by the substance and the ambitions of the Atlantic Alliance, now that the Cold War is over.

In this regard, France may advance her good relations with Moscow (despite problems over Chechnya), and her endeavor for strengthening the links between Russia and the European Union. The question remains asked however in New Delhi: who is defining the rules regarding sovereignty in the Balkans, or for that matter in the world at large? India has not participated in the 1991 Gulf War, and did not appreciate the recourse to referendum in East Timor.

French authorities did their best in offering India a comforting interpretation of the EU-NATO involvement in Kosovo (France was the European country engaging the largest forces in the conflict). They clarified three points, related to (i) the necessity to intervene, (ii) the respective role of Europe and the US, (iii) the lessons to be drawn. To quote the French Minister of Foreign Affairs: 'Even we French agreed to a NATO operation because doing nothing would have been worse. But it wasn't NATO which used us, it was we who used NATO as an instrument. We clearly said at that time that it was an exception and not a precedent.'[63]

India's reading of the NATO and OSCE intervention in Macedonia, in the summer of 2001, appears quite different from what it was two years before, perhaps not just because the sovereignty issue in this case is less a matter of controversy. After September 11, India has not opposed the US intervention in Afghanistan, nor the NATO members' limited forces involvement, the UN resolution permitting them being obviously not the only criterion considered in this regard.

The debates raised by the Kosovo episode drive us to our third point. The Indo-French dialogue is of particular interest for it analyses global issues. Between 1997 and 2002, France happens to have had a Minister of Foreign Affairs who did not 'simply' carry on his task. Hubert Védrine was also engaged, text after text, speech after speech, in shaping a diplomatic doctrine addressing the new configurations and the global challenges faced by the nation states and the multilateral UN system.

At the same time, the BJP-led Indian government was redefining the basis of its own foreign policy. In a recent book, *Defending India*, the Minister of External Affairs, Jaswant Singh, discarded the Nehruvian policy described as 'idealistic romanticism', and preached *realpolitik*.[64] The Indo-French dialogue in foreign affairs is therefore rich in intellectual content, and addresses some of the decisive issues of the present world. If both sides would recognize that the key objective of a foreign policy is the defence or the advancement of national interest, both would admit as well that this concept of national interests can no more be totally self-defined.

France struggles for keeping her rank in the world, but in the meantime works for the emergence of a European pole. India longs for being acknowledged as a global power, which has to be done 'not with arrogance but not with timidity'.[65] Such an ambition calls for an economic strength which is still questioned, and which has to be assessed at the global level, be it on trade or on the impact of growth on the human development index. This also means acknowledging, as Jairam Ramesh does, that 'if India seeks a global role for itself, it must play by global rules'.[66] India may have genuine concerns about the fairness or the double standards of the rules of the game, be it on WTO, on dual technologies, on the UN system. She has to address them internally, but also, obviously, through a constant multifaceted dialogue with others countries, with other powers.

The Indo-French dialogue offers in this regard a number of opportunities, not simply because 'India nurtures a special relationship with France, a country with which (she) shares a commitment to common principles',[67] or because the French relationship with the US may appear relevant to India in the new context developed between New Delhi and Washington.

The value of the Indo-French dialogue owes much to the quality of a relationship 'based on equality and mutual respect'. France makes a point not to hector India, and develop a dialogue 'free from rancour', and not 'dominated by nuclear proliferation and Kashmir',[68] contrary to the post-tests Indo-American dialogue. French and Indian diplomats and policy-makers discuss more than their short-term interests: democracy, human rights, sovereignty, right of interference. On some issues they converge. On other ones their judgements differ. The important point is that the dialogue is carried on. A few examples may be in order.

Hubert Védrine asserts that 'the great political values of democracy and respect for human rights' are universal values, but adds for the benefit of his Indian audience that 'the way in which the Western countries sometimes impose them through threats, or use them for their own purposes, can lead to suspicion and rejection'. He calls for an 'incremental approach to political transformation, because 'democratization is not like conversion, and ideological or religious revelation, but is rather a historical, sociological and economic' process.[69]

Such reflections, developed in the French think-tanks and in the French media (not without controversy) do strike a chord in India herself. These sentiments are echoed by key Indian decision-makers. For example, Brajesh Mishra commented in Paris about the problems raised by 'absolutism in human rights': 'when the West wanted to impose democracy and human rights by employing direct or indirect pressures, India preferred an evolution'. Yes, democracy and human rights ought to be promoted, but 'one must, however, proceed in a very guarded fashion, neither push (them) nor impose (them)'.[70]

If Védrine agrees that NGOs and civil society, whatever their contribution, cannot take over from the state in matter of diplomacy, he does not however preclude the possibility of interfering in special cases. He clarifies: 'We can no longer accept that leaders who perpetrate massacres and atrocities should, in the name of sovereignty, be able to oppose international interventions to protect peoples, provided this has been decided legitimately.'[71]

The standard position of New Delhi in this regard has always been, since the Nehruvian days, to assert the pre-eminence of national sovereignty. However, of late, unorthodox questions are now accepted in India, and even discussed by top-ranking officials. Indian Foreign Secretary Chokila Iyer acknowledged recently that 'the traditional absolutist notions of state sovereignty' is now under challenge. She was not referring only to 'the ongoing process of creation of supranational institutions in Europe', which 'could also impact on strategies and processes in our regions of the world', for 'voluntary surrender of sovereignty … is bound to be an increasingly intense and accepted phenomenon'.

The Foreign Secretary was directly addressing the 'dilemma' raised by 'genocide and egregious human rights violations': 'should the international community watch as a mute spectator, restrained by the sanctity of national sovereignty'? The answer is not yet clear, for the risks of a 'right or responsibility of humanitarian intervention and limits on national sovereignty, even if well-intentioned' could be 'based on the promise that external forces can resolve all problems, in all parts of the world'.[72] But the question has now been raised.

At stake are two related questions raised by Védrine about multipolarity: (i) how to organize a cooperative multipolarity, a positive relationship between the major powers? (ii) how could the poles establish 'an equitable relationship with the whole multilateral system, in other words all the UN member countries'? Védrine's answer may please India. To devise rules enabling 'the necessary humanitarian intervention to be decided on under less difficult conditions than those provided by the UN Charter' (…) is the exercise today assigned to the international community and especially to the permanent members of the Security Council and not just them, but also those destined to join them'.[73]

Could we conclude from the above that India and France share the view that 'community of principle is the basis of [a] multipolar world' as a commentator put it?[74] The hard *realpolitik* favored by the present Indian government may choose nice words sometimes, but might also be direct enough. When Jaswant Singh was asked 'where does (India) find her principal allies, her best friends?', he carefully avoided drawing a merit list, and chose rather to locate himself on ground occupied before by Talleyrand and Kissinger: 'I don't think countries have best friends. Countries have best interests.'[75] Singh had clarified earlier that 'foreign policy (means) the relentless pursuit of one's own national interest and not only the establishment of a just world order'.[76] I am not sure that the present paradigm of the French foreign policy, which does recognize the commanding national interest, would be so blunt regarding the quest for 'a just world order'.

Must we believe therefore that there is 'more hype than substance in the Indo-French relationship', considering the limited progress of economic relations, and the fact that, apart from the quest for a global balance, 'India does not fall within France's direct range of interest'?[77]

Beyond these uncertainties, a few facts must nonetheless be noted. First, the image of India has changed in the past decade. Liberalization and nuclear weapons have drawn French attention to India as never before. The trend does not affect only economic and strategic analysts. Contemporary India is entering the French market not just through government policies or textiles imports. In the field of culture, be it dance, music, cinema or literature, India has now found a larger audience and readership than in the past. Whatever questions may be raised about the sustainability of growth, the pace of reforms, or New Delhi's South Asian policy, this cultural visibility, not just confined to the traditional legacy, is an asset, a testimony of creativity, which have benefited Japan and China when their own images changed decades ago.

The balance sheet, furthermore, must not be evaluated at a bilateral level only. Behind the hyperbole of official speeches celebrating what makes India and France close to each other, their present rapprochement tells us more than a mutual (re)discovery, more than immediate shared interests. It offers a testimony of the new emerging world, where a complex geometry of international relations unfolds itself, still informed by the hegemonic network of the US 'hyperpower' (Védrine), but eager to celebrate 'the global cultural diversity' (Singh). Despite differences, a true comprehensive dialogue is carried on, just as India conducts other dialogues with very diverse countries, from old Russian friend to old Chinese foe. No best friends, only best interests? A cooperative multipolarity serves in fact the interests of all.

This is perhaps the conclusion one may draw from the recent interaction between a 60 million European nation and a billion-plus emerging India. By developing her relations with France, India is not guided only by economic considerations or access to defence technologies. Paris offers to New Delhi not an alternative to the US hegemony, but another way to look at global affairs, and an additional entry point to the European Union. This remains true after a new French government, headed by Jean-Pierre Raffarin, came to power in May 2002, following the re-election of Jacques Chirac as French President. Three months later, the new Minister of Foreign Affairs, Dominique de Villepin, was in South Asia. He reiterated to the Indian Press that the bilateral dialogue was held 'in a climate of great trust and openess'[78] and underlined how it helps 'to forge new strategic balances'.[79] The visit of the new French Prime Minister in India, planned for February 2003, confirms the willingness of both countries to carry on their positive relationship, not affected by the growing closeness between New Delhi and Washington.

The dialogue on international politics is clearly the leading thread between the two countries, stronger than trade interests. This reminds us that ideas, not just power, do matter. Beyond shared interests and an expanding cooperation, the Indo-French relationship, if not one of the most potent internationally, illustrates in its own way the much larger geopolitical quest for global adjustment presently unfolding. Bilateralism keeps its value, of course, but its impact must be assessed in a much more complex, multidirectional geography of relations and perceptions, which today designs the warp and the weft of the new world order.

It remains to be seen, however, which space will be left open to these multidirectional relationships by the growing and powerful assertiveness of the US. In this regard, the Indo-French current dialogue inserts itself in much broader debates, which put under scrutiny the strength of the European Union as a whole, compared to the weight of each of its member countries; the search for equilibrium between the US, Russia and China in the face of the new Asian dynamics; and the uncertain quest for a reformed United Nations system of global regulation.

NOTES

Thanks are due to policymakers, diplomats, defence experts and analysts who have offered me their time and their knowledge, in Paris and in New Delhi. Factual errors or misperceptions, if any, are entirely mine. The Centre for the Study of India and South Asia, CNRS-EHESS, Paris; the Indo-French Programme of Cooperation in Social Sciences (MSH, Paris & UGC, New Delhi); the Centre de Sciences Humaines in New Delhi and the French Institute in Pondicherry have all facilitated, one way or another, my visit and my stay in India.

1. For an assessment of Indo-French relations from Nehru to de Gaulle, see Boquérat (2001).
2. See Francis Doré, Chairman Indo-French Chamber of Commerce and Industry (1998).
3. See V.P. Dutt, 1999, pp.344–50.

4. As per a bilateral agreement coming to an end in 1993, France has supplied enriched uranium to Tarapur Plant from 1982 to 1993. Paris refused to carry on after the expiry of the agreement, for France was now adhering to the NPT, and had joined the Nuclear Suppliers Group set up in 1992.

5. The main litigations affected the HBJ gas pipeline project and the hydroelectric plant project of Dulhasi.

6. Alain Juppé's press conference, New Delhi, 4 April 1994.

7. Dominique de Villepin's father, Senator Xavier de Villepin, was the Chairman of the Senate Commission for Foreign Affairs and Defence until his son became Minister of Foreign Affairs in J.P. Raffarin's government in May 2002, while Jean François-Poncet, who was Minister of Foreign Affairs under President Giscard d'Estaing when Giscard visited India in 1979, is Chairman of the Senate Commission for Economic Affairs. He is also the French co-Chairman of the new Indo-French Initiative Forum set up after Chirac's visit to India. French parliamentarians (including X. de Villepin) have conducted several study tours in India during the 1990s, and Jean François-Poncet has organised at the Senate a seminar on India in 1996. Senator Chaumont's report defined changing India as 'a chance to seize'. See Villepin, 1994; François-Poncet, 1996, 1997; Chaumont, 1999.

8. Foreign policy is usually a matter of large consensus under 'cohabitation'. From de Gaulle onward, the Presidents, besides being head of armed forces as per the Constitution, also grasped a share of authority in foreign affairs. The similarity of views regarding India between the Right and the Left in power is nonetheless remarkable.

9. See Doré on economy, in *Le Figaro*, 22 Jan. 1998, Parmentier on security in *L'Express*, 22 Jan. 1998 and Racine on larger issues in *Le Monde*, 23 Jan. 1998.

10. The list of the delegation members reads as a 'Who is who' in banking, insurance, energy, services, engineering, information technology and aviation. The CEOs of Dassault, Aerospatiale, Thomson and Framatome were present, along with the Finance Minister and the Minister for Research and Technology.

11. Jacques Chirac's speech, Mumbai, 24 Jan. 1998.

12. The Forum defines itself as 'a high-level non-government group of eminent businessmen, scientists, academics, cultural personalities', but works in touch with the foreign affairs ministries of both governments. His Indian co-Chairman has been Dr Karan Singh, then Ramakrishna Hedge, whilst former French Foreign Affairs Minister Jean François-Poncet co-chairs since its inception. The Forum met for the first time in Paris in July 1998.

13. Jacques Chirac's speech, New Delhi, 25 Jan. 1998.

14. K.K. Katyal in *The Hindu*, 27 Jan. 1998.

15. The quote is the title of an unsigned piece published in *The Economic Times* on 14 May 1998.

16. Jasjit Singh's lecture on 'India's Strategic and Security Perspectives', Maison des Sciences de l'Homme, Paris, 2 June 1999.

17. See the symmetrical statements at an Indo-French seminar held in New Delhi in 2000. First, Hubert Védrine: 'in many areas the US engage in unilateral practices, be it the desire to bypass international institutions, in strategic decision-making, or in failing to meet commitments expected by the world community' (Védrine, in CERI & al, 2001, p.199). Then Jaswant Singh: 'The US approach tends to be perceived by other countries as an attempt at imposition of US values and standards – whether on human rights, nuclear and missile proliferation, multilateral trade issues, intellectual property rights (...). Many countries, including notably France and India, as well as Russia and China, have expressed reservations about at least some of these developments' (Singh, in CERI & al, 2001, pp.215–16).

18. See Védrine's interview to *The Hindu* on 15 Feb. 2000: multipolarity 'is all about reinforcing stability and co-operation in to morrow's world amongst all the poles, whatever these poles might be'. Védrine clarified in *Le Monde Diplomatique* issue of Dec. 2000: 'If I did not sign the final declaration, it was (...) because I could not agree that (...) there should be set up a holy alliance of democratic nations exclusively chosen by the State Department on the basis of dubious criteria (...) and taking instructions from that Department as to how vote at the UN'.

19. The IFPCAR has supported since its inception more than 200 research projects in fields as diverse as Life and Health Sciences; Computer and Information Sciences; Pure and Applied

Mathematics, Physics and Chemistry; Environmental Sciences; Instrumentation; Geophysics and Astrophysics.

20. A French ambassador to India has described as follows the Tarapur episode: 'As far as transfer of technology was concerned, France was used by India to by-pass the regulations, restraints or hostility of other industrialised countries like the United States' (Philippe Petit, in Banerjjee, 1994, p.244).

21. Atul Aneja in *The Hindu*, 2 Feb. 1999.

22. The Indo-Russian agreement includes, besides negotiations on the transfer and refitting of aircraft carrier *Admiral Gorshkov*, a deal for assembling in India under licence 200 of the 310 T-90 tanks ordered, and a deal for producing in India no less than 140 Sukhoi-30 MKI aircraft. In this context, the sale of 10 additional Mirage, although described as 'the biggest defence deal between India and France in the past decade' (*India Abroad*, 5 Jan. 2001), is far from challenging the Russian hegemony.

23. Lecture by Air Vice-Marshal Samir K. Sen: 'Technology and National Security, The Case of India', Indian International Centre, New Delhi, 24 July 2001. Among examples of delayed projects, the most quoted are the Arjun Tank and the Light Combat Aircraft. The LCA, expected to offer a substitute to the ageing MiG-21, made its successful test flight in Jan. 2001, 18 years after the programme has been sanctioned. Dassault was at a time associated with it, but withdrew.

24. See S. Kapila's assesment in paper 127 of the South Asia Analysis Group, 2000.

25. As quoted by Seema Sarin in *The Pioneer*, 3 Feb. 2000.

26. Alain Juppé's press conference, New Delhi, 4 April 1994.

27. On 5 Aug. 1999, one month after the Clinton-Sharif joint declaration which prompted the end of the Kargil conflict, Senator X. de Villepin asked the Foreign Minister 'if one could believe that India would be now willing to accept a greater implication of the international community on Kashmir'. He went to add: 'If we accept this assumption, should we not take and give rise to initiatives for transforming the Line of Control into an international boundary?' The answer came directly from the textbook: 'The bilateral dialogue alone could resolve the disagreement on Kashmir, through ways that India and Pakistan have to define, for all mediation proposals by a third party have failed' (*Senate Reports*, dated 16 Sept. 1999, p.3060). Minister Védrine clarified later on in New Delhi, that 'if the US could help moving things the right way, (France) would be very happy' (press conference on 18 Feb. 2000).

28. Alain Juppé's press conference, New Delhi, 4 April 1994.

29. Brajesh Mishra's speech, Lisbon, 13 April 2000.

30. K.R. Narayanan's speech, Paris, 17 April 2000.

31. Rasthrapati Bhavan, press release, 3 Aug. 2000.

32. French Defence Minister Alain Richard's speech at the United Services Institution of India, New Delhi, 19 May 2000.

33. The value of the French Franc has been fixed at FF 6.55957 for 1 Euro. In Jan. 2002, the conversion rate was 1US$ for 1.12 Euro.

34. Note on Indo-French economic relations, Indian Embassy in Paris (2000), see: www.amb-inde/indofrench1.htm

35. C.V. Ranganathan, in Banerjee, 1994, pp.241–2.

36. Audition of Jean-Bernard Ouvrieu, Personal representative of the French Defense Minister to the French Senate Commission for Foreign Affairs and Defense, 1 Dec. 1999. Ambassador Ouvrieu is also the French Head of the Indo-French High Commission for Defense since its inception.

37. Speech of President Chirac at New Delhi, 25 Jan. 1998.

38. Nirmala George in *The Indian Express*, 20 Oct. 1998.

39. Speech of President Chirac at New Delhi, 25 Jan. 1998.

40. 'The signing of the CTBT would clearly facilitate matters, as would its acceptance of more rigorous monitoring by the International Atomic Energy Agency. Another plus point: development of the co-operation we have already embarked on in the area of nuclear safety' Védrine's TV interview on 17 Feb. 2000.

41. Statement by Hubert Védrine during question hour, National Assembly, Paris, on 2 June 1998.

42. Chirac's speech, Paris, 8 July 2001.

43. France would answer here that if she had not diminished the role of nuclear weapons, she has seriously contributed to nuclear disarmament by being 'the first nuclear power to eliminate surface-to-surface missile systems' and for having, 'alone amongst nuclear powers, dismantled its testing centre and its facilities for the production of fissile materials for nuclear weapons', besides having ratified the CTBT in April 1998 (Chirac's speech, Paris, 8 July 2001).
44. Jaswant Singh's statement made in the Indian Parliament, 9 May 2000.
45. Brajesh Mishra's speech at the National Defence Institute, Lisbon, 4 April 2000.
46. Press briefing by the spokeperson of the Indian Ministry of External Affairs, 3 May 2001.
47. Joint Press Conference by Jaswant Singh and Igor Ivanov, 5 May 2001.
48. C. Raja Mohan in *The Hindu*, 7 May 2001.
49. See the Joint statement released by the White House, 21 March 2000.
50. Amitabh Mattoo in *The Hindu*, 5 May 2001.
51. Jaswant Singh's speech on 17 Feb. 2000. Published by CERI & al, 2001, p.217.
52. Hubert Védrine's interview to Doordarshan, Indian TV channel, 17 Feb. 2000.
53. Jaswant Singh's speech on 17 Feb. 2000. Published by CERI & al, 2001, p.213.
54. K.K. Katyal in *The Hindu*, 27 Jan. 1998.
55. K.K. Katyal in *The Hindu*, 22 May 2000.
56. Jairam Ramesh, at the rountable on US-India relations, New York, 1 Nov. 1999.
57. To quote Ramesh's speech again: 'America and India must have a multifaceted relationship which is durable enough to withstand political differences – examples of France and Israel come to my mind'.
58. Jacques Chirac's speech, Paris, 17 April 2000.
59. Alain Richard's speech, New Delhi, 19 May 2000.
60. Jacques Chirac's speech, New Delhi, 25 Jan. 1998.
61. Pakistan is naturally not eager to see India entering the sanctum sanctorum of global affairs. Noting that France's and Great Britain's declarations in favour of India marked 'a radical departure' from the Western appreciation of India's nuclear tests in 1998, a Pakistani analyst argued that 'the immediate reason for the change in the Western attitude seems to have been the American desire to capitalise on the opportunities offered by the Indian economic potential and its 200 million-strong middle class. What the British and the French have done is nothing but join the rat race in the hope of picking up some crumbs' (Ijaz Hussain in *Dawn*, 8 May 2000). The argument is not convincing, for foreign direct investments answer more specific market rationales.
62. A.B. Vajpayee's speech, Lisbon, 26 June 2000.
63. Hubert Védrine's interview to Doordarshan, 17 Feb. 2000.
64. Jaswant Singh, in *Defending India*, 1999, pp.34–5.
65. Jaswant Singh in *The Times of India*, 12 April 2001.
66. Jairam Ramesh's lecture, 1 Nov. 1999.
67. Jaswant Singh, in *World Affairs* 4/2, 2000, p.18.
68. David Fouquet, in *EIAS Bulletin* 4/2, 2000, on the web.
69. Hubert Védrine's speech, New Delhi, 17 Feb. 2000, published by CERI & al, 2001, p.202.
70. Brajesh Mishra's address at IFRI, Paris, 31 Jan. 2001.
71. Hubert Védrine's speech, New Delhi, 17 Feb. 2000, published by CERI & al, 2001, p.203.
72. Chokila Iyer's speech, New Delhi, 23 July 2001.
73. Hubert Védrine's speech, New Delhi, 17 Feb. 2000, published by CERI & al, 2001, p.203.
74. Mary Burdman in *Young India*, 1 April 2000, p.13.
75. Jaswant Singh's interview to SBS Television on 20 June 2001.
76. Jaswant Singh in *Defending India*, 1999, pp.34–5.
77. Vaiju Naravane, in *Frontline*, 2 March 2001.
78. Dominique de Villepin, *The Times of India*, 1 Aug. 2002.
79. Dominique de Villepin, *The Hindu*, 28 Sept. 2002.

REFERENCES

OFFICIAL STATEMENTS AND SPEECHES

Chirac, J. (French President), 'Address to the Indian and French Business Communities', Mumbai, 24 Jan. 1998.

Chirac, J., 'L'Inde et la France: un partenariat pour le XXIè siècle. Discours prononcé à New Delhi, le 25.1998', *Nouvelles de l'Inde*, Paris, No.315, pp.14–16.

Chirac, J., 'Speech delivered on the occasion of the State dinner given in the honour of Mr K.R. Narayanan, President of the Indian Union', Paris: Elysée Palace, 17 April 2000.

Chirac, J., 'Address to the Institute of Higher Defence Studies', Paris: IHEDN, 8 July 2001. See: www.elysee.fr/actus/arch0106:010608b/speech.htm

Iyer, C. (Indian Foreign Secretary), Speech at the International Conference on 'State Sovereignty in the 21st Century. Concept, Relevance and Limits', New Delhi, 23 July 2001.

Juppé, A. (French Minister of Foreign Affairs), 'Press Conference at the End of his Visit to India', New Delhi: French Embassy, 4 April 1994.

Ministry of External Affairs, 'Summary of Press Briefing by Official Spokeperson', New Delhi: Government of India, 3 May 2001.

Ministry of External Affairs, 'Excerpts from the Press Conference held by External Affairs Minister and Russian Foreign Minister Ivanov', New Delhi: Government of India, 5 May 2001.

Mishra, B. (India's National Security Adviser), 'Global Security: an Indian Perspective'. Presentation at the National Defence Institute, Lisbon, 13 April 2000.

Mishra, B., 'India and the Stability of the Asian Continent'. Address at the Institut Français des Relations Internationales, Paris, 31 January 2001, followed by a Q&A session. See: www.meadev.nic.in/govt/brajesh-31jan.htm

Narayanan, K.R. (Indian President), 'Discours prononcé lors du banquet offert par M. Jacques Chirac, Président de la République française', Paris, 17 April 2000.

Rastrapathi Bhavan, 'New Ambassador of France presents credentials', Press release, New Delhi, 3 Aug. 2000.

Richard, A. (French Defense Minister), 'European Defence and the Emergence of a New Multipolar World'. Address at the United Service Institution of India, New Delhi: USI, 19 May 2000.

Singh, J. (Indian Minister of External Affairs), 'Suo motu statement made in the Parliament on the NPT Review Conference', New Delhi: Lok Sabha, 9 May 2000.

Singh, J., Speech at the concluding session of the seminar on 'India and France in a Multipolar World' on 17 Feb. 2000, in CERI, CSH, IIC, *Indian and France in a Multipolar World* (New Delhi: Manohar 2001) pp.213–17.

Vajpayee, A.B. (Indian Prime Minister), 'Speech at the European Union-India Business Summit', Lisbon, 27 June 2000. See: www.amb-inde.fr/PM%20SPEECH.htm

Védrine, H. (French Minister of Foreign Affairs), Speech at the concluding session of the seminar on 'India and France in a Multipolar World' on 17 Feb. 2000, in CERI, CSH, IIC, *Indian and France in a Multipolar World* (New Delhi: Manohar 2001) pp.197–203.

White House, 'US-India Relations. A Vision for the 21st Century', Joint statement, Washington: Office of the Press Secretary, 21 March 2000.

PUBLISHED INTERVIEWS

Singh, J., 'India in a Changing World', *World Affairs* 4/2, 2000, pp.14–20.

Singh, J., 'China, not a factor in Indo-US ties', *The Times of India*, 12 April 2001.

Singh, J., Transcript of the interview given to 'Dateline' program on SBS Television, Australia, 20 June 2001. See: www.meadev.nic.in/govt/eam-australia.htm

Védrine, H., 'We believe in a Multipolar World', *The Hindu*, 12 Feb. 2000.

Védrine, H., Interview to the Televison Channel Doordarshan, 17 Feb. 2000. See: www.diplomatie.gouv.fr/actual/evenements/inde/vedrine6.gb.html

Védrine, H., Entretien avec la presse indienne, 18 Feb. 2000. See: www.diplomatie.gouv.fr/actual/evenements/inde/vedrine5.html

Villepin, D. de, 'Indo-French waltz', *The Times of India*, 1 Aug. 2002.
Villepin D. de, 'India, Pak. must resume dialogue', *The Hindu*, 28 Sept. 2002.

BOOKS, REPORTS, ANALYSES AND ARTICLES

Banerjee, D. (ed.), *Security in the New World Order. An Indo-French Dialogue* (New Delhi: Institute for Defence Studies and Analysis 1994).

Boquérat, G., 'Les relations franco-indiennes de Nehru à de Gaulle', paper presented at the seminar on 'Les relations franco-indiennes de 1693 à nos jours', Nantes University, June 2001.

Burdman, M., 'Community of Principle is the Basis of a Multipolar World', *Young India*, 1 April 2000, pp.13–15.

Chaumont, J., *L'Inde en mouvement. Une chance à saisir pour la France*, Rapport 476, Sénat (Paris: Sénat 1999).

CERI, CSH, IIC, *India and France in a Multipolar World* (New Delhi: Manohar 2001).

Délégation générale pour l'armement, *Rapport au Parlement sur les ventes d'armes de la France* (Paris: Ministère de la Défense 2001).

Dutt, V.P., *India's Foreign Policy in a Changing World* (New Delhi: Vikas 1999).

Fouquet, D., 'France's Védrine marks new links with Indian visit', *European Institute for Asian Studies Bulletin* 4/2 (2000). See: www.eias.org/bulletin.cfm?art_id=156&bul=49

François-Poncet, J. *et al.*, *Le pari indien*. Rapport 390 (Paris: Sénat 1996).

François-Poncet, J. *et al.*, *Le pari indien. II*. Rapport 73 (Paris: Sénat 1997).

Kapila, S., 'South Asia: France moves strategically towards India', South Asia Analysis Group, Paper 127 (2000). See: www.2000saag.org/papers2/paper

Petit, P., 'Indo-French Relations. A French Perspective', in D. Banerjee (ed.), *Security in the New World Order* (New Delhi: Manoahar 1994) pp.243–9.

Ranganathan, P., 'Indo-French Relations. An Indian Perspective', in D. Banerjee (ed.), *Security in the New World Order* (New Delhi: Manohar 1994) pp.239–42.

Ramesh, J., 'Yankee go home, but take me with you', speech at the seminar on USIndia (New York, 1 Nov. 1999). See: www.asiasociety.org/publications/yankeegohome_contents.html

Singh, J., *Defending India* (London: Macmillan 1999).

Villepin, X. de, *et al.* (eds.), *L'Inde, un 'pays-continent en mutation*, Rapport No.314 (Paris: Sénat 1994).

Védrine, H., 'Refonder la politique étrangère française', *Le Monde Diplomatique*, Dec. 2000.

Védrine, H., 'La diplomatie au service de la démocratie', *Le Monde*, 22 Feb. 2001.

Védrine , H. and Moisi, D., *Les cartes de la France à l'heure de la mondialisation* (Paris: Fayard 2000).

PRESS COMMENTS, ANALYSES AND OPINIONS

Agrawal, S., Brussels and Strasbourg, not London, *The Financial Express*, 14 April 2001.
Aneja, A., India, France seek long term defence ties, *The Hindu*, 2 Feb. 1999.
Doré, F., 'La visite de Jacques Chirac en Inde. Resserrer les liens', *Le Figaro*, 22 Jan. 1998.
George, N., 'Returns from the French Connection', *Indian Express*, 20 Oct. 1998.
Hussain, I., 'India's quest for Security Council seat', *Dawn*, 8 May 2000.
Katyal, K.K., 'Chirac visit restores warmth in bilateral ties', *The Hindu*, 27 Jan. 1998.
Katyal, K.K., 'India, France and Germany', *The Hindu*, 22 May 2000.
Mattoo, A., 'India in Bush's 100 days', *The Hindu*, 5 May 2001.
Montbrial, T. de, 'Le poids de l'Inde', *Le Figaro*, 16 Nov. 1996.
Naravane, V., 'A delicate equation', *Frontline*, 2 March 2001.
Padgaonkar, D., 'India, France agree to hold strategic dialogue', *The Times of India*, 3 Sept. 1998.
Parmentier, G., 'Attention à l'Asie du Sud!', *L'Express*, 22 Jan. 1998.
Racine, J.L., 'Les enjeux d'un voyage en Inde', *Le Monde*, 23 Jan. 1998.
Raja Mohan, C., 'India, France start strategic dialogue', *The Hindu*, 30 Sept. 1998.
Raja Mohan, C., 'In praise of diplomatic exuberance', *The Hindu*, 7 May 2001.
Sarin, S., 'India's French connection', *The Pioneer*, 3 Feb. 2000.

8

India and Israel: Emerging Partnership

P.R. KUMARASWAMY

Under normal circumstances, India's relations with a single country should not generate undue controversies, especially if the country in question is not a great power. Bilateral relations are motivated by shared political, economic, cultural or strategic interests and hence the absence of relations between any two sovereign countries would reflect the relative importance the countries in question attach to each another. However, Israel has been a unique case in India's foreign policy. The prolonged Indian reluctance and refusal to establish normal diplomatic relations with the Jewish State had been one of the most controversial dimensions of India's foreign policy. The four decades of non-relations as well as the extent of relations during the past decade have attracted widespread attention, comments and even criticisms.

The newly-found relations between India and Israel should not be dismissed as another example of bilateral relations. It heralded a new phase of assertive independence in India's foreign policy when it bade farewell to past rhetoric and ideological baggage and opted for interest-driven realism. For long, its Israel policy had been a prisoner of various regional pressures and domestic concerns and normalization is a departure from this past.

The establishment of resident missions did not accompany its hesitant recognition in 1950. Initial Indian inclination toward the establishment of normal diplomatic relations was not acted upon and soon it became a hostage to various domestic compulsions and regional apprehensions. As a result, for the next four decades non-relations with Israel became the hallmark of India's Middle East policy. On 29 January 1992, when Prime Minister Narasimha Rao remedied this anomaly and completed the process initiated by Jawaharlal Nehru, India became the last major non-Arab and non-Islamic power to establish diplomatic ties with Israel.

The importance of the changed international climate following the end of the Cold War played a significant role in Rao reversing protracted Indian unfriendliness if not hostility toward Israel. The collapse of the bipolar world order had granted new strategic space for regional powers to define their interests to optimize their security. At the same time, it is possible to argue that by breaking away from the past, Rao also signaled India's aspirations for great power status. Domestic political instability and fluctuations in coalition politics did not inhibit various governments from pursuing closer political as well as security cooperation with Israel. Even those parties such as the Communists, known for past animosity toward Israel, have quietly come around to recognizing and realizing the usefulness of the new situation.

Historical Baggage

The significance of India's newly found relations with a small state in the ever-turbulent Middle East could not be appreciated without a brief understanding of India's traditional position *vis-à-vis* Israel. The roots of this policy can be traced to the beginning of the twentieth century when the Indian nationalists forged a common cause with the Arabs of Palestine against British imperialism.[1] If the Judeo-Christian heritage influenced the West to adopt a sympathetic attitude toward the Jewish political aspirations in Palestine, even before independence, the Indian nationalists viewed the whole question through an Islamic prism.

Despite their sympathy for the centuries of Jewish suffering and subjugation, they were unable to appreciate and endorse the Zionist aspirations for a Jewish national home in Palestine. Mahatma Gandhi aptly summed up this unsympathetic Indian position: 'Palestine belongs to the Arabs in the same since that England belongs to the English and France to the French.'[2]

For his part, Jawaharlal Nehru perceived the Arab–Jewish conflict as part of the larger anti-imperialism that was sweeping the colonies. Rejecting any historical Jewish claims to Palestine, he observed: 'Palestine is essentially an Arab country and no decision can be made without the consent of the Arabs'.[3] Thus, despite half-hearted attempts in 1930s, the Zionists failed to secure the support of the Indian nationalists.[4]

Though important, neither Gandhi's moral arguments nor Nehru's anti-imperialist rhetoric explain India's lack of appreciation of Jewish aspirations. The intensification of Arab–Jewish conflict in Palestine coincided with the rivalry between the Indian National Congress and the Muslim League and this spilled over into the Middle East when the Palestine question was presented as an Islamic agenda. Indian leaders began to view the Jewish claims through an Islamic prism. The Zionist indifference toward India further consolidated this pro-Arab and pro-Islamic orientation of the Indian nationalists.

In 1947, India had the opportunity to articulate its independent position at the international level and thereby influence the course of events in Palestine when the issue came up before the United Nations. Representing Asia at the 11-member United Nations Special Committee on Palestine (UNSCOP), India reflected the orientation of the Indian nationalists and championed the Arab cause in Palestine.

Partly reflecting the Congress party's opposition to the Muslim League's 'two-nation theory', India sought to dismiss the Zionist demands and, supported by Iran and the then Yugoslavia, proposed a minority plan. While the seven-member majority advocated partition of Palestine, the minority plan suggested a federal Palestine with adequate internal autonomy for the Jewish population. When the UN General Assembly endorsed the majority plan on 29 November 1947, India joined the Arab and Islamic countries in opposing partition of Palestine.[5]

Meanwhile, the establishment of Israel and its acceptance by the international community compelled India to respond to new political realities of the Middle East. After much deliberation, Israeli persuasion and domestic pressures emanating from its pro-Arab legacy, on 18 September 1950, India granted *de jure* recognition to the Jewish state.[6] Shortly afterwards, Israel opened a trade office in Bombay (now Mumbai) which gradually transformed into a consular mission and the first Israeli Consul assumed office in June 1953. Though inclined to open a resident mission in Israel, citing financial constraints and scarcity of diplomatic personnel, India postponed any moves toward Israel.

Non-relation

What started as a routine issue soon transformed into a controversial foreign policy question. Nehru's assurances to Israel in early 1952 for normalization had to face domestic opposition, especially from his senior cabinet colleague Abul Kalam Azad.[7] Perceived opposition of the Indian Muslims aside, apprehensions over the Arab position on the Kashmir question played a role in the consolidation of pro-Arab policy.[8] Above all, Pakistani diplomatic efforts in the Middle East, especially Pakistan's campaign for an Islamic bloc sounded alarm bells in New Delhi.

Even though never officially admitted, India's Israel policy became a hostage to India's rivalry with Pakistan for diplomatic influence in the Middle East. In the pre-independent years, the Congress party adopted an unsympathetic position toward the Zionists partly due to its rivalry with the Muslim League and after 1947 India's rivalry with Pakistan shaped its policy toward Israel.

Gradually a host of regional developments and international trends prevented any meaningful interaction and understanding between India and Israel. The absence of ties drew widespread criticisms in both India and abroad. The emerging friendship between Nehru and Egyptian President Gamal Abdul Nasser turned out to be a turning-point in India's attitude toward Israel. Nehru saw the Egyptian leader as a symbol and leader of Arab nationalism and anti-colonial struggle in the Middle East. Nasser's commitment to secularism and socialism and his opposition to US-backed military alliances earned him Nehru's appreciation and support. It was natural that the Israeli invasion of Sinai in 1956 and its collaboration with the colonial powers infuriated Nehru, and for the first time he ruled out diplomatic ties with Israel on the plea that the 'time is not yet ripe'. Since then, this became a standard Indian refrain to explain the absence of diplomatic relations with the Jewish State.

Afterwards matters deteriorated and India moved closer to the Arabs and became less friendly toward Israel. Even occasional Israeli military assistance during India's conflicts with China in 1962 and Pakistan in 1965, did not arrest this downward spiral. India's support for the Arabs during the June 1967 war was a foregone conclusion. Under Mrs Indira Gandhi India found the newly formed Palestine Liberation Organization (PLO) a useful ally in the Middle East and in January 1975 she recognized the PLO as the sole and legitimate representative of the Palestinian people.

Even the *Janata*-led non-Congress government, which came to power in 1977, found it prudent to continue with the Middle East policy structured by Nehru and nourished by his daughter. With the result, the *incognito* visit of Israel's Foreign Minister, Moshe Dayan, during Morarji Desai's tenure proved to be more controversial and not especially fruitful.

In the international arena, opposition and hostility toward Israel was also on the rise. Countries that were neutral, if not friendlier, at the time of Israel's formation began to recognize and capitalize on the political benefits accruing from supporting the Palestinians. Those who benefited from economic and security aid from Israel in the past felt it prudent to adopt an anti-Israeli posture in public.

Since its exclusion from Bandung conference in 1955, the Afro-Asian community and the non-aligned countries were highly critical of Israel. With the Soviet Union and its allies providing a strong ideological foundation, anti-Israeli rhetoric became fashionable and politically correct.

Having aspired for a leadership role in the Afro-Asian world, non-aligned movement and among the Third World countries, India found it prudent and wise to adopt an unfriendly posture *vis-à-vis* Israel and availed itself of every opportunity to condemn Israel and establish its credentials among the Arabs. Neither the advent of Islamic resurgence and religious radicalism following Nasser's defeat in the June 1967 war nor the pro-Pakistan stand taken by principal powers of the Middle East made any significant dent in India's unfriendly policy towards Israel.

When she returned to power in 1980, Indira Gandhi upgraded the Palestinian mission in New Delhi to a fully-fledged embassy and conferred all diplomatic privileges and immunities. At the same time, the Israeli consul languished in Bombay. Even this minimal representation was curtailed following a controversial media interview by Yossef Hasseen, the then Israeli consul, in June 1982 wherein he criticized India for competing with Pakistan to curry favor among the Arabs. Though not off the mark, his comments infuriated the government and in an unprecedented move, Hasseen was declared *persona non grata*. Denials of visas to Israeli participants to international conferences and sports meets hosted by India became regular and in 1983 Israel was explicitly excluded from the Olympic Council of Asia (OCA), the supreme sport body of the continent.[9]

Prelude to Normalization

The arrival of Indira's son, Rajiv, in 1984 signaled a new trend in the Indo-Israeli relations. The ideological rhetoric of the past had no attraction for the young leader who sought to carry forward the country into the next century as a modern and technologically developed country. Abandoning the socialist traditions of the Congress Party, he initiated a policy of economic liberalization and adopted a somewhat non-ideological approach to foreign policy. His desire for freshness and a departure from the past also influenced India's Israel policy.

Moreover, Rajiv was also helped by a changed international climate favoring Israel. Until the outbreak of the Palestinian *intifada* in 1987, the 1980s witnessed a positive and less hostile trend toward Israel. Various countries of the Communist bloc had rekindled their ties with Israel suspended following the June 1967 war and this was followed by some Third World countries reexamining their position *vis-à-vis* Israel.

Despite its peace with Israel, Egypt was gradually readmitted into the Arab and Islamic blocs. Casting aside ideological underpinnings, both the Soviet Union and China have established regular but low-level contacts with Israel. Curiously, India's warming up with Israel coincided with the thaws between Israel and the Soviet Union.

These developments had a positive impact upon Rajiv Gandhi's Israel policy. During his five-year tenure, he initiated some small but significant moves toward normalization of relations with Israel. Unlike some of his immediate predecessors, he openly met with Israeli officials and pro-Israeli circles in the US. Without making any categorical statement on the thorny issue of normalization, he signaled a shift in India's perception of Israel. In some ways, his incremental measures toward Israel became an integral part of his policy *vis-à-vis* Washington. Among others, he restored a full consul in Bombay; extended the consular jurisdiction to the southern state of Kerala; relaxed visa procedures for Israeli passport holders; and abandoned the erstwhile ban on sports contacts with Israel by hosting the Davis Cup tennis event in 1987.[10]

However, certain factors worked against Rajiv Gandhi in seeking a complete normalization of relations with Israel. The outbreak of the *intifada* significantly eroded the gains that Israel made in early 1980s. Even traditional Israeli strongholds in the US found it difficult to endorse the Israeli response to the Palestinian uprising. Under this circumstance normalization became an unthinkable preposition. Rajiv Gandhi also faced a host of problems in the domestic arena, especially following the allegations of bribery in arms deals, which reduced his maneuverability.

However, the progress achieved during Rajiv Gandhi's tenure (1984–89) helped his Foreign Minister Narasimha Rao when the latter became Prime Minister in 1991. Rao began capitalizing on the political uncertainties following Rajiv Gandhi's assassination during the election campaign and the unstable political verdict. Political expediency compelled Rao to continue the policies of his Congress predecessors, especially Indira Gandhi and her son Rajiv. At the same time, the economic crisis, which compelled Rao to seek international financial assistance and introduce economic liberalization, made him recognize the need to modernize and improve foreign policy.

In a major departure from the past, on 16 December 1991 India voted with the majority in repealing the 1975 UN General Assembly resolution that equated Zionism with racism. As India was one of the original supporters of the infamous resolution, Rao's decision signaled a new approach toward Israel. Despite criticisms from opposition ranks over 'abandonment' of the traditional support for the Arabs, Rao continued the path of normalization and initiated formal diplomat contacts with Israel. And pursuing the path to its logical conclusion on 29 January 1992, India announced the establishment of normal diplomatic relations with Israel.

NORMALIZATION AND AFTER

Regional as well as domestic factors enabled Rao to reverse the prolonged unsympathetic attitude toward Israel. The inauguration of the Madrid conference in October 1991 significantly reduced the negative implications of opening up to Israel. The Middle East peace process symbolized the desire of both parties to seek a political solution to the protracted Arab-Israeli conflict through direct negotiations. In certain ways, the Palestinian willingness to co-exist with Israel vindicated India's desire for a peaceful and amicable resolution of the conflict.[11]

When the PLO itself was willing to accept Israel's existence and conduct negotiations with the Zionist state, there was no compelling reason for India to be more Catholic than the Pope. In the 1970s, the Egypt-Israel peace did provide an opportunity for India to reverse its Israel policy but Arab opposition to President Anwar Sadat's separate peace with Israel scuttled any room for maneuver. Matters were rather different in 1992 when even predominantly 'confrontationist' states like Syria had recognized the need to come to terms with Israel and seek a negotiated settlement based on mutual recognition and coexistence.

The end of the Cold War accompanied by the disintegration and eventual disappearance of the Soviet Union also dealt a severe blow to ideological opposition toward Israel. Even though India's anti-Israeli policy had not evolved in the Cold War, the East–West divide provided a strong ideological basis for it. Israel's exclusion and isolation from the Third World, non-aligned movement, Group of 77 and a host of other such forums were the result of perceived Israeli identification with the West as well as due to the ideological opposition of the East.

In the domestic arena, the Communists whose support was vital for Indira Gandhi, especially during her initial tenure (1966–77), provided a strong ideological foundation for the anti-Israeli policy.[12] The end of the Cold War weakened this ideological link within the Indian Left and anti-Israeli rhetoric was no longer coterminous with being pro-Arab.

At another level, forced to introduce economic liberalization, Rao recognized the incongruities of India's Israel policy. The success of the market economy depended heavily upon financial investments and technological cooperation from the West, especially the US. Since the late 1940s, Washington has been pressuring India to modify its policy toward Israel.[13]

As Foreign Minister under Rajiv Gandhi, Rao dealt with repeated American pressures over Israel and some of Rajiv's initiatives toward Israel during that period were indeed friendly gestures toward the US.[14] Even the decision to normalize ties with Israel was announced on the eve of Rao's visit to New York for the summit session of the Security Council and his meeting with President George H.W. Bush.

Though Pakistan still occupies a prominent position in India's foreign policy calculations and maneuvers, by 1990s the influence of Pakistan in determining the Israel policy appeared to be on the decline. Grudgingly India has come to recognize certain realities of the Middle East. Prolonged and consistent Indian support for the Palestinian cause did not endear India in the region, especially in the post-Nasser era. Even the Indian bureaucracy had recognized that during crucial times, a number of Arab and Islamic countries sided with Pakistan.[15] The internal divisions within the Arab world and the Palestinian unpopularity following their pro-Iraq stand during the Kuwait crisis exposed diminishing utility of the Palestinian factor. In short, anti-Israeli rhetoric was far less useful for Rao than for Indira Gandhi.

More to the point, there was a general international sympathy and understanding toward Israel, especially due to the restraint it exercised against the wave of Iraqi Scud missiles. A number of countries began to renew or seek new ties with Israel. The Soviet Union reestablishing diplomatic ties that were broken off in June 1967 preceded the inauguration of the Madrid conference. Casting aside ideological animosity and prolonged hostility, China also moved closer, recognized, and established ties with Israel.[16] India could not remain oblivious to this process.

Lastly, as subsequent events indicated, apprehensions over Muslim sentiments *vis-à-vis* Israel proved to be misplaced. As early as in April 1947 veteran historian, diplomat and Nehru's confidant K. M. Panikkar attributed lack of Indian understanding and sympathy for Jewish political aspirations to the role of the Muslim community in India.[17] Though apprehensive of discussing this question in public,[18] from the times of Nehru every prominent Indian leader had alluded to the role of domestic Muslim population as a major factor in India's Israel policy.[19]

Narasimha Rao, however, enjoyed some tactical advantages. Since the mid-1980s the Congress party has been steadily losing its traditional support among the Muslim electorates and, in the 1991 election, the party did not receive the endorsement and support of the self-styled Muslim leadership which asked its followers to vote for V. P. Singh's Janata Dal. This considerably weakened their leverage *vis-à-vis* the Congress party.

At the same time, Rao's move also evoked negative reactions. A decision that had taken more than four decades to be formulated was called a 'hasty and unprincipled' move. In their view, India should have waited until a comprehensive Middle East peace was in place. According to the conservative circles, so long as the Israeli occupation of Arab territories continued, normalization of ties was an aberration and betrayal of the traditional Indian commitments to the Palestinian cause.

One scholar went to the extent of portraying the normalization move as an 'anti-Muslim' alliance.[20] Such a charge, however, is rather ironic. For decades the erstwhile *Jana Sangh* and its later incarnation the Bharatiya Janata Party (BJP) had consistently advocated normalization. A Congress government formally committed to secularism took the final decision toward such a decision.

There were suggestions that some of the senior colleagues of Rao had reservations over this issue.[21] Repeated Indian reiteration of its support for the Palestinians and frequent denials of any military/security cooperation with the Jewish State were a reflection of the internal pressures and differences over this issue. Moreover, visits by Palestinian leader Yasser Arafat preceded or followed every major development concerning Israel.

With the sole exception of a brief visit by Foreign Minister Shimon Peres in May 1993, in the initial years, the bilateral ties did not see any high-profile contracts or visits. India's problems over the demolition of the controversial but historical mosque at Ayodhya and Israeli deportation of more than 400 suspected *Hamas* activists in December 1992 partly precluded any immediate high visibility in bilateral relations.

However, nearly a decade after Rao's decision, Indo-Israeli relations have been placed on a firm basis. Irrespective of the disagreements over specific issues concerning the Middle East peace process, bilateral relations ceased to be a contentious issue in India's foreign policy. Helped by the decentralization of power brought about by economic liberalization, state governments ruled by various political parties have sought and promoted strong economic ties with Israel.

Even parties which had originally opposed Rao's decision in 1992, such as the Janata Dal, have realized the benefits of economic cooperation with Israel. The visit by veteran communist leader and the then West Bengal Chief Minister Jyoti Basu in summer 2000 was a reminder that normalization enjoys widespread support in India.

From Rhetoric to Substance

If the Congress party was responsible for creating the necessary administrative framework for the promotion of bilateral ties, under the BJP the relations have gathered substance. True to its past record of pro-Israeli sentiments, the BJP has been pursuing an unapologetic foreign policy toward Israel. In mid-2000 the visits of Home Minister L. K. Advani and Foreign Minister Jaswant Singh raised eyebrows both in India and in the Middle East.

Even the negative publicity generated by the outbreak of the second *intifada* later that year did not materially affect the Indian position.[22] While the Israeli handling of the Palestinian uprising did witness the return of pre-1992 hostility and anti-Israeli rhetoric in the media,[23] the Indian government was content with general platitudes and did not join the international chorus in condemning Israeli handling of the violence.[24] As one leading commentator remarked, 'there is little reason for India to return to the old ways of doing diplomatic business in the region'.[25]

On the contrary, in December 2000, right in the middle of the crisis, the periodic meeting of Indian envoys in the Middle East was held in Israel.[26] Even negative media reports over the Indian contingent of the Lebanese-based United Nations Interim Force in Lebanon (UNIFIL) had not prevented India from signing defense contracts with Israel.[27]

There were suggestions and speculations in the media that a number of Arab and Islamic countries have expressed their apprehensions and displeasure over progress in Indo-Israeli ties. At times rescheduling of official visits to the region was attributed to the host's displeasure over India's Israel policy. One unnamed Arab diplomat even drew ideological parallels between BJP's *Hindutava* and Zionism.[28]

A careful perusal of the foreign policy track record of the government, however, indicates that far from antagonizing the Middle East, the Israel policy had induced key players such as Iran and Saudi Arabia to engage actively with India. If the former is rather keen to export oil through pipelines to India, the latter is keen to promote bilateral ties with New Delhi.[29] The Arab and Islamic countries do not appear to keep their bilateral ties with India a hostage to the Arab-Israeli conflict. Indeed, even Iraq was eager to improve its ties with India.[30]

The favorable climate provided by the political establishment in both countries set the tone for economic ties. The bilateral trade had crossed the $1 billion mark in 2000 and Israel has emerged as India's principal trading partner in the region. While the diamond trade still constitutes a substantial portion, its share in the overall trade is declining.[31] Israel is also one of the largest foreign investors in India. State governments, public-sector undertakings and private and individual firms have entered into numerous agreements with their Israeli counterparts. The establishment of direct air links has facilitated economic cooperation as well as increased the flow of Israeli tourists to India. Cultural contacts and exchanges are also on the rise.

However, the real progress in bilateral relations appears to be taking place in an area that both countries are reluctant to discuss: defense collaboration. One can argue that possible defense cooperation was one of the factors, which worked in favor of normalization. The absence of ties did not prevent India from seeking and securing limited military help from Israel in the form of small arms and ammunition.[32]

After some initial hesitation, both countries are actively promoting a whole range of defense-related cooperation. The day the terrorists struck the World Trade Center and the Pentagon, Israeli National Security Adviser Major General Uzi Dayan was holding high-level discussions with top Indian officials in New Delhi on terrorism. The following December a high-level Indian delegation was in Israel to coordinate anti-terrorist strategies.

The fight against Islamic fundamentalism, often mentioned as a possible common adversary, does not seem an attractive and sensible option. Without discounting the use of religion by some terrorist groups operating against India and Israel, both countries have been careful not to present themselves in alliance against militant Islam. Of late India has become a prime target for international and cross-border terrorism and hence it is natural that counter-terrorism is figuring prominently in their interactions, especially during Advani's visit.[33]

Remotely piloted vehicles (RPVs), Barak ship-borne anti-missile systems for the navy, ammunition for the Bofors guns during the Kargil operations, upgrading of MiG jets, and the supply of Phalcon airborne early warning systems are some of the prominent defense deals. In August 2001 after months of negotiations, India signed a series of defense contracts estimated at $2 billion for the supply of long-range surveillance equipment, night-vision hardware and ammunition.[34]

Properly constructed and pursued, such ties can be expanded beyond the cash-and-carry model. In areas such as avionics, aircraft upgrading, modernized weapons and missile systems, Israeli technological expertise can meet most of India's needs. As they are placed in a hostile regional environment, qualitative superiority and technological independence are vital for the long-term security interests of both countries.

India cannot achieve technologic progress and self-sufficiency without external assistance and participation. For its part, the financial viability of the defense industries is vital for Israel's ability to maintain its qualitative edge over its Arab adversaries. Israel enjoys certain unique advantages over other arms suppliers: its experience with weapons and systems of both the former blocs; the no-questions-asked policy that governs its arms trade; and its reputation as a reliable supplier and expertise in technological innovation and upgrading skills.

In short, India's search for technology and Israel's need for economizing defense research are complementary. Numerous strategic programs currently undertaken (or recently shelved) in both countries are complementary; these include Lavi (India's unnamed LCA) aircraft, Merkava (Arjun) tanks, Jericho-I missile (Prithvi), Jericho-II, (Agni) or RPVs. With the exception of the US, major defense frames are no longer built alone and therefore there is no reason why India and Israel cannot pool their resources and economize their defense production. Space and satellite programs offer another attractive area for long-term cooperation.

This potential aside, possible defense cooperation also benefits from Washington's amber-light approach toward the issue. Except for a brief period following India's nuclear tests in May 1998, the US has been indifferent toward Indo-Israeli defense ties. This contrasts with the American attitude toward Israeli-Chinese defense links. In the past, Israel was seen and portrayed as China's backdoor to Western technology.[35] Media reports over possible transfer of American military technology to China by Israel did not induce any public response from the Reagan administration.

Things began to change following the end of the Cold War when senior American officials began to act on suspected Israeli impropriety in its defense ties with China.[36] In a serious and highly controversial move, in early 1992 Israel was accused of illegally transferring Patriot anti-missile technology to China.[37] The controversy, coming in the midst of the ongoing tension between the Bush administration and the right-wing Israeli government under Yitzhak Shamir, led to each side questioning not only the veracity of the respective claims but also the motivations of the other.

Unlike the past, the mainstream American media was actively pursuing the allegation and in an unprecedented move, the Bush administration sent an investigation team to Israel to verify the allegation. Even though the inspection did not formally confirm the allegation, the controversy had done substantial damage to US-Israeli relations and led to the tightening of export regulations and US military aid to Israel. In short, due to technological as well as strategic concerns, the US is no longer willing to ignore Israeli-Chinese military ties.

This position contrasts with Washington's attitude *vis-à-vis* Indo-Israeli defense ties. Even the American sensitivities and subsequent sanctions following India's nuclear tests had not dampened the relations. While the US has been more concerned over speculations of cooperation in the nuclear arena, the general American position has been one of indifference and feigned disquiet. The protracted dialogue over the nuclear question and gradual improvement of the Indo-US relations will only enhance and facilitate Indo-Israeli defence ties.

In short, while India is seen as a potential friend and ally in the strategic calculations in Asia, there is no need for Washington to be apprehensive of such relations. So long as India and Israel dovetail their policies and pronouncements within the ambit of American non-proliferation concerns, the defense cooperation between the two countries is unlikely to figure on American radar screen.

In the foreign policy arena, the normalization was also a signal of India's determined effort to minimize the role of Pakistan in India's Middle East policy. India's obsession with Pakistan comes out clear in its Middle East policy where it allowed its rivalry with Pakistan to cloud its attitudes and approaches toward Israel. Its repeated emphasis on its secular credentials and its pronouncedly pro-Arab policy led to Pakistan becoming India's 'center of gravity' in the Middle East.[38] A host of Indian reactions toward Israel were a direct consequence of this preoccupation.

At the same time, the dividend of this policy has been minimal, especially during crises. Furthermore, by allowing Pakistan to occupy a dominant position in its foreign policy, India has undermined its claims for recognition as a great power. The diminishing appreciation of the Palestinian card also contributed to the weakening of the Pakistani factor.[39] Indeed, during Foreign Minister Jaswant Singh's visit to Saudi Arabia in early 2001, India went out of its way to claim that the bilateral ties were not aimed at Pakistan. Reacting to Pakistani concerns over his visit, Singh declared that such apprehensions 'would be misreading of India's intention and belittling the wisdom of the Saudi leadership'.[40] Growing political interactions and economic cooperation between India and countries such as Iran, Saudi Arabia and Turkey signify a calculated attempt not to make the Middle East policy a hostage to India's relations with Pakistan.

CONCLUSION

Since the normalization, the Indo-Israeli relations have grown considerably, encompassing political, economic, cultural and, above all, security relations. Prolonged neglect and indifference have not diminished the pace of ties. After some initial hesitations and apprehensions, the relationship is firmly in place. While the vagaries of the Middle East peace process and change of regimes in India could influence the pace, the overall direction is promising.

Despite pressures from certain Arab countries, primarily Egypt, India has defined its priorities and pursued a policy that is less rhetorical and more substantial. As a result, far from being a contentious issue, nearly a decade later, normalization enjoys widespread support in India. Even if a government hostile to Israel were to come to power in New Delhi, it would be unable to reverse and nullify the achievements since 1992. In addition to the absence of any bilateral conflicts and disputes, the improvement of the Indo-US relations adds a new and favorable climate to Indo-Israeli relations.

NOTES

1. Among others see, India, Ministry of External Affairs, *India and Palestine: The Evolution of Policy* (New Delhi, nd), M.S. Agwani, 'The Palestine conflict in Asian perspective', in Ibrahim Abu-Laghod (ed.), *The Transformation of Palestine* (Evanston, IL: Northwestern University Press 1971) pp.443–62; and Leonard Gordon, 'Indian nationalist ideas about Palestine and Israel', *Jewish Social Studies* (New York) 37/34 (Summer–Fall 1975) pp.22–134.

2. *Harijan*, 26 Nov. 1938, in *The Collected Works of Mahatma Gandhi* (New Delhi: Publications Divisions, Government of India, 1958 ff.) Vol.68, p.137.

3. Nehru's speech to the Asian Relations Conference in March 1947, *Asian Relations: Report of the proceedings and documentation of the first Asian Relations Conference, New Delhi, March–April 1947* (New Delhi, Asian Relations Organization 1948) p.70.

4. For discussions on Gandhi's position see, Gideon Shimoni, *Gandhi, Satyagraha and the Jews: A Formative Factor in India's Policy toward Israel* (Jerusalem: Leonard Davis Inst. for Int. Relations 1977), P.R. Kumaraswamy, 'Mahatma Gandhi and the Jewish national home', *Asian and African Studies* (Haifa) 26/1 (March 1992) pp.1–13; and Margaret Chatterjee, *Gandhi and His Jewish Friends* (Basingstoke: Macmillan 1992).

5. Indeed, consistent with this position, in May 1949 India voted against the majority when the Assembly approved Israeli application for UN membership. It is essential to remember that India was advocating a plan that it found unsuitable for the subcontinent where the Hindu–Muslim relation was less inimical than the Arab–Jewish ties in Palestine.

6. P.R. Kumaraswamy, 'India's recognition of Israel, September 1950', *Middle Eastern Studies* (London) 31/1 (Jan. 1995) pp.124–38.

7. Michael Brecher, *Nehru: A Political Biography* (London: Oxford 1959) pp.571–2; and *The New States of Asia: A Political Analysis* (London: Oxford, 1968 reprint) p.130.

8. It is often overlooked that at the UN the Kashmir question was discussed at the Security Council where the Arab states did not have a major say.

9. This move permanently excluded Israel from Asian Games even though Israel had participated in a few Games in the past.

10. P.R. Kumaraswamy, 'India and Israel: Prelude to normalization', *Journal of South-Asian and Middle Eastern Studies* (Villanova, PA) 19/2 (Winter 1995) pp.53–66; and 'India, Israel and the Davis Cup tie 1987', *Journal of Indo-Judaic Studies* (forthcoming).

11. Even at the height of anti-Israeli sentiments, India never endorsed the extremist aspirations of the Palestinians against the existence of Israel.

12. Indeed, at one time being a Leftist meant taking an anti-Israeli posture. Reeling under that influence one scholar described Israel as 'the illegitimate offspring of retreating imperialism'.

13. There are suggestions that in 1982 only American pressure prevented the closure of the Israeli consulate.

14. The return of a consul to Bombay and the extension of consular jurisdiction to Kerala were preceded by meetings between Indian leaders and American friends of Israel.

15. For example see Foreign Secretary J.N. Dixit's outspoken interview in *The Week*, 9 Feb. 1992, p.37.

16. Within days after the Chinese move, India followed suit. For a discussion on this linkage see, P.R. Kumaraswamy, 'South Asia and People's Republic of China-Israel diplomatic relations', in Jonathan Goldstein (ed.), *China and Israel, 1948–1998: A Fifty Year Retrospective* (Westport, CO: Praeger 1999) pp.131–52.

17. On the eve of India's independence Panikkar told the Jewish delegation from Palestine: '... once Pakistan is established, Hindu leaders and politicians may well take a pro-Zionist line'. Panikkar quoted in S.H. Bergmann and Yaacov Shimoni, Report on the Inter-Asia Conference, d.17 April 1947, *Central Zionist Archives*, Jerusalem, S25/7485. On 4 April 1947, Panikkar handed over a confidential note titled 'A memorandum on Hindu–Zionist relations' to the visiting delegation. For a discussion on this see, P.R. Kumaraswamy, 'Sardar K.M. Panikkar and India-Israel Relations', *International Studies* (New Delhi) 32/3 (July 1995) pp.327–37.

18. Foreign Minister Jaswant Singh's reference to Indian Muslims shaping India's Israel policy

at a lecture in Jerusalem in June 2000 evoked strong criticisms and rebuke.

19. Eliahu Elath to Moshe Sharett on his meeting with Nehru d. 14 Oct. 1949, *Documents on the Foreign Policy of the State of Israel* (Jerusalem: Israel State Archives) Vol.4, pp.547–8. Declassified Israeli documents frequently mention Indian diplomats referring to the feelings of the Indian Muslim population as a factor.

20. Among other see, Mani Shankar Aiyar, '*Chutzpah*', *Sunday*, 6 June 1993, pp.14–17. Punyapriya Dasgupta, 'Betrayal of India's Israel policy', *Economic and Political Weekly* 27/1516, 11–18 April 1992, pp.767–72; and Bansidhar Pradhan, 'India's policy toward the PLO', in Riyaz Punjabi and A.K. Pasha (ed.), *India and the Islamic World* (New Delhi: Radiant 1998) p.73.

21. According to a former foreign secretary, 'Arjun Singh felt that this decision might affect Muslim support for the Congress and went on to imply that establishing relations with Israel would be a departure from the Nehruvian framework of our foreign policy'. J.N. Dixit, *My South Block Years: Memoirs of a Foreign Secretary* (New Delhi: UBSPD 1996) p.311.

22. Congress leader Natwar Singh highlighted this dilemma of the opposition. While India should maintain good relations with Israel, 'it could not be at the expense of our relations with Palestine people'. *The Hindu*, 22 Oct. 2000.

23. For example see, Sukumar Muralidharan, 'Peace, and war', *Frontline* (Chennai/Madras), 10 Nov. 2000, pp.15–18.

24. K.K. Katyal, 'West Asia crisis tells on foreign policy consensus', *The Hindu*, 18 Oct. 2000.

25. C. Raja Mohan, 'India's West Asian stakes', *The Hindu*, 16 Oct. 2000.

26. *The Hindu*, 4 Dec. 2000.

27. Michael Jansen, 'Indian summer', *Middle East International*, 27 July 2001, pp.10–11.

28. John Cherian, 'India's changing stand', *Frontline*, 10 Nov. 2000, p.14.

29. There were no high-level contacts between the two countries since Indira Gandhi's visit to the kingdom in 1982.

30. Right in the middle of the *intifada*, Iraqi vice-president Taha Yassin Ramadan paid an official visit to India.

31. Likewise, energy resources account for bulk of India's trade with the Middle East.

32. For a detailed discussion see, P.R. Kumaraswamy, *India and Israel: Evolving Security Partnership* (Ramat Gan: BESA Center for Strategic Studies 1998).

33. Thomas Withington, 'Israel and India partner up', *Bulletin of the Atomic Scientists* 57/2 (Jan.–Feb. 2001) pp.18–19.

34. *The Hindu*, 16 Aug. 2001.

35. For a discussion on the military ties see, P.R. Kumaraswamy, 'The star and the dragon: An overview of Israeli-PRC military relations', *Issues and Studies* (Taipei) 30/4, April 1994, pp.36–55. For a skeptical account see, Yitzhak Shichor, 'Israel's Military Transfers to China and Taiwan', *Survival* 40/1 (Spring 1998) pp.68–91.

36. Duncan Clarke, 'Israel's unauthorized arms transfers', *Foreign Policy*, No.99 (Summer 1995) pp.89–109.

37. P.R. Kumaraswamy, 'Israel, China and United States: The Patriot controversy', *Israel Affairs* 3/2 (Winter 1996) pp.12–33.

38. E Sasson to S. Divon, d. 28 Dec. 1950, *Israel State Archives*, Foreign Office file 53/6b.

39. Moreover, despite its public rhetoric against Israel, Pakistan has maintained close contacts with the Jewish state dating back to the partition phase. For a recent discussion see, P.R. Kumaraswamy, *Beyond the Veil: Israel-Pakistan Relations, JCSS Memorandum 55* (Tel Aviv: Jaffee Center for Strategic Studies 2000).

40. *The Hindu*, 22 Jan. 2001.

9

The Political Economy of India's Second-Generation Reforms

SUNILA KALE

For four decades, starting with the implementation of the First Five-Year Plan in 1951, India followed a model of centralized economic planning. The foundational ideas of these planning decades were embodied in 14 pages of text written in 1944–1945 by Jawaharlal Nehru, while imprisoned in Ahmednagar Fort for his participation in nationalist campaigning.[1] In 1991, India's political leaders – descendents of Nehru's own political lineage ensconced in the Congress Party – announced a radical change of policy course: from that point onwards, the government would begin the task of disengaging itself from the economy, leaping off the metaphorical 'commanding heights'.[2]

The immediate impetus for adopting market reforms came from the fiscal and balance of payments crises that beset the country in 1991. As in many other developing countries that embarked on reforms in the 1980s and 1990s, the initial tasks of stabilization were carried out with some speed. Several other more complex tasks like dismantling barriers to trade and foreign capital, and liberalizing the investment regime were carried out in a gradual manner throughout the decade. Yet other reforms, such as privatization, eliminating subsidies, and conducting labour and agrarian reforms, were discussed but not implemented during the first decade of reforms.

Of all the remaining items on the bold new economic agenda announced in 1991, privatization and the scaling back of the public sector have proven to be the least successful and most susceptible to political derailing. Since the first days of reform in 1991, Indian politicians and policymakers have argued that the successful transition from a planned economy to a market economy would hinge on effectively minimizing the role of public sector enterprise and privatization. Despite the periodic professions of continued commitment to undertaking reforms in these areas, little in the way of concrete action has been seen, especially in contrast to the wide-sweeping activity in trade, investment, and financial sector reforms.

Why has India made considerable progress in some areas of reform while other areas of the economy were left largely untouched during the 1990s? And second, why, after trying unsuccessfully to implement a privatization program at myriad points in the 1900s, has the government begun to see limited success in this effort in 2001 and 2002?

In September 2001, the McKinsey Global Institute outlined a 13-pronged strategy to achieve 10 per cent growth of India's gross domestic product (GDP). On their list of recommendations are provisions for eliminating subsidies that distort the product markets in goods and services; reducing barriers that disturb factor markets; minimizing government ownership at both the central and state levels; abolishing the reservation of products for small-scale industries; raising property taxes and tariffs for municipal services; and reforming labor laws.[3] These recommendations echo the suggestions made by advocates of neo-liberal reform inside and outside of the Indian government since the early 1990s.

In this essay, I survey the current status of reforms – both those that have already been completed or are underway and those that are finally being pursued after ten years of false starts – and offer a preliminary explanation for the difference between the two.[4] In doing so, I focus on one reform strategy that the government has had particular difficulty implementing: public sector retrenchment and privatization. I suggest that the growing, though still limited, success with privatization is due in large part to the new institutional environment of competitive investment unleashed by earlier waves of market reform.

In what follows I first briefly situate my argument within a larger debate about the conditions under which market reforms are realized. In the next section I discuss Rajiv Gandhi's attempt to liberalize the economy in the mid-1980s. This is followed by a section describing the crisis of 1991 and the reforms to date.[5] The remainder of the analysis will take up public sector reform and privatization, and draw from the case of the 2001 privatization of one large public sector firm in northern India, the Bharat Aluminium Company Limited (BALCO).

SECOND GENERATION REFORMS AND COMPETITIVE INVESTMENT

Scholars investigating the conditions under which market-oriented reforms are likely, initially posited a relationship between regime-type and reform-mindedness. Some argued that democracy and reform ability are negatively correlated, as leaders in democratic societies are encouraged to provide immediate consumption, thus stealing resources from the pool available for future spending or investment, and making policy goals like balanced budgets and the elimination of subsidies impossible feats.[6]

A second wave of scholars, finding little systematic evidence of a link between regime-type and reform abilities, argued that democracies can be equally good reformers; the spirit of public debate that pervades democratic societies allows democratically elected leaders to build coalitions in support of reform without resorting to the oppressive tactics of authoritarian states.[7]

Neither the first argument – that democracies are inherently deficient reformers – nor the revisionist variant just described, can fully explicate the Indian case. While it is true that democratic governments can engage in reform, the Indian experience suggests that the kind and sequence of the reforms is dramatically affected by electoral exigencies.[8]

In India, the neo-liberal reforms that are perceived to have the most immediate effect in terms of job and wage losses, and thus, the reforms that are most likely to inspire immediate popular opposition, have been for the most part forced off the reform table during the first reform decade. These include public sector retrenchment and privatization, labor reform, measures to curtail government subsidies and other spending, and agrarian reforms. Each of these reforms carries the threat of short-term job and/or welfare losses. They are known collectively by the moniker 'second-generation reforms', and to date, they are a generation that is largely unborn.

When these reforms have been successful, they have been accomplished not because politicians have successfully swayed public opinion to craft coalitions in their support, but often by what Rob Jenkins has described as 'reform by stealth'.[9] The 'unseemly underside of democracy', according to his argument, enables leaders to use savvy political skills in manipulating the circuitry of democratic institutions to deflect attention from reforms, dress reforms in the garb of the status quo, and shift the onus and responsibility for reforms to other levels of government in India's federal system.[10]

As the privatization, or disinvestment as it is called in India, of BALCO suggests, the bifurcation of political power between the state and the center, and the new environment of competitive investment promotion that resulted from opening the economy to private investment, play important roles in simultaneously shaping and delimiting the political strategies available to both incumbent and opposition leaders.

On the one hand, four consecutive democratically elected governments in India in the 1990s were able to pass important legislation that carried India far from its historical moorings in centralized planning and towards a market-oriented system. However, as others have pointed out, the kinds of reforms that India's leaders have enacted had little direct, obvious, or immediate effect on India's masses.[11] In the parlance of economic reform literature, the reforms of India's first decade were met by little organized resistance from the *losers* from reform and important support from a small but influential group of the potential *winners* from reform.

On the other hand, the reforms that have yet to be undertaken are all met by sizeable and organized opposition from those, who stand to lose in the immediate term. Some students of Indian political economy have suggested that the structural adjustments that remain to be attempted may yet require another crisis such as the one faced in 1991 to allow politicians the necessary latitude to execute them.[12] However, the privatization of BALCO suggests that while these reforms are fraught with difficulties and political opposition, some will ultimately prevail partly because the first-generation reforms changed the rules of the game for India's political leaders. Most notably, earlier reforms created an institutional environment that forces current leaders from different states to appear pro-reform in order to compete with each other for investment.

The dynamic of the new institutional environment emerges from the economic and political transformations that India underwent throughout the 1990s that have affected the way states relate to one another and to the central government. This in turn has shaped state-level political economic processes.

Of the many consequences of the economic reforms of the early 1990s in India, one stands out: reform created incentives for the states to compete against each other for investments. Prior to the early 1990s, the central government regulated investment, which included assigning the location and scope of new projects. But after the central government reduced its regulatory load and decreased public investment, states have been increasingly competing to secure private investments.

One result of this transformation is that opposition regional parties – even left-leaning ones like the communist government in West Bengal – have simultaneously implemented neo-liberal policies within their own states that are seen as necessary to be competitive, even while protesting similar reforms at the center. Similarly, members of the Congress party volubly protest economic reforms at the center, where it is the largest opposition party, while at the same time supporting reforms in Congress-led state governments.

Seemingly contradictory policy stances become clear when considered in the light of this double-bind of political leaders, as I will illustrate further with the case study of the privatization of BALCO. First, however, we should understand that the history of the current era of reform begins during Rajiv Gandhi's stewardship.

RAJIV GANDHI'S REFORM EFFORTS

In 1985, without the stimulus of a severe economic crisis or inducements from international financial institutions, the newly elected government headed by Rajiv Gandhi initiated a series of economic reforms, the ultimate goal of which was to open India to the global economy, lift the labyrinthine regulations on economic activity within the country, and eliminate the subsidies and price controls that tied the government to powerful domestic constituencies.

Many scholars of political economy contend that an economic crisis is necessary to create popular acceptance and a strong political coalition in support of often-unpopular reforms.[13] The Gandhi regime's short-lived encounter with reform lends support to this thesis. The Congress government was beset with protest on the streets in the form of strikes and in some cases riots; opposition from rival political parties and from within the Congress party; and disapproval from powerful industrialists close to the government.

The budget for 1985–86, presented by Finance Minister V.P. Singh, took several steps to dismantle elements of the centrally planned economy, particularly in the areas of trade and investment. The proposals included the removal of licensing requirements for a handful of industries, an increase in investment limits, reduction in tariff restrictions on some imports, substitution of tariffs for quantitative restrictions on some goods, and active encouragement of exports through tax concessions. Without specifying a concrete course of action, the government also declared the need for public sector reform. Like the 1985–86 budget, India's Seventh Five-Year Plan, which covered the years 1985–86 to 1989–90, advocated economic liberalization.[14]

In early 1986, the government announced plans to reduce subsidies in order to address fiscal imbalances. The targeted subsidies, which included petroleum, food, fertilizer, and transport, adversely affected the poor and middle class alike, and gave Gandhi's political opponents a popular policy platform from which to criticize the government. The labor strikes and rallies, many of which were organized by opposition political leaders, had the effect of alarming members of the Congress party, who joined the opposition in demanding a reduction in subsidy cuts, a demand with which the government soon complied.

Since the landslide victory in the 1984 elections, in which Congress secured 514 out of 545 seats in the lower house of parliament, the Congress had lost in elections at the state and local levels. Dissidents within the Congress party attributed some of these losses to the dissatisfaction of the majority of Indians with Gandhi's reformist agenda.[15]

Opposition to the reform policies spread to rival political parties who spun Gandhi's pro-reform stance as anti-working class and anti-poor. Not only had the government enacted tax cuts for business, providing powerful fodder for Gandhi's opponents, but the economy did not react positively to the liberalization measures. Inflation remained near 10 per cent and the trade deficit increased.

In addition to opposition from political leaders and unions, Gandhi's liberalization program increasingly drew ire from the business community. While some in the business community approved of the attempts to alleviate licensing requirements, many others were being hurt by unfamiliar foreign competition.

The bulk of Gandhi's success with reform came within the first two years of the regime. Starting in 1986 opposition to reform had magnified enough to make further changes politically difficult, despite the overwhelming majority of the Congress government in parliament. Political disturbances in Punjab and accusations of corruption within Gandhi's inner circle further constrained the government.

A comparison of the 1985–86 budget proposals, described earlier, with the one introduced for 1986–87 reveals the extent to which the Gandhi government backpedaled on liberalization. To counter the effects of being painted as pro-rich, the government responded by levying duties on televisions, air conditioners, cars, and refrigerators, tax-cuts for wage-earners, and an increase in spending on poverty alleviation programs of 65 per cent. These measures together effectively signaled the end of the market-reform effort. Despite this failure, however, the idea of liberalization had taken root in some bureaucratic circles in Delhi. Members of these circles would play an important role in a renewed reform program only five years later, one that was spurred by economic crisis.

THE 1990S: A DECADE OF REFORM

Though the 1990s saw steady economic growth and achievements in economic reform, it began in crisis. A broad confluence of factors contributed to India's economic bind in 1991. Although the Indian economy grew more quickly during the 1980s than it had during previous decades, the proportion of the central government's fiscal deficit grew over the decade as well. By the mid-1980s, the fiscal deficit represented approximately 8 per cent of GDP, and it continued at that volume through the remainder of the 1980s. Inflation also grew over the course of the 1980s, and stood at 10 per cent at the start of the 1990s. The public sector continued to absorb much of the country's investment capital without contributing to the economy proportionately.

Iraq's invasion of Kuwait in August 1990 and the ensuing Gulf War strained India's already precarious economic position. The World Bank asserted that India, along with several other South Asian and East Asian countries, was among the most adversely affected due to the escalation in oil prices, loss of foreign exchange earnings of workers in the Gulf region, displaced workers, and reductions in export profits.[16]

In the culmination of these dynamics, India found itself with foreign exchange reserves adequate to finance only two weeks of necessary imports, a lowered investment rating that made additional loans more costly, and the prospect of defaulting on its international debt payments.[17] The immediate task of the government was to re-establish macroeconomic stability, prevent a default on debt payments, and bring down inflation, all of which the government accomplished despite being one of the most fragile governments since independence.

Since the early days of crisis management, the Indian government has implemented decisive market-oriented reforms in areas of economic life. The most substantial and most visible of these are the reforms made to trade and investment regulations, and financial sector liberalization. For the most part, reforms have been carried out in an incremental fashion, by a gradual lowering of rates and barriers rather than any drastic movements.

The government has implemented measures lifting constraints on private investment, and generally enabling new investments to be determined by market mechanisms rather than by government discretion through centralized plans. Industrial licensing requirements were lifted to allow firms to increase capacity in existing plants and establish new plants without first clearing excessive bureaucratic hurdles. In addition to changes in the licensing regime, the universe of industries reserved for the public sector has periodically contracted.

In 1991, at the start of reforms, 18 industries were reserved for the public sector. The July 1991 industrial policy statement reduced this number to eight, and a subsequent policy in 1993 further decreased the list of reserved industries to six, in which the government would retain at least a 51 per cent controlling stake. The six were coal and lignite; mineral oils; ammunition and defense equipment; atomic energy; radioactive minerals; and railway transport.

In March 1999, these six were further categorized into strategic and non-strategic sectors, and only ammunition and defense equipment, atomic energy, and railway transport were classed in the former category. In these sectors, the government would retain strategic control. For all other public sector firms, the decision to decrease government ownership below 51 per cent would be made on a case-by-case basis.[18]

Like the reform of investment regulations, changes to the trade regime proceeded at a measured pace. In 1991, average Indian tariff rates, on a trade-weighted basis, stood at 87 per cent, a figure that fell gradually over the course of the decade, and hovered around 25 per cent from 1997 to 2001.[19] Similarly, quantitative restrictions (QRs) were decreased throughout of the decade, and were entirely eliminated in April 2001. The government continues to employ other non-tariff barriers as well as tariffs, often at the behest of members of the business community.

In addition to changing the rules of trade and investment, the successive pro-reform governments of the 1990s also significantly changed the regulations governing foreign direct investment, portfolio investment, and the insurance and banking sectors. In tandem with a diminished regulatory load, the Indian government also de-emphasized its investment role. Private interests, in turn, have become far more autonomous in their investment decisions at the same time that their importance for economic growth and expansion has intensified.

Now, not only does the central government try to enhance its attractiveness as a site for foreign direct investment, but state and local governments are also in the business of wooing investment. The stars of Indian politics in this regard have been entrepreneurial politicians like the Chief Minister of Andhra Pradesh, Chandra Baba Naidu, who has traveled abroad and courted foreign businesspeople in India to sell his state's investment potential.

Despite all of the undoubted reform momentum of the 1990s, several areas have been largely untouched. These include agriculture and land reform, labour reform, the elimination of the still substantial barriers to an internal market, and public sector reform and privatization. The latter two in particular have proven to be especially susceptible to political derailing. I address these issues in the remainder of the essay, by discussing first the rise of public enterprise before turning to the recent attempts to shrink the public sector.

Expansion of the Indian Public Sector

The Indian public sector dates back to the days just after independence in 1947. Like Nehru, the majority of Indian leaders were committed from the start to a socialist plan of development and industrialization. In some developing countries there was a sense among leaders that the state was intervening on a temporary basis to protect infant industries, and forming enterprises that would later be turned over to the private sector. In contrast, state-owned enterprises (SOEs) in India were considered viable long-term operations.

The Industrial Policy Resolution of 1948 reserved the manufacture of arms, production of atomic energy, and railway networks for state monopoly, and further identified six basic industries (iron and steel, coal, aircraft manufacture, shipbuilding, mineral oils, and telecommunications) that would be developed by the state. All other sectors were left open to private development.

The Industrial Policy Resolution of 1956 further extended the purview of the public sector and subdivided all sectors into three categories. Seventeen sectors were to be reserved for the public domain, 12 would be occupied by both public and private enterprises, and a third category of industrial activity was considered to be solely the domain of the private sector. Initially, the first and second categories were primarily composed of basic and heavy industries.

The Indian government gave five principal justifications for the creation and expansion of public sector enterprise.[20] First, at the time of the First Five Year Plan, there was a global consensus that spanned the divide between developed and developing countries in favor of state enterprises as a means of achieving economic growth. Second, there was a dearth of capital available in the market to finance large new enterprises. The government was able to maintain high tax rates and engage in deficit spending to marshal the necessary capital to invest in new enterprises. Third, the Indian government used the public sector to protect labour in the private sector, largely by establishing a policy of absorbing 'sick' or failing private sector firms into the public sector. Fourth, state ownership was intended to ensure that certain strategic sectors remained in public hands and worked for general social welfare; and finally, state enterprises were used to develop the economy in terms of diversifying its sectoral output, promoting development in regions that were hitherto industrially backward, creating jobs, and bringing low cost goods to the domestic market.

Government involvement in industry became deeper and broader throughout the subsequent decades. In addition to the handful of strategic sectors that were initially reserved for the public domain, the public sector proliferated due to the creation of new enterprises and the nationalization of private firms. It also diversified its output to the extent of producing textiles, footwear, leather goods, bread, television sets, and bicycles.

In addition to managing myriad large and small SOEs, the government created a regulatory environment, famously described as the 'license-permit Raj', that constrained private capital and tied it to the government as well. The SOE sector continued to expand under the leadership of Nehru's daughter, Indira Gandhi, and it was not until large-scale fiscal and balance of payments crises erupted in the late 1980s that the governing élites took steps to limit the construction of new public sector units.

Even from some stalwart proponents of market-reform there is a grudging recognition that the Indian public sector was successful in accomplishing a handful of the tasks for which it was intended. In a matter of a few decades the Indian economy had developed large industries and multiplied the number of goods produced domestically. On the other hand, critics suggest that some items on the agenda, like protecting labor, were almost too successfully accomplished. Unfortunately, the result was the creation of a labor aristocracy in the public sector that did not contribute to any meaningful redistribution and stunted job growth.

Table 1 provides data on the growth of public enterprises under the direct control of the central government. What becomes clear from examining the growth trajectory of the public sector is that the decision to privatize was a sudden one; the public sector continued to grow in terms of investments and number of firms until one year after the new economic agenda was unveiled in 1991. Since the adoption of the new policies, the public sector has stagnated, and although the central government publicly advocated liberalization, privatization in India has not proceeded apace.

The multiplication of public sector enterprises under the direct control of the central government proceeded in tandem with the development of public enterprises at the state level. Estimates of the total number of state level public enterprises range from 755 to 954 to 1,100.[21] The data on state level public enterprises (SLPEs) are far more sparse and unreliable than those available for CPEs. However, the general perception of state level enterprises is that they under-perform relative to the central units. While the

TABLE 1

INVESTMENT IN CENTRAL PUBLIC SECTOR ENTERPRISES (CPEs)

Time period	Total Investment (Rs crore)	Number of CPEs
Start of the 1st Five-Year Plan, 1951	29	5
Start of the 2nd Five-Year Plan, 1956	81	21
Start of the 3rd Five-Year Plan, 1961	948	47
End of the 3rd Five-Year Plan, 1966	2,410	73
Start of the 4th Five-Year Plan, 1969	3,897	84
Start of the 5th Five-Year Plan, 1974	6,237	122
End of the 5th Five-Year Plan, 1979	15,534	169
Start of the 6th Five-Year Plan, 1980	18,150	179
Start of the 7th Five-Year Plan, 1985	42,673	215
End of the 7th Five-Year Plan, 1990	99,329	244
Start of the 8th Five-Year Plan, 1992	135,445	246
End of the 8th Five-Year Plan, 1997	213,610	242
1998	231,024	240
1999	239,167	240
2000	252,554	240

Source: Ministry of Disinvestment, Government of India, 'Annual Report 2000–2001'.

central government has had great difficulty building political coalitions in support of restructuring and privatizing, some state governments seem to be making limited progress.

Privatization

Even now, despite rhetorical support for privatization, there remains disunity within the government, and many bureaucrats continue to support the idea of public enterprise. Two government bureaucracies that are involved in the public sector and efforts at privatization are the Ministry of Disinvestment, formed in December 1999, and the Department of Public Enterprises, housed in the Ministry of Heavy Industries and Public Enterprises. Public statements from these two nodal agencies reveal clearly that there is a wide range of opinion on the utility of public enterprises and the effectiveness of privatization within the state apparatus itself. While the former agency emphasizes the progress in privatization, the latter organization calls attention to the improved performance that has resulted from enterprise restructuring and operational reforms.

Those who deem public sector reform and disinvestment to be critical for India's economic health argue that these methods constitute the best hope for reducing the fiscal deficits of the center and states, which combined stand at approximately 10 per cent of GDP. For example, the

International Monetary Fund has suggested that it is largely the fiscal deficit that bars the way of India achieving 8 per cent to 9 per cent GDP growth rates.[22]

These views are supported by an extensive theoretical and empirical literature concerning the greater economic efficiency of the market relative to the state. The state, it is argued, should extricate itself from all business and confine itself to the provision of a handful of public goods.

The market-oriented policies begun in 1991 were sold politically on the promise that neither workers and farmers nor small business people would be hurt.[23] To the extent that the reforms of the early years did negatively impact these groups, the situation was tolerated because the economic crises of 1991 created a coalition in support of reform. Many of the so-called second-generation reforms that are next on the government's agenda, in contrast, are perceived to threaten the immediate welfare of core political constituencies. Meanwhile, the unifying impact of the crisis has long since dissipated.

Opposition to privatization and labor reforms in particular, and growing dissatisfaction with neoliberal reforms in general, has been exacerbated and strengthened by several other characteristics of the reform decade: economic growth has been perceived to be uneven by region and by sector, causing those who lost out in the process to resist further changes.

On 29 November 1991, workers in India's sprawling public sector staged a one-day strike in response to government announcements that loss-making public sector units would be shut down.[24] In sectors of the economy that are primarily filled by public sector enterprises, like banking, air transport, insurance, and energy, the strike successfully brought operations to a halt, although it had a less dramatic effect on sectors that are also populated by private firms. The strike was the first response by Indian labor to the economic reform plans of the Rao government. Not surprisingly, the cause of the protest was the government's announcements to begin privatization and public sector closures, rather than any of the other stabilization and liberalization elements of the new economic policies of 1991.

Once the call for a strike was made in early November, the Rao government responded by announcing, during a meeting of the World Economic Forum in New Delhi, that India would not begin privatization, and that even discussing privatization was premature at the current time. A measured pace of action in these issue areas, Rao contended, was required to maintain political and social stability within the country.[25]

In 1998, on 10 and 11 December, workers in all of the central public sector units again went on strike to protest a reinstated commitment to privatization and the imminent closure of eight sick public units. Spearheading the strike was the Centre of India Trade Unions, which is allied to the Communist Party of India (Marxist). The federation of trade unions allied to the Bharatiya Janata Party (BJP), the Bharatiya Mazdoor Sangh (BMS), did not participate in the strike, accusing the organizers of having political rather than union motivations.[26] On 16 December, a week after the first wave of strikes, 200,000 workers in India's state-owned insurance companies staged a one-day strike to protest the introduction of legislation to privatize the insurance sector and open it to foreign investment.

Throughout the decade, each instance of government officials affirming their intentions to privatize was met by organized resistance and then followed by a quick announcement of policy reversal by political leaders. As a consequence, the governments' aspirations to raise hundreds of crores through sales of public assets have been largely unrealized (see Table 2). As of mid-2000, the government had managed to reduce its equity in approximately 39 of the 240 central public enterprises, but had successfully sold a controlling stake, or a percentage in excess of 51 per cent, in only two units. BALCO was slated to become the third. In seven of the past nine years, the government failed to reach the target for revenue through privatization that it established at the outset of each year.

The Strained Disinvestment of BALCO

The privatization of India's Bharat Aluminium Company Limited, the country's third largest aluminum producer located in the newly created state of Chhatisgarh, is emblematic of the high political hurdles that the government faces in privatization and the joint role that labor and political

TABLE 2
DISINVESTMENT IN PUBLIC SECTOR UNDERTAKINGS

Year	Target (Rs crore)	Achievement (Rs crore)
1991–92	2500	3038
1992–93	2500	1913
1993–94	3500	Nil
1994–95	4000	4843
1995–96	7000	362
1996–97	5000	380
1997–98	4800	902
1998–99	5000	5371
1999–2000	10000	1821

Source: Ministry of Finance, Government of India, 'Economic Survey, 2000–2001'.

opposition play in forestalling disinvestment. What the central government's Ministry of Disinvestment intended as a model of the disinvestment process that would inaugurate a string of other large disinvestment plans instead turned into a two-year, highly contentious episode that involved opposition political parties, labor unions, the state government of Chhatisgarh, the Supreme Court, several central government ministries, and accusations that the disinvestment betrayed the constitutionally-protected rights of the tribal residents and workers of Chhatisgarh. The resolution of the BALCO controversy is also illustrative of the reasons that privatization and other second-generation reforms may ultimately succeed, albeit in a piecemeal and protracted fashion.

In 2000, the government announced that BALCO had been chosen for disinvestment. It was to be the first significant sale of a controlling stake in a public sector unit.[27] A 1997 report of the now-defunct Disinvestment Commission, which suggested that the government sell 40 per cent of equity in BALCO, was revised in 1998 in favor of a proposal to dispense with a 51 per cent stake.[28] After a year of negotiations with interested domestic and foreign parties, the government finalized the sale of BALCO on 2 May 2001 to the Indian company Sterlite Industries for Rs. 551.5 crore.

While the negotiations were proceeding, the seven principal labour unions that are active among the 7,500 workers of BALCO, fearful of labour retrenchment by the new ownership, lodged their dissent with management and bureaucracy in the state. In February, the seven unions, opposition political parties, and the Chhatisgarh Chamber of Commerce joined to form the Virodhi Samyukta Samiti (Anti-Privatization Front). On 3 March the unions went on an indefinite strike, calling for a reversal of the disinvestment project. Chhatisgarh Chief Minister Ajit Jogi, a member of the Congress party, supported the unions vociferously, although the central government's Ministry of Disinvestment claimed that the state elite, and Jogi in particular, were consulted during all of the privatization negotiations.[29]

Jogi and the unions leveled three charges against the disinvestment proceedings.[30] First, the opposition claimed that the value of assets owned by BALCO, including real estate, equipment, inventory and raw materials, and a power plant, far exceeded, the price paid by Sterlite. And because the government sold a controlling interest in the unit, it would be difficult to prevent the new owners from liquidating assets. That BALCO was debt-free and had earned profits in recent years also inspired opposition from those who claimed that the government should be selling enterprises that incurred losses rather than profitable ones.[31] Second, Jogi claimed that the government did not consult the state political elite in the negotiations. Third, Jogi alleged that the sale of BALCO violated constitutional protections of tribal lands. The government took the lands on which BALCO sits from several villages in 1971, with the specific intent of being used for public purposes. The sale of those lands to private holders, the opposition asserted, violated the terms of the initial transfer.[32]

The state government of Chhatisgarh filed petitions with the Delhi and Chhatisgarh High Courts, which the Supreme Court stayed and had transferred to itself. BALCO workers returned to work in early May, after two months of strikes and negotiations between Sterlite and the unions that ended with Sterlite accepting the bulk of union proposals.[33] By September, the output of the plant had yet to return to pre-disinvestment levels. In December 2001, the Supreme Court issued a ruling that the courts were not the appropriate venues for judging the valuation of public assets, and that the courts were not the proper authority to weigh the merits of the government's economic policies. The Court also condemned the role played by the Chhatisgarh's Chief Minister and the state government.

By the end of the two-month strike Chief Minister Jogi had reversed his stance, and actively encouraged the workers from the plant to return to their posts. Jogi's abrupt about-face on the issue of BALCO's privatization ceases to be puzzling when viewed in the context of his contradictory needs as a politician. On the one hand, Jogi was able to bolster his image as a pro-labor and pro-tribal politician by supporting the BALCO workers' strike. On the other hand, the development needs of his state required that he attract foreign and domestic private capital, a task to which Jogi seemed committed.[34]

Indeed, since taking office in 2000, Jogi's government established a strategic management group to encourage and facilitate foreign investment in the state, particularly in infrastructure development. The Supreme Court, after taking up the case filed by Jogi, inquired why his government simultaneously accused the BALCO sale of trampling on the rights of Chhatisgarh's tribal citizens, but negotiated the establishment of plants by Daewoo Power and Essar Steel on formerly-tribal lands.

Although the BALCO disinvestment was ultimately realized, and the judiciary endorsed the manner in which the central government proceeded, the BALCO controversy revealed the extent of the cracks in the political and social landscape on the sensitive issue of privatization. Popular discontent with privatization enabled politicians from rival parties to leverage the issue for their political advantage, a phenomenon that characterizes much of the political posturing over other second-generation reforms.

Nevertheless, as in the case of BALCO, there seem to be equally vital forces curtailing the extent of political opposition. For example, Congress leaders at the center, where the party represent the largest opposition party, are voluble in their criticism of the government's market-reform agenda. However, various Congress-led state governments, like those of Karnataka, Maharashtra, and even Chhatisgarh, have been active in endorsing and initiating economic reforms at the state level, and aggressively seeking domestic and international investment.[35] In the case of BALCO, this need to attract investment is what ultimately constrained the political opposition and allowed the sale to proceed.

The publicly owned international airline, Air India, was also put up for sale in 2001, and may have suffered some of the consequences of BALCO. For several reasons Air India represents an ideal candidate for privatization. It has been losing money for six years and due to capital scarcity, does not have adequate aircraft to take advantage of all of the air routes to which it has rights.[36] Tata Sons and Singapore Airlines had jointly bid for the airline in 2001, but the latter retreated from the competition on 1 September 2001. In its press release announcing the withdrawal of its bid, Singapore Airlines said that it 'was surprised by the intensity of opposition to the privatization of Air India from various quarters including certain sections of political groups, trade unions and of the media'.[37]

In contrast to the divisive experiences with BALCO and Air India, the government was able to successfully negotiate the sale of a 51 per cent stake in Computer Maintenance Corporation (CMC) to Tata Sons in October 2001. CMC is located in a growing industry, and unlike the BALCO employees, the workers in CMC favored the sale.[38] The contrast between the unproblematic sale of CMC and the case of BALCO illustrates the extent to which labor opposition and political and public criticism delayed privatization in the latter case. This will be particularly problematic for the privatization of India's old-economy industrial plants that are often characterized by excess labor, low productivity, and debt.

CONCLUSION

India firmly joined the ranks of liberalizing countries during the 1990s. Changes to the trade, investment, and financial regimes have had a tremendous impact on economic functions in the state, and on the interactions of the state and the economy. Nevertheless, several items on the reform agenda were not addressed during the first decade of reform.

Foremost among these is privatization. While reforming and retrenching the public sector, were often brought up during the 1990s, popular and political opposition successfully forestalled implementation of the plans. The disinvestment of BALCO suggests that while popular opposition to privatization continues, there are definite limits to the extent of political opposition. Political leaders, whether members of the national ruling coalition or members of the opposition, have a similar need to attract foreign investment to their home state.

In the analysis of BALCO's privatization, I have suggested that while electoral pressures first compelled Jogi to support the workers in their strike efforts, his need to present his state as an attractive site for investment in the end forced him to quietly withdraw his support of the strike. Lower levels of public investment and a reduced regulatory role for the government have forced states to seek out investment to finance economic growth. In this context the Chief Minister of Chhatisgarh Ajit Jogi's initial vocal opposition to BALCO's sale and his subsequent tacit approval are not surprising. Rather, his actions reveal his dual needs to play the role of opposition politician at the center and the role of incumbent within his own state, a role in which politicians from across the ideological spectrum will increasingly find themselves.

NOTES

1. Jean Waelbroeck, 'Half a Century of Development Economics: A Review Based on the *Handbook of Development Economics*' *World Bank Economic Review* 12 (1999) pp.323–52.
2. The 'commanding heights', a phrase first used by Lenin to describe his New Economic Policy in 1922, is also a stock phrase in the lexicon of scholars of Indian state socialism.
3. 'McKinsey Suggests Action Plan for 10 Per Cent GDP Growth', *Financial Express*, 7 Sept. 2001; 'India Urged to Cut Red Tape to Boost Growth', *Financial Times*, 7 Sept. 2001.
4. It is beyond the scope of this paper to address questions of the efficacy of different kinds of neo-liberal reforms or the impact they have upon development.
5. These three topics – Gandhi's reform attempts, the 1991 crisis, and the decade of reform – have generated extensive articles and book-length treatments. For information on Gandhi's reform efforts, see Vijay Joshi and I.M.D. Little *India: Macroeconomics and Political Economy, 1964–1991* (Washington DC: World Bank 1994); Atul Kohli, 'The Politics of Liberalisation in India', *World Development* 17/3 (1989). For information on the 1991 crisis and the immediate response of the Indian government, see Jagdish Bhagwati, *India in Transition: Freeing the Economy* (Oxford: Clarendon Press 1993); Bimal Jalan *India's Economic Crisis: The Way Ahead* (New Delhi: Oxford University Press 1991); Bimal Jalan *The Indian Economy: Problems and Prospects* (New Delhi: Viking 1992); Kaushik Basu, 'Structural Reform in India, 1991–1993', *Economic and Political Weekly* 28/48, 27 Nov. 1993; T.N. Srinivasan, 'Reform of Industrial and Trade Policies', *Economic and Political Weekly* 26/37 14 Sept. 1991. For information on India's economic reforms during the 1990s, see Isher Judge Ahluwalia and I.M.D. Little (eds.), *India's Economic Reforms and Development: Essays for Manmohan Singh* (New Delhi: Oxford University Press 1998); Vijay Joshi and I.M.D. Little, *India's Economic Reforms, 1991–2001* (Oxford: Oxford University Press 1996); Jeffrey D. Sachs, Ashutosh Varshney and Nirupam Bajpai (eds.), *India in the Era of Economic Reforms* (New Delhi: Oxford University Press 1999); Deepak Nayyar, *Economic Liberalization in India: Analytics, Experience and Lessons* (Hyderabad:

Orient Longman 1996); World Bank, *India 1998 Macroeconomic Update: Reforming for Growth and Poverty Reduction* (Washington DC: World Bank 1998).

6. The arguments linking regime type to reform ability are reviewed in Adam Przeworski and Fernando Limongi, 'Political Regimes and Economic Growth', *Journal of Economic Perspectives* 7 (Summer 1993) pp.51–69.

7. Barbara Geddes, 'Challenging the Conventional Wisdom' in Larry Diamond and Marc F. Plattner (eds.), *Economic Reform and Democracy* (Baltimore: Johns Hopkins Press 1995); Nicolas van de Walle, 'Crisis and Opportunity in Africa', in Larry Diamond and Marc F. Plattner (eds.), *Economic Reform and Democracy* (Baltimore: Johns Hopkins Press 1995) pp.155–7.

8. Vijay Joshi and I.M.D. Little, *India's Economic Reforms, 1991–2001* (New York: Oxford University Press 1996). The importance of political economic perspectives in explaining India's reforms is underscored in the work of these prominent economists. On page 4, the authors argue that 'economic arguments do not seem to explain either pace of reform or the areas of progress and neglect. Political explanation is required'.

9. Rob Jenkins, *Democratic Politics and Economic Reform in India* (Cambridge: Cambridge University Press 1999) pp.172–207.

10. Ibid. p.4.

11. Ashutosh Varshney, 'Mass Politics or Elite Politics? India's Economic Reforms in Comparative Perspective', in Jeffrey D. Sachs, Ashutosh Varshney and Nirupam Bajpai (eds.), *India in the Era of Economic Reforms* (New Delhi: Oxford University Press 1999) pp.249–57.

12. Vijay Joshi and I.M.D. Little, *India's Economic Reforms 1991–2001* (Oxford: Oxford University Press 1996) p.249.

13. Stephen Haggard and Robert R. Kaufman (eds.), *The Politics of Economic Adjustment*. (Princeton: Princeton University Press 1992); John Williamson and Stephen Haggard, 'The Political Conditions for Economic Reform', in John Williamson (ed.), *The Political Economy of Policy Reform* (Washington DC: Institute for International Economics 1994).

14. See John P. Lewis, 'The Economy' in Marshall M. Bouton (ed.), *India Briefing, 1987* (Boulder, CO: Westview Press 1987) pp.90–92 for a discussion of the Seventh Five-Year Plan.

15. Walter Tayoler, 'End of Gandhi's Honeymoon' *US News and World Report*, 15 Sept. 1986.

16. Gene Kramer, 'World Bank says India, Philippines, Sri Lanka, Bangladesh Worst Off', *Associated Press* 20 Sept. 1990.

17. Deena Khatkhate, 'India on an Economic Reform Trajectory', in Leonard A. Gordon and Philip Oldenburg (eds.) *India Briefing, 1992* (Boulder: Westview Press 1992).

18. 'Ministry of Disinvestment Annual Report 2000–2001', Government of India, 2001.

19. 'India: Recent Economic Developments and Selected Issues', Washington DC, *International Monetary Fund*, 2001.

20. Ministry of Disinvestment, Government of India, *Annual Report 2000–2001*, 2001. Chapter 2 of the report, which discusses the rationale for the public sector, is available at: <www.divest.nic.in/annureport/chapter2.htm>.

21. The first figure is taken from the Ministry of Disinvestment, Government of India, 'Disinvestment in States', which is available online at: <www.divest.nic.in/disistates4.htm>. The second figure comes from data assembled by the Institute of Public Enterprise, Hyderabad, India, and was quoted in the report of a project funded by the United Nations Development Project, 'Corporate Management: Restructuring Selected Public Sector Units'. The third, and largest estimate is contained in Ram Kumar Mishra, 'Competitiveness of Public Sector in India' (Birmingham: International Association of Schools and Institutes of Administration 1999). The UNDP report suggests that some of the reasons for the wide variation in data are due to the divergent ways that states count and measure their SLPEs. For example, some states do not count the state electricity boards as SLPEs due to their status as statutory corporations, while other states do include their electricity boards and other such units in the list of SLPEs. See Ram Kumar Mishra, 'Competitiveness of Public Sector in India' (Birmingham: International Association of Schools and Institutes of Administration 1999).

22. 'IMF Exudes 89 Per Cent Growth for India', *Times of India*, 22 Jan. 2002.
23. Abhijit Sen, 'An Argument for Further Reform', *Frontline* 18/6, 17–30 March 2001.
24. Steve Coll, 'One-Day Strike in India Cripples Some Industries', *Washington Post*, 30 Nov. 1991; Derek Brown, 'India's Air And Train Services Disrupted By Political Strike', *The Guardian*, 30 Nov. 1991; 'Indian Strike Gets Underway, Nearly 300 Arrested', *Agence France Presse*, 29 Nov. 1991.
25. David Housego, 'Delhi to Retain Control of Public Sector Industry', *Financial Times*, 19 Nov. 1991.
26. Arun Kumar, 'Protest Strikes Target BJP Government's Economic Policies', *World Socialist Web Site*, 17 Dec. 1998. Available at: <www.wsws.org/workers/1998/dec1998/ind-d17.shtml>.
27. The central government's sale of a 74 per cent stake in Lagan Jute Machinery to Murlidhar Ratanlal Exports in July 2000, and of a 74 per cent stake in Modern Food Industries to Hindustan Lever in February 2000 are less consequential in terms of the much smaller size of the two operations relative to BALCO.
28. V. Sridhar, 'Blocking Privatisation', *Frontline* 18/9, 11 May 2001.
29. V. Sridhar, 'Battle over Balco', *Frontline* 18/6, 30 March 2001.
30. Ibid.
31. Khozem Merchant, 'End to Balco Strike Opens Way For Ambitious Expansion Plans', *Financial Times*, 15 June 2001.
32. V. Sridhar, 'The Balco Struggle', *Frontline* 18/8, 27 April 2001.
33. 'Festive Look at Balco Plant as Workers Resume Duty', *Times of India*, 10 May 2001.
34. C.R.L. Narasimhan, 'The Supreme Court and Economic Governance', *The Hindu*, 24 Dec. 2001.
35. Tyagaraj Sharma, 'Congress Flip-flop', *The Statesman*, 20 June 2001; Anju Sharma, 'Jogi Dons New Role to Attract Investors', *Hindustan Times*, 21 May 2001; Namita Devidayal, 'Maharasthra's PSU Sell-Off Model', *Times of India*, 2 Nov. 2001.
36. 'Unproductive', *The Economist*, 8 Sept. 2001.
37. Press Release, Singapore Airlines, 'Air India', 1 Sept. 2001. Available online at: <www.singaporeair.com/saa/app/saa>.
38. Parthasarathi Swami and Roy Pinto, 'A Painless Privatization', *Business India*, 28 Oct. 2001.

Abstracts

The US-India Courtship: From Clinton to Bush
ROBERT M. HATHAWAY
While a considerable thaw in Indo-US relations bequeathed by the Cold War took place under Clinton, there are still factors, even after 11 September 2001, which have hindered a relationship with common strategic interests. These factors involve divergences on nuclear proliferation, the emergence of China as a world power, the pace of India's economic liberalisation, and Indo-Pakistan tension. A strategic partnership is achievable, but India will need to keep US interests constantly in focus.

India, Pakistan and Kashmir
STEPHEN PHILIP COHEN
The India–Pakistan conflict has taken a new, nuclear turn, making South Asia one of the most dangerous places in the world. The Kashmir dispute is only one aspect of the larger struggle between the two states. Their conflict is hard to manage, and may prove impossible to resolve, because it is a 'paired minority' conflict in which each side views itself as threatened and vulnerable, and thus resists negotiation and compromise.

Toward a 'Force-in-Being': The Logic, Structure and Utility of India's Emerging Nuclear Posture
ASHLEY J. TELLIS
Defined as a 'force-in-being', this nuclear posture exhibits a deterrent capability based on available but dispersed components capable of being constituted into usable nuclear weapon systems during a supreme emergency, and even after enduring an enemy nuclear strike. On current plans, New Delhi's force-in-being will be limited in size, separated in geographical disposition, and centralized in control.

Asymmetrical Indian and Chinese Threat Perceptions
JOHN W. GARVER

India tends to be deeply apprehensive of threats from China, while China appears comparatively unconcerned about threats from India, and finds it difficult to understand why India might perceive China as a threat. Two explanations of this asymmetry are (1) a deliberate and systematic understatement of Chinese concerns about India, resulting from the mobilization function of China's public media, and (2) the greater effectiveness of China's application of power over the past 50 years.

Indo-Russian Strategic Relations: New Choices and Constraints
DEEPA OLLAPALLY

Three levels of analysis are applied: bilateral, regional and global. While the bilateral level has been critical in the past, global compulsions are becoming less intense, and regional dynamics now hold the key to future relations.

The Indo-French Strategic Dialogue: Bilateralism and World Perceptions
JEAN-LUC RACINE

Shared willingness to develop a stronger relationship, articulated by President Chirac during his visit to India in 1998, was not weakened by India's ensuing nuclear tests. Looking for enhanced power and global recognition, India and France share a common approach to *realpolitik*, and India's foreign policy is still searching for fresh opportunities to maximize influence in a new global order.

India and Israel: Emerging Partnership
P. R. KUMARASWAMY

The absence of formal diplomatic relations between India and Israel from India's hesitant recognition of Israel in 1950 and the establishment of full relations in January 1992, was the result of a complex interplay between two sets of tensions. The first involved the Arab–Israeli dispute, and India's sympathies with a post-colonial Arab world and with the Non-Aligned Movement; the second involved accommodating Muslim opinion within India. Normalization has proceeded more strongly as the growth of Hindu nationalism has weakened Muslim leverage on Indian foreign policy.

The Political Economy of India's Second-Generation Reforms
SUNILA KALE

The essay analyses the broad failure of India's attempts to deregulate its economy in the 1990s and the comparative success of privatisation efforts since 2000, and suggests that the growing, though still limited, success with privatisation is due largely to the new institutional environment of competitive investment unleashed by earlier waves of market reform.

About the Contributors

Sumit Ganguly is Professor of Asian Studies, University of Texas at Austin.

Robert M. Hathaway is Director of the Asia Program at the Woodrow Wilson International Center for Scholars, Washington DC.

Stephen Philip Cohen is Senior Fellow at the Brookings Institution, Washington DC.

Ashley J. Tellis is Senior Advisor at the American Embassy, New Delhi.

John W. Garver is Professor at the Sam Nunn School of International Affairs, Georgia Institute of Technology, and Associate of the China Research Center.

Deepa Ollapally is Program Officer at the United States Institute of Peace, and Senior Fellow at the Center for the Advanced Study of India, University of Pennsylvania.

Jean-Luc Racine is Senior Fellow at the Centre for the Study of India and South Asia, Ecole des Hautes Etudes en Sciences Sociales, Paris.

P.R. Kumaraswamy is Associate Professor, School of International Studies, Jawaharlal Nehru University, New Delhi.

Sunila Kale is PhD candidate in the Department of Government at the University of Texas at Austin.

Index